hotels • restaurants • spas • shops
chinachic

For regular updates on our special offers, register at

www.thechiccollection.com

hotels • restaurants • spas • shops

chinachic

text paul mooney • brent hannon • sherisse pham • sofia a. suárez • kerry o'neill • elena nichols

·K·U·P·E·R·A·R·D·

executive editor
melisa teo

editors
sharon yap • laura jeanne gobal

assistant editors
li yuemin • priscilla chua

designers
felicia wong • wong hean meng

production manager
sin kam cheong

sales and marketing director
antoine monod

regional sales and marketing manager
new bee yong

sales and marketing consultant
james mcleod

designed and produced by
editions didier millet pte ltd
121 telok ayer street, #03-01
singapore 068590
telephone : +65.6324 9260
facsimile : +65.6324 9261
email : edm@edmbooks.com.sg
website : www.edmbooks.com

first published in great britain 2008 by
kuperard
59 hutton grove, london n12 8ds
telephone : +44 (0) 20 8446 2440
facsimile : +44 (0) 20 8446 2441
email : sales@kuperard.co.uk
website : www.kuperard.co.uk

Kuperard is an imprint of Bravo Ltd.

©2008 editions didier millet pte ltd

Printed in Singapore.

All rights reserved. No part of this publication may be reproduced, stored in a retrieval system, or transmitted in any form or by any means, electronic, electrostatic, magnetic tape, mechanical, photocopying, recording or otherwise, without prior written permission from the publisher.

isbn: 978-1-85733-424-1

COVER CAPTIONS:
1: *A juxtaposition of old and new in Beijing.*
2: *Spa luxury at the Crown Macau.*
3: *Try the signature Moorish martini at the glamorous OPIA in JIA Hong Kong.*
4: *Red lanterns herald the Chinese New Year.*
5: *A detail of a Forbidden City palace.*
6: *The striking new National Stadium, home to the 2008 Beijing Olympics.*
7: *Contemporary Chinese art has captured the imagination of art lovers worldwide.*
8: *Exquisitely designed boutiques enhance the shopping experience.*
9: *Ornate gates bring a touch of Old World Shanghainese glamour to 88 Xintiandi.*
10: *An exhibition of ancient artefacts at one of China's numerous museums.*
11: *A Chinese junk on one of Jiangsu's rivers.*
12: *The Great Wall, China's most recognisable and enduring symbol.*
13: *See and be seen at Bar Rouge, one of Shanghai's hottest nightspots.*
14: *Comfort and contemporary design at The Opposite House.*
15: *The intriguing face of contemporary Chinese art.*
16: *Ceremonial vessels catch the attention of a museum visitor in Shanghai.*

THIS PAGE: *A worker repairing a palace window in the Forbidden City.*

OPPOSITE: *Auspicious red lanterns adorn a tree during Chinese Lunar New Year celebrations.*

PAGE 2: *The iconic Great Wall of China silhouetted at sunrise.*

PAGE 8 AND 9: *The National Grand Theatre in Beijing (foreground) is a modern counterpoint to the city's ancient architecture.*

contents

map of china 10 • introduction 12

beijing 18

map of beijing 20 • introduction 21 • beijing: dining out 24 • beijing's nightlife 28 • beijing: a shopping sensation 30 • spas in beijing 32 • beijing galleries + museums 34 • peking opera 36 • best views of beijing 38

Bayhood No. 9 40 • Commune by the Great Wall Kempinski 44 • Grand Hyatt Beijing 46 • JW Marriott Hotel Beijing 48 • Raffles Beijing Hotel 50 • The Shangri-La Hotel, Beijing 52 • Shangri-La's Kerry Centre Hotel, Beijing 56 • The Opposite House 60 • Jaan at Raffles Beijing Hotel 62 • My Humble House at China Central Place 64 • My Humble House at The Oriental Plaza 66 • Cottage Boutique 68 • Cottage Warehouse 70 • The Village at Sanlitun 72 • Zenspa 74

shanghai 76

map of shanghai 78 • introduction 79 • shanghai: dining out 82 • shanghai's nightlife 86 • shanghai: a shopping sensation 88 • spas in shanghai 92 • shanghai galleries + museums 94 • best views of shanghai 96

88 Xintiandi 98 • Four Seasons Hotel, Shanghai 100 • Hyatt on the Bund 102 • JIA Shanghai 106 • JW Marriott Shanghai 108 • Parkyard Hotel Shanghai 110 • URBN Hotels Shanghai 112 • Kathleen's 5 Rooftop Restaurant + Bar 114 • Simply The Group 116 • Annabel Lee Shanghai 120 • Annly's China 122 • Bund18 124 • Hu + Hu 128

130 suzhou+nanjing

map of suzhou + nanjing 132 • introduction 133 • suzhou + nanjing: dining out 136 • suzhou + nanjing: a shopping sensation 138 • best views of suzhou + nanjing 140

Kayumanis Nanjing 142 • Kempinski Hotel Suzhou 144 • Sheraton Suzhou Hotel + Towers 148

150 hainan

map of hainan 152 • introduction 153 • hainan: dining out 156 • hainan's great outdoors 158 • best views of hainan 160

Mandarin Oriental, Sanya 162 • Sanya Marriott Resort + Spa 164

166 hongkong

map of hong kong 168 • introduction 169 • hong kong: dining out 172 • hong kong's nightlife 176 • hong kong: a shopping sensation 178 • spas in hong kong 182 • hong kong galleries + museums 184

Four Seasons Hotel Hong Kong 186 • Grand Hyatt Hong Kong 188 • JIA Hong Kong 192 • JW Marriott Hong Kong 194 • Lan Kwai Fong Hotel 196 • Hotel Le Méridien Cyberport 198 • KEE Club 200 • Shanghai Tang 202

204 macau

map of macau 206 • introduction 207 • macau: dining out 210 • macau's nightlife 212 • macau: a shopping sensation 214 • spas in macau 216 • macau's casino scene 218

Crown Macau 220 • Sofitel Macau at Ponte 16 226 • Wynn Macau 228

index 232 • picture credits 234 • directory 234

introduction

new china rising

China is bulldozing its way into the 21st century. New skyscrapers, glitzy malls, and posh hotels are rising in cities around the country; cars are clogging newly paved highways and roads once dominated by bicycles. Beijing and Shanghai have become hotspots of creativity and style, while contemporary Chinese art is in demand around the globe on an unprecedented scale. Chinese cinema—in the form of both independent art flicks and big-budget blockbusters—has impressed itself on the international psyche; Chinese architecture and design, dressed up in post-modern sensibilities, is suddenly the rage again.

Despite the wrenching changes brought about by modernisation in the past few decades, however, wherever you travel in China, the past is always with you—from the popular historical dramas that play each day on TV and emanate from taxi radios, to the ancient imperial palaces, serene temples, classic gardens, and old city walls that are scattered around the country. The history of China goes back several millennia, making it the longest continuous civilisation in the world, and this may explain the Chinese people's intimate feelings for the past.

a brief history

The earliest Chinese dynasty for which written records exist is the Shang dynasty (1766–1122 BCE). It was followed by the Zhou dynasty (1145–256 BCE), which left seven 'Warring States' in its wake. The Qin dynasty (221–206 BCE) came to prominence when the future Qinshi Huangdi (first Qin emperor) systematically defeated the six other states. By 221 BCE, he had unified China. He built the Great Wall, and developed an efficient bureaucratic system that was adopted and improved upon by subsequent dynasties. The succeeding Han dynasty significantly extended China's borders and transformed Confucianism into a state ideology. The Tang (618–907) and Song (960–1279) dynasties followed, both high points of art, economic prosperity, and neo-Confucianism. The Mongol-ruled Yuan dynasty (1279–1368) reigned briefly thereafter, promoting trade with the Europeans before being unseated by peasant rebellions, which resulted in the establishment of the Ming dynasty (1368–1644).

In 1644, Li Zicheng, a bandit leader, overthrew the Ming dynasty but was forced to flee after Manchu soldiers slipped through a hole in the Great Wall and poured into the capital to establish the Qing dynasty (1644–1911). The Manchus maintained the traditional Chinese political system and during their first 150 years provided order and prosperity before entering a period of decline. The dynasty collapsed in 1911, the last emperor abdicated, and the Republic of China was born in March 1912. Much of the next three decades was marked by chaos as the Nationalist government battled warlord armies, the Japanese military, and the Communists.

THIS PAGE (FROM TOP): Shanghai's Pudong skyline is anchored by the iconic Oriental Pearl Tower; the once-ubiquitous bicycle is being overtaken as the most common form of transport by motorised vehicles.
OPPOSITE: The expansive geometric glass roof of the Beijing Capital International Airport's Terminal Three, one of the country's key projects ahead of the 2008 Olympics.

THIS PAGE (FROM TOP): *A delegate snaps away during a conference at the Great Hall of the People in Beijing; old buildings are making way for new ones in preparation for the 2008 Olympics.*

OPPOSITE (FROM TOP): *Reputedly the largest 'sky screen' in the world at one of Beijing's immense new shopping malls; contemporary Chinese art is the hottest new addition to collections worldwide.*

In 1949, the Communist Party of China (CPC) claimed victory over the Nationalists and in October that year, Communist leader Chairman Mao Zedong stood at the Gate of Heavenly Peace and declared the birth of the People's Republic of China. The first few years of New China were exhilarating as life slowly returned to normal. Vehicles began rolling off of production lines, industry was booming, and harvests were plentiful. For the first time, the country seemed poised to step on the road to modernisation. Unfortunately, Mao would launch a series of damaging political campaigns over the next 20 years. During the Cultural Revolution (1966–1976), factories and schools were shut down, the arts ground to a halt, and rampaging Red Guards carried out a massive wave of violence, wantonly persecuting people and destroying everything from books and art to temples and imperial palaces. Students, artists, doctors, scientists, and intellectuals were trucked off to the countryside and factories to do manual work and to 'learn' from the peasants and workers.

Mao passed away in 1976, and Deng Xiaoping, a veteran Communist revolutionary, claimed de facto power. He promoted his 'black cat, white cat' theory, which held that it did not matter what economic system was used as long as it produced results. While just 20 years earlier Mao had boasted about cutting off capitalist tails, countless Chinese began to xiahai, or jump into the sea of private business, opening everything from market stalls to factories. 'To get rich is glorious' was the new national battle cry, and capitalism returned with a vengeance.

Today, the Chinese have more disposable income than ever before and the once sparse shop shelves are now overloaded with both local and imported goods, while produce markets are piled high with abundant supplies of fruit, vegetables, and meat. While many Chinese have yet to equally share the benefits of China's economic miracle, there's probably never been a more prosperous period in the country's history. The 2008 Olympics has long been heralded as Beijing's coming out party, with 2008 marking the advent of China's emergence as a global power. The coming decade promises to be even more exciting than the last as China continues its long march back to the future.

chinese art

For decades after liberation in 1949, Chinese art took a backseat to politics as it stayed true to Mao Zedong's 1942 commandment that 'art must serve politics'. Art was but a propaganda tool for 'guiding' the masses. No more. Chinese artists are today guided by market dictates, rather than political ones, a trend that is encouraging an artistic leap forward in creativity and diversity. Chinese art encompasses Plexiglas sculptures of Beijing's working class people, innovative installation art, pop art, satiric portraits of Chairman Mao, outrageous performance art, and

cynical realist depictions of modern society. And it is starting to pay handsomely.

Seemingly overnight, the world has discovered contemporary Chinese artists. The demand from abroad, and from increasingly wealthy and savvy local buyers, appears to be insatiable. As galleries from Hong Kong to New York scramble to purchase the best works for their collections, prices being paid for works by top Chinese artists—some barely known outside of China five years ago—have doubled, tripled, and quadrupled in recent years. One gallery owner has likened the frenzy over new Chinese art to a gold rush. Some critics fear the success may have come too quick and easy, and others complain that too much contemporary art panders to the export market, and that form is more important than quality. But there is no indication that this trend will fade any time soon. Contemporary Chinese art today offers one of the best returns on investment. Those who were smart enough a few years ago to start collecting the works of modern Chinese artists have chalked up considerable bang for their buck. Based on recent auction results, some collectors have seen their investment appreciate at a respectable compound annual return of about 125 per cent.

cinema

As with other arts in China, the Chinese cinema industry was little more than a channel for propaganda following the Communist rise to power, turning out films about bigger-than-life worker, soldier, and peasant-class heroes performing superhuman feats. But things began to change in the 1980s, when reform and the opening up of the country brought far-reaching changes to the movie industry, most notably the rise of the Fifth Generation of Chinese filmmakers, such as Zhang Yimou and Chen Kaige. The first graduates of the Beijing Film Academy after it reopened following the Cultural Revolution, they began to produce non-orthodox films with the country's fertile past and present as a backdrop. Chen's *Yellow Earth*, with Zhang behind the camera, marked the arrival of this group. Zhang, a former factory worker-turned-cinematographer-turned-director, made the classic *Red Sorghum*, and then went on to produce other hits such as *Raise the Red Lantern*, *Ju Dou*, *To Live*, and *Hero*. Chen, on his part, made

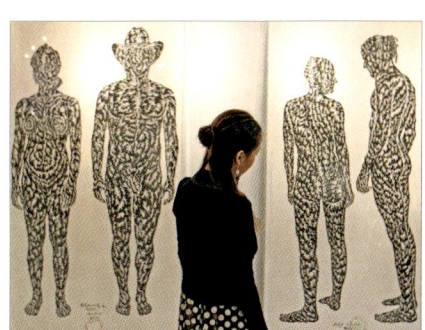

THIS PAGE: *Even the stairway at the National Grand Theatre in Beijing exudes style as the city transforms its urban landscape with daring designs by world-renowned architects.*

OPPOSITE: *The controversial but distinctive National Stadium, dubbed the 'Bird's Nest' because of its construction with interlaced steel, will host the 2008 Olympics in Beijing.*

the moving *Farewell My Concubine*. The more rebellious Sixth Generation filmmakers, such as Zhang Yuan (*Seventeen Years*), Jia Zhangke (*Still Life*), and Wang Xiaoshuai (*Beijing Bicycle*), began to grab the spotlight at international film festivals in the 1990s for their individualistic and unromantic portrayals of modern life in China. More often than not, these films, which focused on the negative by-product of China's rise, won accolades overseas, but were deemed cinema non grata at home. The most recent trend has been the Fifth Generation Chinese blockbuster, such as Chen's *The Promise* and Zhang's mega hits *Hero*, nominated for an Oscar in 2003, and *Curse of the Golden Flower*, which have helped to introduce Chinese cinema to a much wider international audience. Critics, however, say that they pander to Western stereotypes and that they eclipse the work of some of China's more thoughtful, but less well-funded, filmmakers.

design

In addition to art and cinema, China is fast becoming a global creative hotspot for design. Everyone appears to be obsessed with innovation, and almost all of a sudden, design has become a national priority. Among young Chinese, design is one of the hottest major degrees in the country, with no less than 400 schools offering design programmes, and impressive new facilities springing up to meet the demand.

But no where is this trend more evident than in the architectural transformation taking place in major Chinese cities. The world's top architects are falling over one another to scoop up China's offering of some of the most ambitious building projects in the world. In *Time's* 2007 list of the world's top ten new 'Architectural Marvels', three were going up in Beijing: the National Stadium designed for the Olympics by Swiss firm Herzog & de Meuron; the CCTV Tower created by hot Dutch architect Rem Koolhaas, a tetrahedronal structure that *Time* said 'will be the most radically reimagined tall building in the world'; and the Linked Hybrid, an office complex by the American firm Steven Holl Architects that will have sky bridges connecting its eight towers.

Meanwhile, Chinese architects are starting to transform other cities. The Beijing firm MAD Office, for example, won a competition in Toronto with its space age concept of an imposing 56-storey tower spiralling and twisting into the sky. Back at home and closer to the ground, cutting-edge architecture can be seen in trendy eateries and boutique hotels, often exhibiting a mix of oriental and occidental influences. Countless others are renovating century-old courtyard houses, turning them into interesting restaurants, cafés, bars, and inns. This is not to say that China does not still have a long way to go. Schools continue to focus on rote memorisation and creativity is still a notch or two below other innovative countries in the world. But it is well on the way, and part of the fun and excitement is in watching as it works its way into the future.

...some of the most ambitious building projects in the world.

beijing

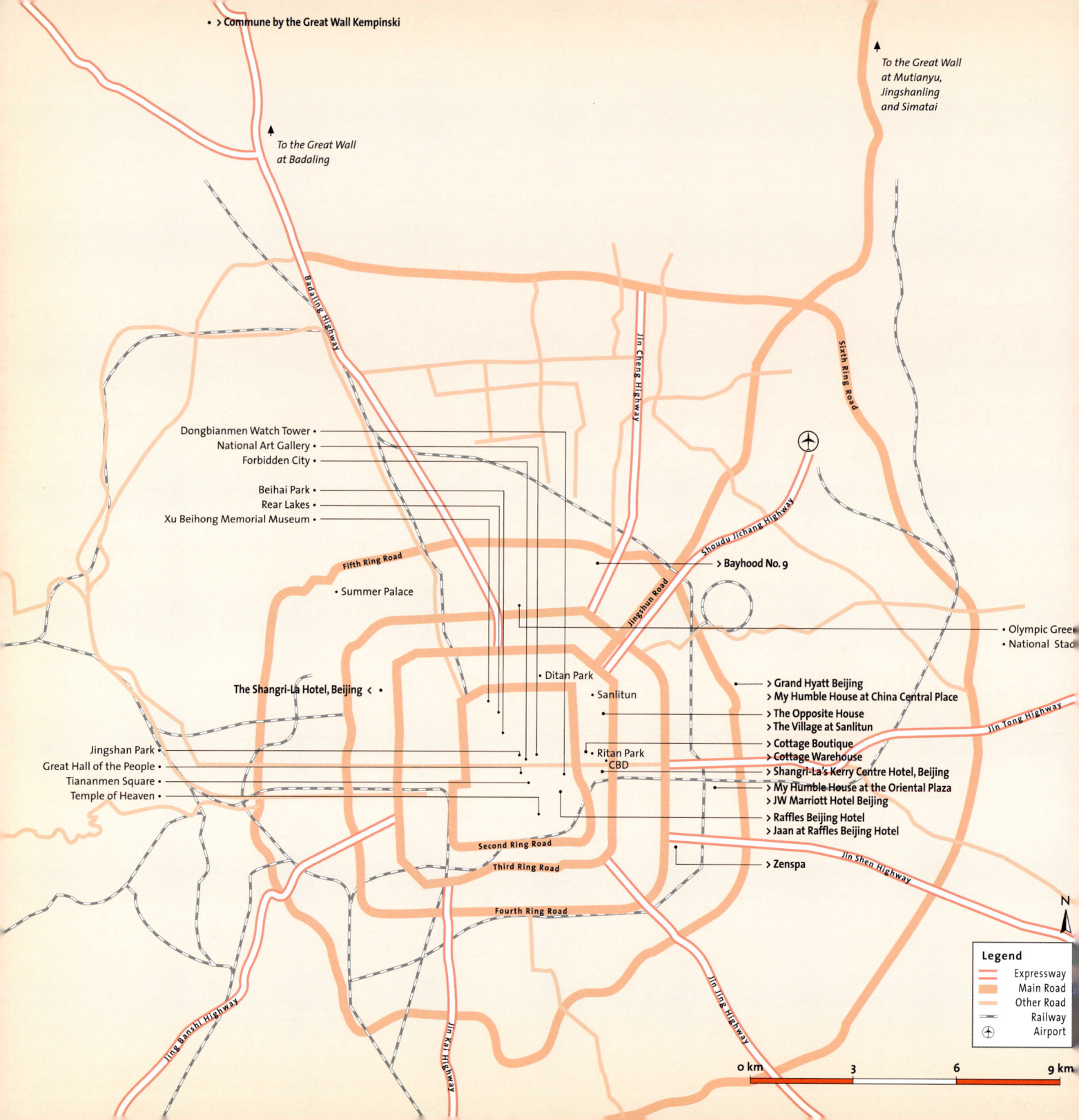

a balance of tradition and modernity

Anyone who has admired old black-and-white photographs of Beijing's magnificent city walls, wandered through its disappearing hutongs, or read the stirring memoirs of those who lived in this great city a century ago, would share the sentiments of Edmund N. Bacon, the renowned American city planner, when he wrote that, very possibly, 'the greatest single work of man on the face of the earth is Peking'. Bacon was especially influenced by the imposing city walls and the Forbidden City, which he said 'taught me that city planning is about movement through space, an architectural sequence of sensors and stimuli, up and down, light and dark, colour and rhythm'. It is against this enduring and magnificent backdrop that Beijing, with its strikingly modern skyline today, continues to leave an indelible impression on visitors.

the beijing of old

Numerous settlements have existed on or near the site of present-day Beijing for the past 3,000 years. The early settlers were not Han Chinese but tribes from the north. The Khitan, the Jurchen, and the Mongols all had their capitals here, each ruler building on the foundation of the previous one. The Ming Emperor Yongle expanded the city beyond the boundaries of the grand Mongol capital. He constructed the magnificent Forbidden City and the Temple of Heaven, the best remaining example of religious architecture in China. The Manchu rulers of the Qing dynasty subsequently added to the grandeur of the Forbidden City and greatly contributed to the city's architectural heritage—many of the historical buildings we see today date back to that golden period.

The city went into a period of decline following the fall of the Qing dynasty in 1911, as it came under the rule of a string of marauding warlord governments and then the Japanese during the Second World War. The Japanese withdrew from China in 1945 after surrendering to Allied Forces, opening the way for the nationalist Kuomintang (KMT) government to resume a bitter civil war with the Communists. The KMT was defeated and the victorious Red Army marched into Beijing. The city became the capital of New China on October 1, 1949, when the leader of the Communist Party of China (CPC), Chairman Mao Zedong, declared at the rostrum of the Gate of Heavenly Peace, 'The Chinese people have stood up!' Over the next few decades, the city underwent wrenching changes. Ancient structures made way for bland, box-like Soviet-style architecture, and the city walls were torn down to make way for a new ring road, a subway, and a massive underground bomb shelter. The Cultural Revolution (1966–1976) was the most destructive

PAGE 18: *The luminous National Aquatics Centre is part of the new urban design that is changing the face of the city ahead of the 2008 Olympics.*

THIS PAGE (FROM TOP): *A vendor delivers coal to households along a traditional hutong; a vivid display of the Chinese national flag at the Military Museum of Chinese People's Revolution.*

period of all: rampaging Red Guards damaged temples and historical sites beyond repair. A sea change came with the passing of Chairman Mao in 1976. Deng Xiaoping, an early member of the Communist Party and a veteran of the epic Long March, emerged as the new strong man. Under his leadership, economic development took precedence and vast measures were implemented to effect a new era of growth.

a new golden era

By the early 1990s, the Chinese had begun making up for lost time. Making their mark in a cultural landscape that had once been stark in its severity, the world's top designer labels found homes in Beijing's new malls and wealthy Chinese traded their staid Mao jackets for North Face and Armani, while Christian Dior and Nina Ricci crowded the main floors of the city's gleaming new department stores. The streets were soon crowded with a steady stream of cars—from the locally produced Geely to Audis, BMWs, and the occasional Hummer—pushing the once ubiquitous bicycle closer to extinction. In the evenings, Chinese and foreign businessmen could be found talking business in the city's hip new fusion restaurants, while students, diplomats, office girls, and the nouveau riche mixed it up on the dance floor at the latest bars and clubs.

A turning point came in 2001 when Beijing won the right to host the 2008 Olympics, setting the city off on one of the most ambitious urban makeovers the world has ever seen. To prepare for the Olympic throng, new highways are being built, new subway lines dug, historical sites dusted off, and patches of green are appearing all over the city. Leading international architects are today household names in the capital, known for their daring designs for both Olympic facilities and new high-rises, including the National Stadium, dubbed the 'Bird's Nest' because of its twig-like structure, and the National Aquatics Centre, known locally as the 'Water Cube'.

Perhaps because of the jarring changes the city has experienced in such a short time, Beijingers are seeking comfort in the things of the past. But to be fair, true Beijingers never really abandoned their traditions. The city's parks have always been crowded in the mornings with people, some practising martial arts, sword-fighting, and taijiquan, some simply kicking a shuttlecock around. Elderly Beijing men still fly their kites, raise crickets, play chess on the streets, or hang their ornate birdcages from tree branches, much as their ancestors have done for hundreds of years. A Beijing writer once lamented that there was no longer any place in the city to hang one's birdcage, a sad reminder of the effects rapid urbanisation has had on the city. But there are increasing signs that the city will find a way to balance tradition and modernity, and that there will be a branch to hang that birdcage on for a few more years to come.

THIS PAGE (FROM TOP): *An imperial rites ceremony being staged at the Temple of Heaven, the best remaining example of religious architecture in China; sports, fashion, and branded goods are big business in this increasingly style-savvy city.*

OPPOSITE: *Pedestrians take a peek through a cut-out in a large billboard fronting Qianmen Street for a glimpse of the renovations being carried out. The old shopping district is being rejuvenated ahead of the 2008 Beijing Olympics.*

...'the greatest single work of man on the face of the earth is Peking'.

beijing: dining out

The dining experience in the Beijing of today is a world away from that of Beijing a decade ago, when most of the city's restaurants were drab affairs. Today, the capital is a Mecca for foodies, a place where one can sample a myriad of cuisines from every province of China—and practically every country in the world—without ever having to leave the city. And restaurants have spiffed up their look with innovative designs, making eating out both visually and gastronomically pleasing.

chinese cuisine

Sample dim sum in a beautiful setting at **Huang Ting** (The Peninsula Beijing, 8 Jinyu Hutong, Wangfujing), where the pan-fried turnip cake in X.O. sauce, deep-fried taro, and steamed pork buns, and steamed rice flour crepe with dough sticks come highly recommended. The interior design is based on Beijing's fading traditional courtyard houses. The walls are built of bricks taken from centuries-old courtyard houses that were destroyed, while the pine floorboards and beams are from a large mansion in Suzhou. **Tiandi Yijia** (140 Nanchizi Avenue), a few minutes' walk from the Forbidden City, also has a courtyard theme. The menu is pan-Chinese cuisine, offering classic dishes from Guangdong, Beijing, and Sichuan.

For a dining experience at a real courtyard house, try **Red Capital Club** (66 Dongsi Jiutiao), the restaurant that kicked off American entrepreneur Lawrence Brahm's so-called Beijing retro movement a decade ago. The restaurant serves what Brahm has termed

24 chinachic

Zhongnanhai cuisine—a reference to both the compound where China's top leaders all once lived and their favourite dishes.

Dine like royalty at **Gugong Yushan** (Room 620, Wangfu Century Building, 55 Dong'anmen Avenue), an imperial restaurant located in the former living quarters of Qing court concubines in the Forbidden City. The dishes, researched by scholars who consulted ancient palace records, are the same ones enjoyed by the Emperor Qianlong. Bookings are required three days in advance.

The delicate and flavoursome cuisine of Jiangsu and Zhejiang provinces, better known by its abbreviated name Jiangzhe cai, is becoming increasingly popular. **Din Tai Fung** (22 Hujiayuan, Yibei Building) of Taipei fame opened its first branch in Beijing several years ago and was an immediate hit. The contemporary venue specialises in xiaolong bao, juicy meat-filled buns cooked in a bamboo steamer, and amazing cairou zhengjiao, steamed dumplings packed with green leaf bok choy and a small amount of minced pork.

At innovative chef Michael Chen's **Kong Yiji Shangyan** (8 Chaoyang Park Road), Jiangzhe cuisine is given a new look. The cuisine here originates in Shaoxing—an idyllic canal town in Zhejiang—but is given a modern twist. Kumquat with shrimps and Jiaxing crispy duck are among the innovative dishes. With its viewing pavilion and indoor waterways lined with baskets and pottery, the restaurant has a pleasant and charming ambience reminiscent of China's old canal towns.

The duck at **Dadong Kaoya** (1–2 Nanxincang Guoji Dasha, 22A Dongsi Shitiao) is roasted to perfection the old-fashioned way—in ovens burning wood from fruit trees until the duck turns the color of molasses. The restaurant's location is a plus—it overlooks the beautifully restored Nanxincang, Beijing's last remaining granary, which dates back to the Ming dynasty and is now converted to galleries, restaurants and bars.

The **Sichuan Huiguan** (2/F, Guohua Touzi Daxia, 3 Dongzhimen South Avenue) has given new meaning to this province's humble fare. Situated in one of Beijing's new sleek glass towers, the restaurant offers refined Sichuan dishes that have just the right amount of spices. This is arguably the best Sichuan restaurant in Beijing.

THIS PAGE (FROM TOP): The innovative sushi keeps the crowd hungry for more at Hatsune; dine in style and comfort at My Humble House where creative contemporary Chinese cuisine is on the menu.
OPPOSITE: Savour a slice of Italy while enjoying Beijing's ancient architecture at Da Giorgio.

beijing:diningout 25

beijing: dining out

Located in a nicely renovated century-old courtyard house decorated with artwork and traditional Chinese furniture, **The Source** (14 Banchang Hutong, Kuanjie) is the brainchild of popular Chinese artist Bing Bing. The restaurant has a moderately priced set menu that changes every week, with a focus on light Sichuan cuisine.

Trendy **Bellagio** (6 Gongti East Road)—the place for people-watching in Beijing—serves Taiwanese cuisine and Sichuan dishes with a Taiwan twist. The Taiwan-style crushed ices covered with toppings are popular. Open until 4 am to serve Beijing's hip after-hours clubbing crowd, this is a perfect place for a late night snack.

Chef Guo Xinjun, a veteran of the Beijing Hotel, has prepared state banquets for US Presidents Nixon and Clinton, and Chinese leaders such as Deng Xiaoping. More importantly, he is the fourth generation of his family to specialise in tanjia or Tan family cuisine, a style of cooking created by an official of the Qing dynasty who combined the delicacies of several regions. Guo runs the kitchen at **Guo Yao Xiaoju** (58 Bei Santiao, Jiaodao Kou, Andingmennei Avenue), a definite contender for best Beijing restaurant.

Made in China (1/F, Grand Hyatt Beijing, 1 East Chang'an Avenue) proudly proclaims its affiliation and inspiration. The restaurant specialises in northern Chinese cuisine.

People come to **Lan** (4/F, Twin Towers, B-12 Jianguomenwai Avenue) for its unique fusion cuisine, but it is the outrageous interior—reminiscent of the palace in the animated movie *Beauty and the Beast*—that people talk about. The décor is the work of French designer Philippe Starck, and consists of a clutter of art scattered about, including European art hanging upside down from the ceilings, huge framed mirrors on the walls, and oversized armchairs. The menu runs the gamut from raw oysters to Japanese sushi to Chinese fusion and good old-fashioned Sichuan favourites.

When describing either the food or the décor at **My Humble House at Oriental Plaza** (W307 Oriental Plaza, 1 East Chang'an Avenue), 'humble' would probably not be the first adjective to come to mind! This chic restaurant is part of the series created by Indonesian-Chinese gourmand Andrew Tjioe. Tjioe eschews the term fusion, preferring to call his style of cooking—which creatively marries Eastern and Western ingredients—contemporary Chinese.

East-meets-West is also the theme at **East 33** (Block E, Raffles Beijing Hotel, 33 East Chang'an Avenue), where diners will be delighted by a diverse menu that features both quintessential Beijing dishes like Peking Duck and Italian favourites, such as wood-fired pizzas.

It almost seems like the owners of **People 8** (18 Jianguomenwai Avenue) don't want you to find the place. Its door is somewhat hidden behind bamboo on a side street, and the interior is fashionably cloaked in darkness. But if you can grope your way to a table, you'll be pleased by the delicious food. The spare ribs with plum sauce and spicy bean curd cooked in a paper cup over a small flame are especially good.

asian cuisine

The expat crowd lines up at **Hatsune** (2/F, Heqiao Building. C, 8A Guanghua Road) for its New World sushi rolls, such as the California sushi filled with crab and avocado topped with sesame seeds, and the '119 roll', a combination of bright red tuna rolls topped with spicy-and-sweet sauce. Reservations are advised.

Yotsuba (2 Xinzhong Jie Xili), has its seafood flown in daily from Tokyo's famous Tsukiji market. Try to get a seat at the sushi counter for a ringside view of the chef as he deftly runs a sharp knife through the fish. Yostuba is open only for dinner.

international

The richly decorated **Aria** (2/F, China World Hotel, 1 Jianguomenwai Avenue), with its polished wooden furnishings and European art, has the feel of an aristocratic businessman's club. The best deal here is the excellent business lunch.

Le Pré Lenôtre (Sofitel Wanda Beijing, Tower C, Wanda Plaza, 93 Jianguo Road) was inspired by Lenôtre's 3-Michelin star rated Le Pré Catelan. With Lenôtre chef de cuisine Frederic Meynard at the helm, the restaurant brings an exclusive Parisian touch to Beijing's culinary scene.

Mare (14 Xindong Road) is known for its tapas with more than 30 choices available. The menu also features a selection of authentic Spanish dishes and a tempting range of desserts.

The hearty menu and subtle flavours of **Da Giorgio** (Grand Hyatt Beijing, 1 East Chang'an Avenue) captures the essence of Italy in a rustic dining atmosphere.

THIS PAGE (FROM TOP): Parisian chic rules the day at Le Pré Lenôtre; Made in China's dining spaces feature authentic touches of Chinese architecture.

OPPOSITE: The lively open kitchen of East 33, seen through a screen of Chinese motifs, invites curious diners to step in for a closer look — and a taste of its diverse East-meets-West menu.

beijing's nightlife

Many newcomers to China think Shanghai—with its pre-liberation reputation as the 'Paris of the East'—is where the action is. However, hip Beijing clubbers will tell you the ancient Chinese capital has the most exciting nightlife. Beijing has more budding bands than any other city in China, and a bevy of ku (cool) bars and clubs are opening all over the city to accommodate the growing demand for fun after sundown. Decades of staid Marxism and Maoism are giving way to Beijing rocking the night away.

Whoever said hotel lobby bars lack atmosphere? **Centro** (1/F, Shangri-La's Kerry Centre Hotel Beijing, 1 Guanghua Road), one of Beijing's sleekest cocktail lounges, has been going strong for four years and remains one of the places to be seen. This is no doubt due to the contemporary interiors, excellent cocktails, imported live jazz in the evenings, and the chance to rub shoulders with Beijing's who's who.

Step into **Face** (26 Dongcao Yuan, Gongti South Road) and be immediately transported into a whole different world. Think Orwell's *Burmese Days*. Chinese, Indian, and Southeast Asian artistic pieces are pleasingly placed around the walls, colonial furniture tucked away in the corners. Face has a subdued and seductively dark atmosphere, making it almost temple-like. This is a good 'mood' place for a drink before or after dinner. There are Thai, Indian, and Chinese restaurants just upstairs.

M Bar (6/F, Sofitel Wanda Beijing, Tower C, Wanda Plaza, 93 Jianguo Road) is situated in the stylish new Sofitel Hotel. This French-designed bar is known for its cocktails. There are some 16 different concoctions mixed with Moët & Chandon, and other creative combinations, such as the Vellini, a champagne cocktail made with vanilla vodka and strawberry liqueur.

Located in a corner of the restaurant of the same name, **Lan Club** (4/F, Twin Towers, B-12 Jianguomenwai Avenue) is Beijing's grooviest bar. Its eclectic design is the work of unconventional French designer Philippe Starck. In addition to an excellent collection of imported New World and European wines, live entertainment, and DJs in the evenings, Lan Club also has an oyster bar, cocktail lounge, cigar divan, and 45 private and VIP rooms.

Red Moon (1/F, Grand Hyatt Beijing, 1 East Chang'an Avenue), with its dark red interior and Asian touches, is one of Beijing's most chic hangouts. It has a sushi bar, a wine bar, and a cigar bar, and is stocked with an impressive selection of wines and premium whiskies. The mixed drinks are wonderful. Chinese musicians playing modern music on traditional Chinese instruments are a nice change from the usual lounge music.

The people over at **The World of Suzie Wong** (1A South Nongzhanguan Road, West Gate, Chaoyang Park) must be doing something right. Named after the 1950s Hong Kong love story, which starred William Holden and Nancy Kwan in the movie version, this is one of the few nightspots that has managed to stay hot over the years. Suzie Wong's attracts a loyal clientele with its old Peking furnishings, opium beds, dance floor, and large patio.

THIS PAGE (FROM TOP): *Beijing's hottest clubs play host to a stylish new elite of young big-spenders; the atmospheric Face.*
OPPOSITE: *The décor at Red Moon showcases its collection of fine wines and premium whiskies—and its dedication to those who enjoy a good drink.*

beijing's nightlife 29

beijing: a shopping sensation

Shopping has always been one of the best parts of a trip to Beijing, and there has never been a better time to shop here. Visitors who were once limited to a small number of shops selling pretty much the same things can now enjoy a wide variety of choices—from well-restored furniture and old porcelain in antique shops, to modern fashion items inspired by traditional Chinese designs, and outdoor flea markets, which offer surprisingly interesting items culled from all over China. Remember, however, that the city is knee-deep in factory-fresh antiques, so unless you are a leading expert on Qing dynasty porcelain, leave that Forbidden City vase where you saw it.

Bargaining is a way of life in all but the better-established shops and high-end shopping malls. Don't hesitate to offer an embarrassingly low price—even up to 70 per cent lower than the asking price.

malls

Beijing's newest and hippest mall is **Shinkong Place** (87 Jianguo Road), which offers the biggest collection of well-known luxury brands in the city, including **Chloé**, **Juicy Couture**, and **Marc Jacobs**.

The city's first real shopping centre was **The Malls at Oriental Plaza** (1 East Chang'an Avenue), just a few blocks west of the Forbidden City. Oriental Plaza features a wide variety of foreign brands as well as the better-known Chinese name brands. An added attraction is a cinema that screens both Western blockbusters and the best movies by China's directors.

The Place (9A Guanghua Road), located in the central business district, is probably as well-known for its enormous overhead digital screen, which broadcasts amazing and colourful graphics, as for the international brands it houses, such as **Zara**, **Mango**, **MAC** and **Apple**. It is also home to one of the city's few English-language bookstores.

specialist stores

Beijing Curio City (21 Dongsanhuan South Road) has four floors of more than 250 individual shops selling jewellery, porcelain, teapots, Buddhist

30 chinachic

statues, furniture, and a lot of kitsch. Many of the dealers here are themselves collectors, and the Beijing Curio City is supervised by the Beijing Cultural Relics Bureau. Be prepared to bargain hard and be on the look out for fakes.

C.L. Ma Furniture (Room 109–110, Building. 4, 6 Chaoyang Park South Road) sells both unrestored and restored antique Chinese tables, chairs, cabinets, and screens obtained from all over China, as well as nicely reproduced pieces. The company, which has its own professional restoration workshop, is owned by C.L. Ma, a well-respected furniture dealer and expert who has written several glossy books on traditional Chinese furniture. The company has been in business for more than 20 years.

Qianxiangyi (5 Zhubaoshi, Qianmen Avenue) has been in the silk business since 1840 and is the largest silk store in China. The shop carries a wide selection of silk bolts on its main floor, with tailors in house to custom-make clothing. Ready-made silk items can be purchased on the second floor. Another famous old silk dealer in the neighbourhood is **Ruifuxiang** (5 Dashilan Street, Qianmen Wai). Although it is the new kid on the block in this area, Ruifuxiang has been selling silk and other materials by the yard since 1893. It also offers a tailoring service. A qi pao takes about one week with several fittings. An express service is available for a slightly higher price.

Genuine hand-woven Tibetan rugs, based on traditional designs, can be purchased at the **Torana** Gallery (Lobby, Kempinski Hotel Beijing, 50 Liangmaqiao Road). These colourful rugs are made from sheep's wool in a factory in Lhasa. The high natural lanolin content of the wool, taken from sheep inhabiting areas above 4,570 m (15,000 ft), explains why the rugs are so soft, stain-resistant and resilient. Torana also sells antique rugs and textiles from Tibet and Xinjiang. These rugs are not cheap, but they are among the most beautiful items you can buy in China.

markets

Panjiayuan Market (18 Huawei Li, Panjiayuan Road) is Beijing's biggest outdoor market with some 3,000 vendors selling here. You'll find interesting pieces floating within this sea of factory-fresh antiques, such as porcelain, traditional paintings, snuff bottles, and woven baskets. The real stuff here, however, is gathered from all over China. There are quaint lanterns, wooden grain boxes carved with Chinese characters, porcelain, Tibetan cabinets, Tankas, paintings, ethnic outfits, and Mao memorabilia. There are small buildings ringing the outdoor market that sell high-end items, such as antique furniture and beautifully restored Chinese doors.

If you're looking for freshwater pearls, go to the **Hongqiao Market** (46 Tiantan East Road), which is just a few minutes' walk from the East Gate of the Temple of Heaven. The market sells a variety of freshwater pearls on the third and fourth floors. In addition to ready-made strands of freshwater pearls, you can also have pearls custom-strung or buy them separately.

THIS PAGE (FROM TOP): *Dazzling multi-hued pearls at one of Beijing's colourful outdoor street markets; Beijing is a shopper's paradise, offering everything from traditional silk handicrafts (left) to the latest fashion (below).*
OPPOSITE: *The popular Wangfujing pedestrianised shopping strip; shoppers will find a good mix of local and foreign designer boutiques in Beijing.*

spas in beijing

Until recently, if you wanted to enjoy a real spa, you would have had to jump on a plane for Hong Kong, Phuket, or Bali. No more. Beijing has seen an explosion in the number of spas around the city, the result of the large number of new world-class hotels arriving in Beijing, and the large-scale renovation of existing hotels gearing up for the Olympics.

a five-star experience

CHI, The Spa (Shangri-La Hotel, Beijing, 29 Zizhuyuan Road), located in the new Valley Wing of the Shangri-La, offers treatments and spa rituals inspired by ancient healing philosophies from China and the Himalayas. The CHI Balance treatment is just one of a range of signature therapies available.

Club Oasis (Grand Hyatt Beijing, 1 East Chang'an Avenue) features massage facilities, spa pools, and a solarium, among other amenities. The variety of facial and body treatments offered draw inspiration from the local environment and culture, and use Chinese natural ingredients.

For a Thai spa experience, visit **I-Spa** (InterContinental Beijing, 11 Financial Street). Exotic treatments, such as the Herbal Mud & Moor Body Wrap, complement traditional offerings like Shiatsu and foot reflexology. The signature experience, the InterContinental, combines traditional Chinese massage with Western aromatherapy techniques.

The new **Peninsula Spa by ESPA** (The Peninsula Beijing, 8 Jinyu Hutong, Wangfujing), Beijing's largest spa facility, boasts 12 state-of-the-art treatment rooms. Treatments include traditional Chinese, therapeutic aroma massage, gentle exfoliating body treatment, sports massage, and foot reflexology.

Occupying an entire floor of the hotel, **The Ritz-Carlton Spa** (The Ritz-Carlton Beijing, 1 Jinchengfang East Street) offers soothing relaxation lounges and 11 treatment rooms, including a signature suite featuring aquatherapy, an exclusive couples' suite with an Ann Sack soaking tub, two specially designed rooms for Thai massage, and three facial rooms.

Beijing's first luxury spa, the **St Regis Spa and Club** (St Regis Beijing, 21 Jianguomenwai Avenue), offers body massages, detoxifying therapies, rejuvenating facials, and more. Its jacuzzi uses natural hot spring water pumped up from deep beneath the hotel. Try the St. Regis signature treatment, a holistic combination of a full body deep-tissue massage and a revitalising facial, topped off with a nutritious meal.

small + personal

For a less expensive spa experience but in surroundings that are just as nice, visit **Oriental Taipan** (Sunjoy Mansion, 6 Ritan Road), which offers aromatic oil massages, facials, manicures and pedicures, and the popular foot massage.

Or, for a luxurious experience outside the realm of hotels, visit the award-winning **Zenspa** (House 1, 8A Xiaowuji Road), which offers full-day treatments in the tranquil setting of a traditional courtyard house. Its treatments include a four-handed massage, and its signature Burmese Thanaka facial.

THIS PAGE (CLOCKWISE FROM LEFT): *Warm and contemplative, CHI, The Spa, is based on a modern interpretation of a Tibetan temple; indulge in rest and relaxation—five-star spa-style—while in Beijing; Zenspa blends ancient architecture and modern minimalism to wonderful effect.*
OPPOSITE: *Club Oasis offers a welcome respite for the senses.*

beijing galleries + museums

Contemporary Chinese art is enjoying an unprecedented popularity. Young new Chinese artists, relatively unknown a few years ago, have become the hottest thing in the art world. With some individual works fetching more than US$2 million, entrepreneurs are rushing to meet the growing demand by opening galleries all over the city.

galleries

The **Dashanzi Art District** (4 Jiuxianqiao Road, Dashanzi), more popularly known as the 798 Factory, is home to galleries, cafés, and restaurants set up in a complex of old Bauhaus-style factories. Once occupied by manufacturers, the premises were taken over in the 1990s by a number of Beijing's finest artists attracted by the abundant space, low rent, and natural light flooding in via the large overhead windows. Today, there are regular exhibitions of installation art, ceramics, oil paintings, sculpture, performance art, and more. The annual Dashanzi International Art Festival is held in May.

CAAW (East End Art District, Nangao Road, Caochangdi Village), or the Chinese Art and Archives Warehouse, is the work of well-known artist Ai Weiwei, one of China's most innovative and outspoken artists. The gallery concentrates on cutting-edge young Chinese artists.

Expatriates have also been active in the local art scene. **One Moon Gallery** (Ditan Park, Andingmenwai), which sits in a beautiful Ming dynasty complex, was established by American Jan Leaming to promote the work of lesser-known contemporary Chinese artists who have not been exhibited before. Exhibitions change every two months. **Pékin Fine Arts** (241 Cui Ge Zhuang Xiang, Caochangdi Village) was opened by Meg Maggio, a long-time connoisseur of the Beijing art scene, to display the works of Asia's best and most creative artists. Visitors can experience both history and contemporary art at **Red Gate Gallery** (1/F and 4/F, Dongbianmen Watchtower, Chongwenmen), which is located in Beijing's sole remaining

tower from the Ming dynasty. Red Gate frequently shows the works of contemporary Chinese artists, while its second and third floors introduce the history of the surrounding Chongwen District. Red Gate is owned by Brian Wallace, who has been in the art business in China for some two decades.

museums

For a long time, museums in China were largely dusty displays of ancient archaeological finds sitting in dimly-lit glass cases. Today, they are going state-of-the-art and featuring a wider array of the country's exciting culture, past and present.

The privately-run **Beijing Mumingtang Ancient Porcelain Museum** (1 Huashi Beili) is a hidden gem. Its collection of some 50,000 pieces of ancient porcelain includes valuable pieces that were fired in the Ru kiln, once one of the five famous kilns in China, which dates back to the late Northern Song dynasty (960–1127) when porcelain-firing technology first emerged.

The **Beijing Planning Exhibition Hall** (20 Qianmen East Avenue) tells the story of urban planning in Beijing. Of particular interest is a scale model of the entire city—you can pick out your own hotel and the places you've visited—with photographs of outlying parts laid down on a photographic glass floor that can be walked on.

Previously a tiny hall tucked away on the side of the Confucius Temple, the new **Capital Museum** (16 Fuxingmenwai Road) has seven floors showcasing the colourful history and culture of ancient Beijing.

The **National Art Museum of China** (1 Wusi Road) is a state-run museum set up to exhibit and research the work of contemporary Chinese artists. It also frequently has large exhibitions of important art from around the world. Original paintings may be purchased here.

The **Poly Art Museum** (9/F, New Poly Plaza, 1 Chaoyangmen North Street) was founded in 1998 to bring important Chinese art back home to China. The museum concentrates on the acquisition of ancient bronzes, sculpture, and painting that are on sale around the world. The collection is divided into two galleries: early Chinese bronzes, and Buddhist scriptures carved in stone. On display are four bronze animal heads that were stolen from the Old Summer Palace by marauding British and French soldiers during the late Qing dynasty. The pieces were acquired for a hefty sum a few years ago at an international auction in Hong Kong.

The small **Xu Beihong Memorial Museum** (53 Xinjiekou North Road) is dedicated to the work of one of China's best-loved contemporary artists, Xu Beihong (1895–1953), best known for his life-like Chinese-style paintings of charging horses. The museum has an interesting collection of some of Xu's best works—oil paintings, watercolours, and sketches.

THIS PAGE (FROM TOP): *Contemporary Chinese art has captured the imagination of the art world; sculptures welcome visitors to a contemporary art exhibition held during an art festival in Beijing.*

OPPOSITE (FROM TOP): *Beijing's many art shows and photography exhibitions (below) attract people of all ages and from all walks of life.*

peking opera

There is probably no other art form in the world as versatile as Peking opera. An offshoot of pre-existing opera schools, jingxi, or the 'theatre of the capital', combines a mixture of skills, requiring artists to be part-gymnast, part-mime artist, part-singer and part-actor. Fans call it the quintessential Chinese art form. According to an old Chinese saying, 'Each word is a song, each movement a dance'.

Unfortunately, Peking opera today plays to half-empty theatres. Proponents of this ancient art form are not willing to concede defeat, but are seeking new ways to energise it in order to compete against new forms of entertainment.

Some opera troupes have been performing at schools, hoping to cultivate new ximi, or opera fans. Some troupes are putting on smaller performances, and even get into costume and make-up in front of the audience. Opera troupes are also borrowing techniques from the more popular modern theatre, TV and cinema. A few years ago, for example, the Beijing Opera Troupe won acclaim for its performance of *Water Thrown Before the Horse* by incorporating mime—a first in Peking opera. In 2007, another company staged an opera on the life of opera legend Mei Lanfang (1894–1961), and an opera troupe from Taiwan adapted Cao Yu's theatre classic *The Wilderness* for the opera stage, both using modern dress, acting techniques and props more commonly found on a Western stage. The two operas were performed in front of large and enthusiastic audiences.

performances

For those interested in enjoying the magical acrobatics and unique vocal style of Peking opera, there are a number of theatres around town with regular performances. These theatres all claim to offer English subtitles flashed stageside, but it is best to call ahead to check.

The clean and comfortable **Chang'an Grand Theatre** (7 Jianguomen Nei Road) stages authentic Peking opera, starring some of the city's top performers, for serious theatre-goers. All the legendary stars of Peking opera have also appeared on the stage at the **Huguang Guildhall** (3 Hufang Road), Beijing's oldest opera hall, which has been staging opera performances since 1807. The theatre was renovated recently to restore its original look. There is also an adjoining museum and a restaurant on the premises.

The **Mei Lanfang Grand Theatre** (32 Ping'anli West Road, north end of Financial Street, southeast corner of Guanyuan Bridge), named after China's most famous opera star, opened in November 2007. The three-storey theatre—the first modern hall specifically designed for opera performances—has state-of-the-art sound equipment and facilities, and special seating for the handicapped.

Visitors can enjoy the whole repertoire of Chinese folk art performances at the **Laoshe Tea House** (3 Qianmen West Road), named for Beijing's most beloved author. This teahouse puts on easily digested snippets of opera, martial arts, acrobatics and comedy catering to foreign audiences. Matinée and evening performances are held every day, and you can order simple snacks and tea at your table.

Most foreign tourists are introduced to Peking opera at **Liyuan Theatre** (Qianmen Hotel, 175 Yongan Road). This venue specialises in stories adapted from the classic *Journey to the West*, starring the amazing acrobatic feats of the Monkey King. A plus is that you can watch the performers apply their intricate make-up before the show.

For a feel of old Beijing, visit **Tianqiao Happy Tea House** (A1 Beiwei Road), a traditional theatre in the old opera district. The audience is seated at tables on the main floor and on the balcony overlooking the stage. Traditional snacks and tea are served during performances, which include operas and shows by acrobats, jugglers and contortionists.

museums

Those looking for a more leisurely experience of Peking opera can visit the fourth floor of the **Capital Museum** (16 Fuxingmenwai Road), which has exhibits on Peking opera, with a miniature opera stage and musical instruments on display. There is also the eponymous **Mei Lanfang Museum** (9 Huguosi Street), located in the beautiful former courtyard home of the famous Peking opera star, who excelled in his performance of the huadan role in Peking opera, where all female roles were played by male performers. The museum exhibits the actor's colourful costumes, personal effects, and beautiful black-and-white photos from his many performances.

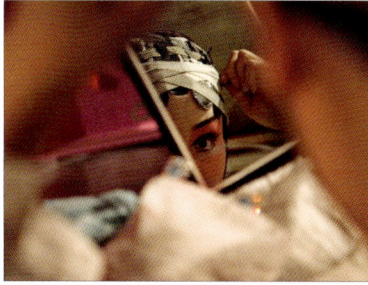

THIS PAGE (FROM TOP): Feathered headdresses, a spectacular feature of Peking opera costume; a performer painstakingly removes her elaborate costume; musicians playing traditional Chinese instruments provide the music behind the scenes.
OPPOSITE (FROM TOP): A contemporary opera performance utilising modern stage production values; the state-of-the-art Mei Lanfang Grand Opera Theatre.

peking opera 37

best views of beijing

There is no shortage of photo opportunities in Beijing, and wandering the city's old hutongs, imperial parks and temples in search of that perfect photo is all part of the fun. If you're lucky enough to be here on a snowy winter's day, you'll be able to photograph romantic snow-covered eaves on the roofs of temple buildings and courtyard houses.

In preparation for the 2008 Olympics, many aging sites have been given a much-needed makeover, so there's never been a better time to snap away in the city. Here is a list of hot spots to get you on your way to shooting the best mix of the old and the new that Beijing has to offer.

Without a doubt, the centuries-old **Forbidden City** (Chang'an Avenue, north of Tiananmen Square) is one of the city's premier spots for photo-taking. The complex, with its many varied vistas and its 9,999 imperial halls topped with golden tiles, is the best example of the ancient capital's imperial architecture. On a clear day, catch wonderful views of these rooftops from the top of **Jingshan Park** (Jingshan Qianjie) north of the Forbidden City.

Once the playground of the royal family, **Beihai Park** (1 Wenjin Street) has many interesting Qing dynasty structures and temples, all with a sprawling lake as a backdrop. For a great vantage point, take a short hike up a set of steps just north of the south gate to the top of **Hortensia Isle**.

The idyllic **Rear Lakes** area has quaint scenes of small boats on the water and people from the neighbourhood fishing and swimming—even in the winter months, when intrepid Beijingers cut out a large swatch of ice for their daily brisk swim. In the winter, you'll also find people skating on the lake or whisking their children across the ice in little sleds.

In the hutongs just off the lakes, one can find a treasure trove of bits and pieces of the city's wonderful old architecture. Keep an eye open for interesting old doors, a few rare ones still with Chinese couplets carved on them, and mendun, intricately carved stones for bracing the doors, which are decorated with auspicious motifs, such as dragons, lions, flowers and fruit. Panels over the doors also often have wood and stone carvings with traditional symbols.

Students of architecture will find a collection of old European buildings along the former **Legation Quarter** (Dongjiao Minxiang), the foreign ghetto at the turn of the 19th century. Especially interesting here are **St. Michael's Catholic Church** (13 Dongjiao Minxiang) the former **Bank of New York** (36 Dongjiao Minxiang) and the **Yokohama Species Bank** (corner of Dongjiao Minxiang and Zhengyi Road).

The sprawling **Temple of Heaven** (Tiantan East Road) houses the finest collection of religious architecture in China. This is also a great place for a bit of local colour: each morning the Chinese head here to practice taijiquan, sword fighting, and other forms of martial arts, as well as ribbon dancing, and mass ballroom and disco dancing. You'll also find a number of amateur Peking opera singers and musicians singing away under the corridors. Similar scenes can also be found in other imperial parks dating back to the Ming dynasty, such as **Ritan Park** (6 Ritan Road), or the Sun Altar Park, and **Ditan Park** (Andingmenwai Avenue), or the Earth Altar Park.

The sprawling **Summer Palace** (Yiheyuan Road), once a warm weather retreat for the emperors and entourage, is filled with Qing dynasty architecture, imperial halls, temples, arched bridges and beautiful lake views, which are especially picturesque when the sun sets. Enjoy amazing vistas from the top of **Longevity Hill**. The nearby **Old Summer Palace** (28 Qinghua Road) has the look of Greek or Roman ruins, with large Greek columns, stone water fountains, and arches turned over on their sides, left exactly as they were in the Qing dynasty, when marauding British and French troops rampaged through the palace.

If you are hoping to capture spectacular day and night views of shiny steel and glass structures in the **Central Business District**, you won't be disappointed with a visit to the bar on the 65th-floor of the new **Park Hyatt** (2 Jianguomenwai Avenue). One of the most impressive pieces of architecture that can be seen from here, or just about any place in this neighbourhood, is the new **CCTV Tower** (East Third Ring Road, just north of Jianguomenwai Avenue), comprising two L-shaped steel towers that join each other at a turned angle high above the ground.

Traditional scenes of the Great Wall rolling over the mountainside like a curling dragon can be had at **Mutianyu** or **Badaling**, two of the most popular tourist spots for viewing this ancient structure. To see the less renovated parts of the wall, go further out to **Simatai**, **Jinshanling** and **Huanghuacheng**.

For a look at rural China without going too far out of your way, visit the old Ming dynasty village of **Cuandixia**, about a two-hour drive outside of Beijing in Mentougou. This walled village has over 100 old farmhouses, and some of the walls still have fading slogans from the Cultural Revolution. Beautiful panoramic views of the village and valley can be seen from a hill overlooking the village.

THIS PAGE (FROM TOP): *The Hall of Supreme Harmony stands at the heart of the Forbidden City; a guard surveying the grounds of the Summer Palace; the awe-inspiring Temple of Heaven is the best remaining example of religious architecture in China.*

OPPOSITE: *A romantic picture of winter in Beijing—the city offers beautiful views in every season.*

bestviewsofbeijing 39

bayhood no. 9

THIS PAGE: *Private driving stations combine the best of golfing facilities with a luxurious setting.*
OPPOSITE: *Watch the action at the 18th hole from the clubhouse balcony.*

Considering Beijing's fame as a booming metropolis filled with towering skyscrapers and bustling streets, it is hard to imagine the existence of a spectacular 18-hole golf course only 30 minutes from the central business district. Yet, as of March 2007, a sprawling green has indeed sprung up in the luxurious guise of Bayhood No. 9.

The first Professional Golf Association-operated (PGA) course and academy in Asia, Bayhood No. 9 possesses a prestige and distinction that only the PGA brand affords.

Located in Beihu, the golf resort is set against a lush background of thick pine forests and placid lakes. Beihu was the site of a former imperial garden as well as an imperial hunting ground, and has a rich history that spans across more than 600 years. With such illustrious surroundings, teeing off at Bayhood No. 9 is an experience golfing enthusiasts cannot afford to miss.

It is easy to see why the prestigious magazine *Golfer's Digest* deems Bayhood No. 9 'one of the most impressive new resorts in the Far East'. Designed by renowned Canadian firm Nelson & Howarth Golf Course Architects, the championship course stretches across 80 hectares (198 acres), and promises to challenge even the most seasoned golfers. Manicured fairways meander through rolling hills and alongside plentiful water features, giving the course an open, countryside feel despite its close proximity to the city.

Understanding that focus is key in a good game of golf, players are accompanied by two trained caddies who attend to every need. State-of-the-art global positioning system (GPS) devices are also provided, placing Bayhood No. 9 at the forefront of golfing technology. Accurate to within one metre, the GPS system is used to indicate the exact distance between the player and upcoming obstacles, be it the bunker, the dog-leg, or the hole itself. With the owners of Bayhood No. 9 going to such lengths, each individual can be assured that their maximum potential will be achieved during the game.

...promises to challenge even the most seasoned golfers.

The golf academy is a world-class operation that utilises the expertise of the PGA and three highly trained, certified professionals. Coaching programmes are tailor-made for players of all abilities and ages, including children. Housed within the awe-inspiring, two-level driving range, the academy includes a short game area, with a par 3 course and two putting greens. The lower floor incorporates 40 driving stations, while the upper floor features 22 exclusive VIP suites. Each suite comes with double-bay driving stations out on the terrace and a stylishly decorated room to relax in. Flat-screen TVs, high-speed Internet access, and dining facilities are just some of the amenities offered within, providing guests with the utmost in style and comfort. Unrivalled in its sophistication, Bayhood No. 9 offers golf fanatics opportunites to practice their swing while enjoying the company of friends in supremely luxurious surroundings.

Also part of the academy are four high-tech indoor swing studios, fully equipped with cutting-edge gadgetry to detect faults and improve one's swing. These include The Trackman, a ball tracking device that uses radar technology to measure the movement of the club and the ball's subsequent flight, and the Dartfish, an advanced programme that compares movement and swing through video analysis and comes up with an in-depth study of a player's technical performance. Clearly, Bayhood No. 9 is unsurpassed when

The spacious lounge adds a dash of colour with its vibrant red cushions, while full-length windows flanking the building allow sunlight to stream in and bathe the entire clubhouse in a warm, golden glow. Guests seeking fresh air can partake light refreshments on the expansive balcony while appreciating the golf resort's sprawling green compound.

Having a meal at The Dining Room is an experience in itself. The restaurant is divided into 18 private dining rooms, each decorated with a theme that celebrates different aspects of Chinese culture and history. Designer lighting fixtures combine with contemporary oriental furnishings to create chic, sophisticated rooms. Accentuated by the impressive backdrop of the golf course, the versatility of each room makes the restaurant an ideal location for intimate dinner affairs as well as high-end product launches, glitzy exhibitions, and large-scale banquets.

A tantalising mix of Cantonese and Sichuan cuisines, The Dining Room's delectable menu is created by highly acclaimed chef Xu Longguo. Throughout his illustrious career, Chef Xu has served a long list of dignitaries, including Nelson Mandela and Jiang Zemin. Aesthetics is an important aspect of Chef Xu's signature style, and each dish is crafted and presented in such a way that nothing short of a culinary work of art is presented at the table. With such imaginative cuisine, any meal at The Dining Room is sure to be a multi-sensory gastronomic affair.

it comes to the various ways and means of improving one's game, setting the benchmark for future golfing developments in China.

The extraordinary golf course and academy are complemented by the lavish clubhouse and restaurant. A dynamic, neoclassical structure, the clubhouse is located at the 18th hole. Its strong, modern lines present a dynamic contrast to the serene lake and trees. No expense has been spared in making the clubhouse perfect for that post-game drink or get-together. Cool stone floors and timber beams create an air of calm, while gilt accents in the reception areas exude a stately elegance.

THIS PAGE: The lofty neo-oriental interiors of the clubhouse.

OPPOSITE (FROM LEFT): The restaurant's private rooms can be converted into function halls; Bayhood No. 9's world-class championship course.

...a host of good reasons to pay a visit to this verdant golf resort.

The luxurious spa is yet another way to enjoy the golf resort's lush grounds. With an extensive menu of facial and body treatments in store for both ladies and men, spa-goers will be delighted to know that all treatment products used are organic and specially blended for Bayhood No. 9.

Just a stone's throw away from the busy streets of Beijing, there are a host of good reasons to pay a visit to this verdant golf resort. However, with a boutique hotel, and fitness centre to be added to the golf resort's premises, there will soon be many more reasons to make a trip to Bayhood No. 9.

features
18-hole golf course • PGA golf academy • 40 driving stations • 9-hole night course • 2 putting greens • 22 VIP suites • clubhouse • high-speed Internet access • two-storey driving range

food
The Dining Room: Chinese fusion

drink
clubhouse lounge

nearby
Badaling • Forbidden City • Ming Tombs • Summer Palace

contact
9 Anwai Beihu, Chaoyang District, Beijing 100012 •
telephone: +86.10.6491 8888 •
facsimile: +86.10.6498 0078 •
email: info@bayhood9.com •
website: www.bayhood9.com

commune by the great wall kempinski

THIS PAGE (FROM LEFT): *A combination of luxury and nature will put the senses at ease; the surrounding beauty of the Commune.*

OPPOSITE (FROM LEFT): *Full-length windows open out to dramatic vistas; children will find much to enjoy with features like pool slides.*

Set in 8 sq km (3 sq miles) of private land in the Badaling Mountains near the Shuiguan section of the Great Wall, Commune by the Great Wall Kempinski is a remarkable collection of contemporary architecture. Designed by 12 renowned Asian architects, 46 exclusive villas are dramatically studded across the steep slopes of the valley, each offering panoramic views of the Great Wall as well as the lush greenery of the mountains.

An hour from Beijing, the Commune guarantees a unique and luxurious experience in a rural setting. The Commune's scenic landscape is ideal for a romantic getaway, a cosy holiday with family or friends, even a private party or corporate event. Originally comprising 11 villas and Presidential Suites ranging in size from 300 to 700 sq m (3,230 to 7,530 sq ft), each is individually designed by architects from across Asia. The Commune also recently opened an additional 31 villas based on four of its most popular designs.

One such design is the Suitcase House. Created by architect Gary Chang, the structure exhibits a humorous yet practical approach to modern living. Having entered the main chamber, guests might need a little help in finding their way around. The bedroom, bathroom, kitchen, and sauna are beneath floor hatches, leaving an expansive, open space unhindered by conventions of interior design. The roof terrace is also accessible via a pull-down staircase.

Another design is the Bamboo House. With four bedrooms, a glass-encased sitting room, and a sleek kitchen, this semi-rustic structure is inspired by the geometries of bamboo scaffolding. Bamboo slats cast evocative shadows across the slate floor and water features throughout the house.

...head out and experience firsthand the peace and beauty of rural China.

rooms
187 rooms • 3 suites • 32 villas

food
24 Café: light meals • Courtyard Restaurant: Chinese • The Terrace Lounge: Chinese and Western

drink
Pink Bar and Lounge • The Terrace Lounge

features
Anantara Spa • 24-hour butler service • clubhouse • fitness centre • helipad • high-speed Internet access • kids' club • pool • private road to the Great Wall

business
ballroom • 24-hour business centre • conference facilities • function hall • multilingual staff

nearby
Great Wall • Ming Tombs

contact
The Great Wall Exit at Shuiguan, Badaling Highway, Beijing 100022 • telephone: +86.10.8118 1888 • facsimile: +86.10.8118 1866 • email: reservations.thegreatwall@kempinski.com website: www.commune.com.cn

To cater to single guests and large groups, villas can be reserved by the room or as an entire group.

Roof terraces and lawns with breathtaking views of the Great Wall offer picturesque settings for reading and resting. The clubhouse includes a library, lounge, function hall, and pool, while the hotel's restaurants serve Chinese and Western cuisine using a wide range of locally grown organic produce. In addition, the world-famous Anantara Spa offers 15 treatment suites overlooking the mountains.

Without leaving their luxurious rooms, guests can stay connected to the world outside with satellite TV, DVD players, high-speed Internet access, and 24-hour butler service. However, with a private road leading direct from the hotel to the Great Wall, visitors may decide instead to head out and experience firsthand the peace and beauty of rural China.

Without a doubt, Commune by the Great Wall Kempinski offers an unsurpassed experience of one of China's most iconic, and magnificent historical sights.

grand hyatt beijing

The vibrant city reflected in its sleek glass windows, Grand Hyatt Beijing asserts a commanding presence at the intersection of Chang'an and Wangfujing avenues, where it is housed within Oriental Plaza—China's single largest commercial complex. Even as the hotel sits in the midst of China's surging commerce and strengthens its stake on modernity, it is also just five minutes from the Forbidden City, the seat of Imperial power during the great Qing dynasty. Such is the allure of Grand Hyatt Beijing, conveniently placed between old and new worlds.

Upon entering, visitors are greeted by the spacious lobby with its high ceilings, natural colours, and warm lighting. From there, guests are whisked off to one of the hotel's 11 luxurious room categories. Of note is the exclusive Presidential suite, with its marble floors, full-length windows and even a fireplace. There is also the newly refurbished Grand Executive suites, which offer a luxurious bedroom, spacious study, and kitchenette. If that is not enough, the Diplomat suites, which come with a full view over the Forbidden City, are bound to take one's breath away. Needless to say, all rooms provide goose-down duvets, crisp bedlinen, and marbled bathrooms, while furniture crafted from rich woods is complemented by local contemporary artwork.

Cuisine-wise, the hotel boasts a host of fine-dining restaurants to tickle the palate. Noble Court serves refined Cantonese fare, while Made In China is known for its signature northern Chinese dishes. Guests looking for a hearty Italian meal can head to Da Giorgio, while an international spread can be found at the Grand Café. Last but not least, Redmoon restaurant and bar offers various lunch menus and a multitude of cocktails to choose from.

THIS PAGE (FROM TOP): Experience the best of northern Chinese cuisine at Made In China; Relax in comfort and luxury by the hotel's tranquil pool.

OPPOSITE (FROM LEFT): The elegantly appointed Diplomat suites give guests an impressive view of the Forbidden City; the Fountain Lounge is ideal for informal gatherings.

...enjoy the best of high living in the historic city.

For physical and mental rejuvenation, the Club Oasis fitness centre is outfitted with a gym, spa pools, and massage services. The 55-m- (180-ft-) long indoor pool is a must-see. Swimmers will be enthralled by the pool's virtual sky, which features varying weather phenomena, while lounging about in a climate-controlled environment. To add to the illusion, lush palm trees and piped underwater music create a private tropical paradise in the middle of China's capital.

Grand Hyatt Beijing's stellar conference and banquet facilities will meet all social and business needs. Function rooms of varying sizes cater to all occasions, from receptions to meetings. The hotel also offers 'the residence', a unique concept that integrates three meeting rooms, two showcase coffee bars, a lounge area, and a private office into a comfortable and versatile function space. Exquisite Chinese artwork and dark wood interiors give a tasteful touch to any high-profile event.

Since its launch in 2001, the Grand Hyatt Beijing has received multiple accolades from both international and domestic media, including *Business Traveller China's* 'Best Business Hotel in Beijing' award in 2006 and 2007. With such an impressive reputation for assurance, guests can expect nothing less than the best of high living in the historic city.

rooms
707 rooms • 118 suites

food
Da Giorgio: Italian • Fountain Lounge: afternoon tea • Grand Café: international • Made In China: Chinese • Noble Court: Cantonese • Redmoon: sushi bar • The Patisserie: cakes and pastries

drink
Fountain Lounge • Redmoon: bar

features
Grand Club Lounge • high-speed Internet and Wi-Fi access • gym • indoor pool • massage services • spa pools

business
ballroom • business centre • limousine service • meeting and function rooms • secretarial services

nearby
National Grand Theatre • Forbidden City • Tiananmen Square

contact
1 East Chang'an Avenue, Beijing 100738 • telephone: +86.10.8518 1234 • facsimile: + 86.10.8518 0000 • email: grandhyattbeijing@hyatt.com • website: beijing.grand.hyatt.com

jw marriott hotel beijing

THIS PAGE: *Savour prime cuts within CRU Steakhouse's dramatic interiors.*

OPPOSITE (FROM LEFT): *Rooms are elegantly furnished in soothing colours; the Quan Spa is a luxurious retreat.*

With Beijing developing at a fast and furious pace, visitors to the city are becoming spoilt for choice when it comes to selecting a place to stay. There is one name, however, that stands out from the crowd for its exceptional service, attention to detail and supreme luxury—the JW Marriott Hotel Beijing.

With a prime location at China Central Place in the Chaoyang district, the hotel stands amid premium residential properties and world-class shopping malls. Housed in an eye-catching steel and glass edifice, the JW Marriott Hotel Beijing's interiors are a shining example of style and comfort. The soaring ceilings of the sleek, sumptuously appointed lobby provide a foretaste of the refined elegance to be found throughout the hotel. The rooms' contemporary feel is reflected in the natural wood and pressed leather furnishings, while crisp bedlinen and plump feather pillows promise a peaceful slumber.

As understated as the rooms might look, expect nothing less than state-of-the-art technology. High-speed Internet access and touch screen phones make working after-hours a breeze. DVD players, 42-inch LCD TVs, and rainfall showers entice guests to spend a quiet evening in.

...a shining example of style and comfort.

To banish the stresses of the day, a visit to the Quan Spa is indispensable. Focusing on the curative and cleansing properties of water, this haven of tranquillity offers a range of face and body therapies. Drawing on contemporary techniques and ancient Chinese beauty rituals, the spa is committed to ensuring guests' total relaxation.

Equally tantalising is the inspiring array of dining possibilities on offer, which are sure to delight demanding epicureans. Asia Bistro incorporates the very best of Asian cuisine, with four open kitchens serving mouth-watering specialities from China, India, Thailand, and Vietnam.

At CRU Steakhouse, gourmands can enjoy juicy steaks as well as a variety of the freshest seafood. With a cutting-edge meat aging room, chefs can ensure that all selected cuts are optimally aged and fully flavoured. For French food lovers, paradise comes in the form of the Pinot Brasserie. Here, traditional fare with an imaginative slant is served up in a casual, ebullient dining atmosphere.

And who could imagine a more ideal setting than the Loong Bar to unwind in at the end of the day? A sip on the signature Snafu Loong cocktail is guaranteed to set the senses alight with another memorable evening spent at the JW Marriott Hotel Beijing.

rooms
549 rooms • 39 suites

food
Asia Bistro: Asian • CRU Steakhouse: Western • Pinot Brasserie: French

drink
Lobby Lounge • Loong Bar

features
Quan Spa • health club • high-speed Internet access • pool • satellite TV

business
business centre • conference facilities

nearby
China Central Place • Beijing CBD International Golf Club • Forbidden City

contact
83 Jianguo Road, China Central Place, Chaoyang District, Beijing 100025 •
telephone: +86.10.5908 6688 •
facsimile: +86.10.5908 6699 •
email: mhrs.bjsjw.sr.reservation1@marriott.com •
website: www.jwmarriottbeijing.com

raffles beijing hotel

THIS PAGE: *Luxury, romance and glamour abound at the Raffles Beijing Hotel.*

OPPOSITE (FROM TOP): *Dining at East 33 is elegantly fashionable; oriental details accentuate the hotel's classic interior.*

The Raffles Beijing Hotel belongs to a handful of hotels in the world whose fascinating history is entwined with that of its city's. Constructed in 1917, the hotel has been the centre of Beijing's political, social, and cultural scene. This stunning beaux arts structure reopened in 2006 as part of Raffles Hotels and Resorts, and is now one of Asia's most celebrated hotels. A finer headquarters for exploring the city's treasures simply does not exist—the Forbidden City and Tiananmen Square are practically next door, making Raffles Beijing Hotel the favourite of celebrities and dignitaries alike.

Rooms here are the epitome of refined elegance, with sumptuous four-poster beds and polished timber floors off-set by rich,

A finer headquarters for exploring the city's treasures simply does not exist…

colourful fabrics and original oil paintings of old Beijing. Cleverly concealed in this palatial setting are high-tech fittings ranging from LCD TVs to high-speed Internet access, keeping guests in touch and entertained. There is even an on-call valet service to ensure guests' needs are attended to—yet another example of the outstanding service that has earned the hotel numerous illustrious awards from *Condé Nast Traveler* and other distinguished publications.

The Raffles Inc. executive suites may appeal to the business traveller, with added benefits such as complimentary refreshments and access to a private lounge. Meanwhile, the RafflesAmrita fitness centre offers the perfect opportunity to unwind before sampling the culinary delights of the hotel's restaurants.

East 33 is fast becoming one of Beijing's most fashionable eateries, with its mix of Chinese and Italian fare served from the central show kitchen's interactive display stations. Afternoon tea is served at La Vie, where all manner of pastries and cakes are accompanied by an impressive selection of teas. However, it is the fine French cuisine of Jaan that has everyone talking, and since it appeared on *Condé Nast Traveler*'s list of 'Hot Tables 2007', epicureans are travelling from far and wide to savour its sublime menu.

Perhaps it is the atmospheric Writers Bar, serving oysters, caviar, and the signature Beijing sling, that captures the true essence of Raffles Beijing Hotel—sophisticated, imbued with historical significance, and truly unforgettable.

rooms
147 rooms • 24 suites

food
East 33: Chinese and Italian • Jaan: contemporary French • La Vie: afternoon tea

drink
La Vie: tea lounge • Writers Bar

features
RafflesAmrita fitness centre • high-speed Internet access • indoor pool • LCD TV • on-call valet service

business
banquet and conference facilities • business centre • limousine service

nearby
Forbidden City • Silk Street Market • Tiananmen Square

contact
33 East Chang'an Avenue, Dongcheng District, Beijing 100004 •
telephone: +86.10.6526 3388 •
facsimile: +86.10.6527 3838 •
email: beijing@raffles.com •
website: www.beijing.raffles.com

the shangri-la hotel, beijing

With a prime location near Beijing's bustling business district, Shangri-La Hotel, Beijing is immensely popular with vacationers and business travellers alike. Voted one of 'the best hotels in Beijing' by the *Asiamoney Travel Poll* in 2008, it was also listed on *Condé Nast Traveller's* 2007 Gold List as one of the 'Top 75 Hotels in Asia' and recognised as 'The Best Business Hotel in China' by *Trend's National Geographic Traveler* in 2007.

In March 2007, the hotel completed its US$50-million expansion project. Located in a 17-storey glass tower, the new Valley Wing was unveiled, bringing its total number of rooms to 670. Guests residing in the Valley Wing can enjoy a host of benefits, beginning with exclusive access to the grand Valley Wing Lounge, the largest executive lounge among Shangri-La Hotels and Resorts worldwide. Complimentary breakfast is served here, followed by champagne, wines, and canapés, made available throughout the day. Other benefits include the complimentary use of meeting rooms and computers, while guests with their own laptops can enjoy free, unlimited wireless Internet access throughout the building.

THIS PAGE: *Plush comforts and swish luxury at Shangri-La Hotel, Beijing.*
OPPOSITE: *The lofty rooms at the new Valley Wing.*

...immensely popular with vacationers and business travellers alike.

The Valley Wing's premier rooms offer views of the capital's cityscape, or the hotel's expansive Chinese garden. Decorated along contemporary Asian lines, bedrooms feature a walk-in wardrobe, an en-suite bathroom, an adjoining lounge area, satellite TV, DVD players, and high-speed Internet access. Suites offer additional features such as iHome units and an in-room fax and copying machine for the convenience of hotel guests, while the exclusive Presidential Suite comes complete with personal butler service, a separate studio, and a private exercise area.

The original Shangri-La building—now named the Garden Wing—also offers many services and benefits. Rooms and suites enjoy views of the city or garden, and offer amenities that cater to its leisure and business travellers. The Garden Wing's Horizon Club, the exclusive club lounge for Horizon Club Room guests, features benefits ranging from complimentary food and beverages, to express check-in and check-out services.

CHI, The Spa, is another brand-new facility at the hotel. Covering 1,000 sq m (10,764 sq ft), it is equipped with 11 luxurious private suites. Treatment rooms are modern interpretations of a Tibetan temple and showcase Himalayan art. The combination of shimmering light, scented incense, and music from Tibetan singing bowls adds to the spa's serene atmosphere.

THIS PAGE: *Blu Lobster entices with its chic décor and innovative menu.*

OPPOSITE (FROM LEFT): *The soothing interiors of CHI, The Spa; the hotel's garden are styled on traditional Chinese design.*

All treatments are inspired by traditional Asian healing philosophies, targeted at restoring the balance between mind and body. The signature Himalayan Healing Stone Massage is particularly appealing to tired senses: a combination of hot stones heated in oils and herbs are used to restore vitality to the body, followed by a cool stone massage to de-stress the mind. Exercise enthusiasts can opt for the health club, where they will be spoilt for choice with the wide variety of fitness facilities, which includes the 25-m (82-ft) heated indoor pool, whirlpool, sauna, and steam rooms.

For an appreciation of Beijing's natural beauty, guests can embark on an hour-long cruise on the River Dragon. Commissioned exclusively by Shangri-La Hotel, Beijing, this 11-m- (36-ft-) long, traditionally-designed, 38-seat barge heads along the Chang River towards the Summer Palace, recreating the Imperial route that only members of the Chinese royalty had access to. The river tour offers picturesque views of ancient temples and charming courtyard houses by the riverbanks, and ends with a guided tour of the stunning, historical palace.

This feast of the senses continues within the hotel's dining establishments. The contemporary restaurant and cocktail lounge Blu Lobster enhances the dining experience with its inventive Western cuisine and its collection of one of the finest selection of Bordeaux wines in Beijing. Rated one of the 'Top 50 restaurants in China' by *Food and Wine* magazine, a meal at this sophisticated restaurant is guaranteed to be nothing short of an unforgettable experience.

The award-winning Shang Palace focuses on authentic Cantonese specialities. Lunch is an especially popular affair here,

...majestic surroundings and trademark Shangri-La hospitality...

with diners sampling the wide range of fresh dim sum while looking out over the hotel's immaculate gardens.

If a taste of the world is what one desires, head for Café Cha's all-day international buffet spread. The restaurant's open kitchen concept allows diners to view the talented chefs at work while awaiting their orders. Last but not least, the newly renovated Nishimura allows guests to savour Japanese favourites such as sushi, teppanyaki, and robatayaki in its private rooms and traditional tatami rooms, and to choose from the largest selection of sake in Beijing.

Less formal but no less charming are the Lobby Lounge and Cloud Nine Bar, where an extensive list of beverages and signature cocktails are served in a relaxed atmosphere accompanied by live entertainment. The Garden Bar and Terrace located in the hotel garden is set amid koi ponds and Chinese pavilions, offering a stunning view of the hotel's landscaped gardens, along with a variety of snacks and refreshments.

With its majestic surroundings and trademark Shangri-La hospitality, a stay at the Shangri-La Hotel, Beijing is bound to be a memorable experience.

rooms
640 rooms • 30 suites

food
Blu Lobster: contemporary Western • Café Cha: international • Nishimura: Japanese • Shang Palace: Cantonese

drink
Cloud Nine Bar • Lobby Lounge • The Garden Bar and Terrace

features
CHI, The Spa • executive club • health club • high-speed Internet access • indoor pool • satellite TV

business
airport butler • business centre • conference facilities • limousine service • meeting rooms

nearby
River Dragon Cruise • Houhai hutongs • Summer Palace

contact
29 Zizhuyuan Road, Haidian District, Beijing 100089 •
telephone: +86.10.6841 2211 •
facsimile: +86.10.6841 8002/3 •
email: slb@shangri-la.com •
website: www.shangri-la.com

shangri-la's kerry centre hotel, beijing

THIS PAGE: *Rooms are warmly decorated and come with high-speed Internet access.*

OPPOSITE: *The lobby's artful lighting and wood finishes emphasise its welcoming atmosphere.*

Located in Beijing's Chaoyang district, Shangri-La's Kerry Centre Hotel, Beijing sits at the heart of the city's diplomatic, commercial, and financial centre. With easy access to many of the capital's historic attractions, including the Forbidden City and Temple of Heavenly Peace, the stately hotel is an ideal base for both business and leisure travellers. Many sightseeing spots are also within walking distance. Guests can stroll among the tranquil greenery of Ritan Park, the lively bars along Workers' Stadium, and the bustling streets of the Silk Market.

Since its opening in 1999, Shangri-La's Kerry Centre Hotel, Beijing has received numerous accolades. Voted one of the 'Top Five Hotels' in Beijing by *Euromoney* in 2001, it has since garnered many prestigious awards, including *Travel + Leisure (China)* magazine's award as one of 'China's Top Hotels in 2007'.

...fuses signature hospitality with contemporary style.

As part of the Shangri-La group, the establishment fuses signature hospitality with contemporary style. Elegantly appointed rooms create a serene respite from the frenetic city outside. High ceilings, wood finishes, neutral tones, and Asian details form a stylish and modern haven for unwinding and recharging. Full-length windows with a dramatic view of Beijing's cityscape allow guests to embrace their spectacular surroundings in one of the world's most exciting cities. An expansive marble bathroom, DVD entertainment system, separate sitting area, 24-hour butler service, and even a menu offering various pillows make certain that no requirement goes unattended. High-speed Internet access, in-room fax machines, and large-screen televisions also keep guests up to speed in this fast moving city.

Sprawled across three floors and 6,000 sq m (64,560 sq ft), the hotel's Kerry Sports fitness centre impresses with its state-of-the-art facilities. Visitors can enjoy the five-lane 35-m (115-ft) indoor heated pool, relax in the luxurious jacuzzi, steam room, and sauna. For the children's entertainment, there is a dedicated plunge pool, and both indoor and outdoor playgrounds complete with slides, climbing frames, and playhouses.

Leisure activities aside, Kerry Sports is first and foremost a sanctuary for fitness enthusiasts. In addition to a fully-equipped gym, the fitness centre is fitted with an outdoor jogging and rollerblading track, indoor squash and tennis courts, an aerobics studio, and a recreation room for billiards, snooker, and table-tennis. A multi-function studio area incorporating an NBA-compliant basketball court can also double up as badminton courts, with a spectator seating capacity of 100.

As much the ideal accommodation for business travellers as it is for holiday-goers, Shangri-La's Kerry Centre Hotel, Beijing excels in providing unparalleled business support for its business guests. The comprehensive business centre provides full secretarial services along with private boardrooms for conducting important conference calls or meetings. One of the largest in the city, the Grand Ballroom, with its hi-tech audio-visual fittings provides ample space for conferences and functions.

Guests will be spoilt for choice with the hotel's various dining options. The stylish Bento & Berries is ideal for an informal, refreshing lunch, where a delicious array of Japanese deli items, freshly made sandwiches, and baked treats are served. The Coffee Garden's international buffet selection is a definite crowd-puller. Its spectacular open kitchen showcases an irresistible mix of sights and aromas, allowing diners to interact with the talented chefs while awaiting their expertly prepared orders. Throughout the restaurant, large potted trees, tall ceilings and huge open windows create a charming 'courtyard' atmosphere for both romantic dinners and warm gatherings.

Promising an authentic Chinese dining experience, The Horizon Chinese Restaurant excels in Cantonese and Sichuan dishes. Delicious dim sum, fresh seafood, and flavourful soups are just a foretaste of the exquisite menu that has enchanted diners worldwide. Antique furniture, intricate wooden screens, and silk cushions complete the look, emphasising the strong oriental theme of the establishment.

THIS PAGE (FROM LEFT): *Relax at Centro Bar and Lounge; it's sunny at the pool all year round.*
OPPOSITE (FROM LEFT): *Delectable cuisine is served at The Horizon Chinese Restaurant; stylish martinis at Shangri-La's Kerry Centre Hotel, Beijing.*

Attracting the city's most stylish and discerning residents...

For guests looking to engage in retail therapy, the adjoining Kerry Centre complex offers two levels and 13,000 sq m (139,931 sq ft) of high-end shopping. With direct access from the hotel, shopaholics can enjoy convenient access to designer boutiques, sports stores, custom tailors, jewellers, and cafés. The shopping centre's calming water garden will be sure to soothe guests after an intensive bout of shopping.

In the evening, head to one of Beijing's most popular nightlife spots—Shangri-La's Kerry Centre Hotel, Beijing's Centro Bar and Lounge. Attracting the city's most stylish and discerning residents, Centro Bar and Lounge is famous for its commitment to bringing in the best international music talents. Designed by Darryl W. Goveas of Pure Creative Asia, the fashionable bar is set against a funky interior of vivid pink and red hues. The bar itself is inset with lights and encased in a glass frame, creating a dramatic centrepiece at which guests can sample the vast selection of wines, cocktails, and spirits on display. Recently rated as one of 'The World's Seven Best Hotel Bars' by award-winning financial website TheStreet.com, Inc, the 24-hour, contemporary establishment serves as a hip setting for both daytime meetings and late night entertainment.

With its tasteful décor, exceptional service, and enjoyable amenities, Shangri-La's Kerry Centre Hotel, Beijing offers the perfect combination of sophistication and comfort for work, rest, and play.

rooms
464 rooms • 23 suites

food
Bento and Berries: delicatessen • Coffee Garden: international • The Horizon Chinese Restaurant: Cantonese and Sichuan

drink
Centro Bar and Lounge

features
aerobics studio • high-speed Internet access • indoor pool • indoor tennis courts • jacuzzi • multi-function studio • outdoor jogging and roller-blading track • recreation room • sauna • squash courts

business
ballroom • boardrooms • business centre • secretarial services

nearby
Silk Street Market • Ritan Park • Tuanjiehu Park

contact
1 Guanghua Road, Chaoyang District, Beijing 100020 •
telephone: +86.10.6561 8833 •
facsimile: +86.10.6561 2626 •
email: hbkc@shangri-la.com •
website: www.shangri-la.com

the opposite house

THIS PAGE: *The use of curtains give rooms a soft, flowing aesthetic.*
OPPOSITE (FROM LEFT): *Lush bedding, designer amenities, and abundant light promise guests a relaxing stay; oriental accents give furniture a subtle sophistication.*

Located in The Village at Sanlitun, the district's latest open-plan shopping development, The Opposite House promises to be a breath of fresh air among the other commercial establishments in the city. This boutique hotel has been designed to minimise all conventional boundaries: many of its walls and partitions have been replaced with screens and translucent materials, allowing an abundance of light and air to flow unhindered throughout the property.

Colour, texture, and materials used for the hotel's décor and furnishings are also chosen to appeal to the senses. Unpolished wood and stone are softened by the natural element of flowing water. Glass, mesh, and stainless steel provide complementary contrasts, evoking a quiet urbane feel that reflects the sophistication of new Beijing.

The Opposite House offers 89 studios, nine suites, and a penthouse. Designed by renowned Japanese architect Kengo Kuma, the hotel features modern comforts and conveniences that include luxurious bedding and premium bath essentials, LCD TVs, high-speed Internet access, and iPod docking stations. The complimentary well-stocked mini bar will be an added bonus for guests, while the hotel's emphasis on stellar service is evident from its flexible check-in and check-out policies.

Dining and entertainment choices abound at The Opposite House. Using only the freshest seasonal produce, international favourites are served up at the Village Café. The all-day dining establishment's partially open kitchen allows guests to watch the talented chefs work their magic as their meals are being prepared.

Seafood and hand-made pastas take centre stage at Sureño, a contemporary, casual Mediterranean restaurant. Its inviting dining atmosphere is accentuated by a large wood-fired oven in the centre. Sureño's authentic, delectable creations are inspired by carefully sourced ingredients from the cuisines of southern Europe.

For avant-garde renditions of Japanese, northern Chinese, and Korean cuisine, head to Bei. Expect the unexpected as traditional Asian dishes are given modern reinterpretations. Armed with exquisite knife skills, the itamae at the raw bar offer the finest sashimi. Presented with style and flare, Bei's menu presents the finest in contemporary Asian cuisine.

The sophisticated Mesh is the place where the fashionable gather to see and be seen. Excess comes in small doses here with innovative cocktails served in little sets, a foretaste of the bar's extensive drinks list. Over at Punk, edgy luxury is amplified by a dark, lush interior. Only the coolest underground beats spin on its decks, making the club one of the hippest in the capital.

Sanlitun is famous for its concentration of bars and clubs, inviting guests to go out and explore Beijing's social scene. For a refined dose of urban culture, however, look within The Opposite House.

...evoking a quiet urbane feel that reflects the sophistication of new Beijing.

rooms
89 studios • 9 suites • 1 penthouse

food
Bei: North Asian • Sureño: Mediterranean • Village Café: international

drink
Punk: club • Mesh: bar

features
flexible check-in and check-out policies • gym • high-speed Internet access • massage treatment rooms • paperless check-in • private dining rooms

business
event space • limousine service

nearby
The Village at Sanlitun • central business district

contact
Building 1, 11 Sanlitun Road
Beijing 100027 •
telephone: +86.10.6417 6688 •
facsimile: +86.10.6417 7799 •
email: answers@theoppositehouse.com •
website: www.theoppositehouse.com

jaan at raffles beijing hotel

THIS PAGE: *Contemporary touches update the restaurant's classical layout.*

OPPOSITE (CLOCKWISE FROM LEFT): *Culinary creations that please both the eye and palate; only the finest cutlery and glassware grace Jaan's tables.*

Already an establishment of legendary repute, the magnificent Raffles Beijing Hotel reopened its doors in 2006 after extensive restoration. Peerless in customer service, luxury and attention to detail, this hotel par excellence has swept Beijing by storm. However, it is the fine French cuisine served at its signature Jaan restaurant that has caused a commotion with international food critics, who rank it among the world's top restaurants.

Serving 'the city's finest French cuisine', Jaan was elected by *Condé Nast Traveler* for inclusion in its highly prestigious 'Hot Tables 2007' list, making it one of the world's 95 best eateries. This achievement is all the more impressive considering that the magazine's reporters travel incognito to evaluate new restaurants across a staggering 30 countries. It is no coincidence that the Raffles Beijing Hotel itself was also selected as one of the world's 65 best new hotels.

It is not surprising that the Raffles Beijing Hotel serves exquisite French food. When it first opened in 1917, it rapidly acquired a reputation for being the 'number one hotel in the Far East', and housed a first-class French restaurant. In a gesture aimed at recapturing the mystique and sophistication of bygone days, today's Jaan occupies the very same majestic space within the hotel, overlooking the glorious Chang'an Avenue and retaining many of its historic features. For example, the timber-sprung dance floor that made the hotel the focal point of entertainment for the city's glitterati during the 1920s has been faithfully restored, while the century-old Bösendorfer piano retains pride of place as the restaurant's centrepiece.

An atmosphere of refined elegance pervades Jaan: diners sit beneath the high, vaulted ceiling hung with period chandeliers, amid gilt, antique details that evoke the glitz and glamour of another era. This classical setting also has a contemporary flair—cream

...inspired by tradition, yet extremely imaginative.

marble floors and crisp linen tablecloths contrast with the rich silks and damasks of upholstered seats, creating a dining ambience that is both sophisticated and timeless.

It goes without saying that the food served at Jaan is nothing short of exceptional. With an emphasis on seafood, the seasonal à la carte lunch and dinner menus combine modern French and Mediterranean cuisines to create meals that are both light and innovative. In addition, a spectacular six-course dégustation menu brings together sublime culinary craftsmanship with premium wines.

Using the freshest and finest ingredients, Jaan's talented team of chefs create succulent dishes that are inspired by tradition, yet extremely imaginative. The subtle textures, flavours and colours of every dish are carefully taken into consideration and artistically styled. The result is a visual and culinary sensation rarely experienced. Displayed in the restaurant's glass wine cellar, Jaan's extensive selection of prestigious French and New World vintages offer diners the perfect complement to every unforgettable meal.

Beijing may not be the most obvious place to dine on French cuisine. However there are few places in the world that can compare to Jaan. The original French restaurant was a personal favourite among historical personalities such as Henri Cartier-Bresson, Charles De Gaulle and Dr Sun Yat-sen. With its culinary expertise and excellent service, Jaan has effortlessly carried on this tradition of excellence and surpassed it by being a destination restaurant in its own right.

seats
64

food
contemporary French

drink
French and New World wines

features
colonial setting • open kitchen • elegant design

nearby
Forbidden City • Silk Street Market • Tiananmen Square

contact
Raffles Beijing Hotel, 33 East Chang'an Avenue, Dongcheng District, Beijing 100004 •
telephone: +86.10.6526 3388 •
facsimile: +86.10.6527 3838 •
email: beijing@raffles.com •
website: www.beijing.raffles.com

my humble house at china central place

THIS PAGE: *The hip, stylish interiors of My Humble House at China Central Place.*

OPPOSITE (FROM LEFT): *An artistic dining ambience is bound to whet guests' appetites; creations at My Humble House taste as good as they look.*

Located in Beijing's Xicheng district on the west of Houhai Lake, China Central Place is one of the capital's newest and most prestigious landmarks. This vibrant commercial and business development is also home to the luxury hotels of the Ritz-Carlton and JW Marriott groups, state-of-the-art offices as well as a sprawling shopping complex. Easy access to Beijing's most celebrated sights seals its position as one of the must-visit locales in the city.

My Humble House at China Central Place is one of the top restaurants here. It opened in February 2006, following the success of My Humble House at The Oriental Plaza, also in Beijing. Like its sister restaurant, My

...a delightful juxtaposition of traditional Chinese and contemporary elements.

Humble House at China Central Place has also been presented with the prestigious 'International Star Diamond Award' by the American Academy of Hospitality Sciences. Both restaurants are part of the award-winning, Singapore-based Tung Lok Group of restaurants that can now be found in 30 locations across Asia, including Singapore, China, Indonesia, Japan, and India.

Instead of the Zen-like minimalism of My Humble House at The Oriental Plaza, the China Central Place outlet exudes a sultry, urban sophistication. Dark woods and sombre hues contribute to a sense of intimacy and warmth. Chrome stools and leather sofas create a cosy den for stylish pre- or post-dinner drinks at the bar. Discreet booths behind elegant screens of bright chrome give diners greater privacy. Vast windows overlook the lush greenery of a small park below, allowing natural light to stream into the richly furnished interior.

Innovative lighting systems are used to their full advantage throughout the space. Designer lighting by Swiss-based Belux and German designer Ingo Maurer—including his signature Zettel, Birdie, and Jinken lamps—are carefully placed in a zigzag pattern, further adding to the sense of stylish intimacy.

Inspired by ingredients from around the world, the talented chefs at My Humble House use traditional and modern Chinese cooking methods to create a mouth-watering menu of new Chinese cuisine that has become renowned for both its inventive taste and dramatic presentation. Interesting appetisers include Tuna Tartar with Mango Salsa in a Popiah Cone, and Lime Sherbet in Lemongrass Jelly. Main dishes feature delicacies such as the ever popular Bamboo and Wine-Marinated Chicken with Honshimeiji and Asparagus.

While the restaurant sees a steady stream of guests for lunch and dinner, the afternoons cater especially to hardcore dim sum fans. The exquisite flavours of its traditional dim sum dishes alone is enough to make My Humble House a celebrated restaurant.

My Humble House at China Central Place is a delightful juxtaposition of traditional Chinese and contemporary elements, setting the trend for fine-dining in Beijing. Diners are sure to revel in the exceptional dining experience that My Humble House offers.

seats
150

food
contemporary Chinese

drink
extensive wine list • cocktails

features
bar and lounge area • semi-private dining rooms

nearby
China Central Place • Houhai Lake • Xicheng

contact
2/F Club House, Block 19, China Central Place, 89 Jianguo Road, Chaoyang District, Beijing 100025 •
telephone: +86.10.6530 7770 •
facsimile: +86.10.6530 7771 •
email: mhh2@tunglok.com •
website: www.tunglok.com

my humble house at the oriental plaza

THIS PAGE: *The spectacular glass roof allows guests to dine under the stars.*

OPPOSITE (FROM LEFT): *Artistic lighting gives the restaurant its distinctive character; innovative Chinese cuisine at My Humble House.*

Regularly featured in the media, My Humble House at The Oriental Plaza has been the recipient of numerous awards and accolades as one of China's best restaurants—the latest award being the prestigious and coveted 'International Star Diamond Award', bestowed by the American Academy of Hospitality Sciences.

My Humble House has become a favourite for tourists, expatriates, and locals seeking a unique dining experience in Beijing. There are two locations in the capital, each distinct from the other. The one perched atop The Oriental Plaza—China's largest shopping mall—is a minimalist gem. My Humble House at The Oriental Plaza is

...uniquely Chinese in taste, yet global in its appeal.

also a moment's walk from some of the city's most visited sights, such as the Forbidden City and Tiananmen Square.

The restaurant was opened in Beijing by the Singapore-based Tung Lok Group in November 2004, following the success of My Humble House in Singapore. This award-winning restaurant concept can now be found in major cities across Asia.

Designed by Japanese architect S. Miura, My Humble House at The Oriental Plaza lies beneath a spectacular arched glass roof. This imposing structure is accentuated by the pastel colours of the interior, creating a spacious and inviting dining atmosphere. Glass wine cabinets displaying Old and New World vintages partition the restaurant, creating private dining areas that allow for cosy, intimate meals.

Although minimalist in design, extravagant accents give the restaurant an irreverent touch. Embroidered cushions adorn leather armchairs, while the restaurant's custom-made tableware is eclectic in terms of shape and design. In one corner, an alcove has been transformed into a library, displaying lifestyle and cookery books for guests to browse through as they await friends.

In the day, light streams through the full-length windows, giving the restaurant a light and airy atmosphere. High-flying executives gather for business lunches as socialites take their time savouring the various culinary delights. As evening falls and candles are lit, romantic dinners and lively celebrations take centrestage, set against the stunning backdrop of the night sky.

My Humble House offers new Chinese cuisine—uniquely Chinese in taste, yet global in its appeal. Traditional and modern cooking methods are fused with fresh ingredients sourced from all over the world. Priding itself on its exceptional creations, the restaurant ensures that its food presentation is nothing short of a refined art form. The result is a meal that is appealing to both the eye and the palate.

From its refreshing, innovative cuisine to its sleek interiors, the versatility that My Humble House at The Oriental Plaza is known for promises diners a memorable experience, again and again.

seats
120

food
modern Chinese

drink
extensive wine list • cocktails

features
bar • library • private dining rooms • showpiece glass roof

nearby
Oriental Plaza • Forbidden City • Temple of Heaven • Tiananmen Square

contact
Beijing Oriental Plaza, Podium Level, W3, #01-07, 1 East Chang'an Avenue, Dongcheng District, Beijing 100738 • telephone: +86.10.8518 8811 • facsimile: +86.10.8518 6249 • email: mhh@tunglok.com • website: www.tunglok.com

cottage boutique

THIS PAGE: *The Cottage Boutique's eclectic furnishings give the shop a whimsical charm.*

OPPOSITE (FROM LEFT): *The showoom is decorated to resemble actual living spaces; charming dinnerware gives an exotic touch to table settings.*

Beautifully decorated and offering everything imaginable for the home, Cottage Boutique is a shopper's haven. Designed to resemble a house, visitors can wander through the impeccably furnished rooms to discover a treasure trove of Asia's antiques. A stroll through will give visitors an insight into China's vibrant past.

Previously situated in Silk Street Market, the shop was named after its original location, which occupied a space of just 20 sq m (215 sq ft). Its present, and larger, premises are in Chaoyang district, the heart of Beijing's diplomatic, commercial, and financial centre.

The antique shop combines a stunning showroom with intricate furniture, and uses vibrant colours and tactile fabrics to enhance its eye-catching pieces. On hand is owner Rebecca Hsu, whose expertise and infectious enthusiasm will instil a passion for antiques in even the most jaded shopper. Visitors are welcome to enjoy a cup of tea with Rebecca as she relates anecdotes of the various pieces collected over the years.

Each room is beautifully designed, with the walls, shelves, floor, and even ceiling overflowing with artefacts. Beautifully restored antique chests, chairs, screens, and tables abound, while silk cushions, throws, and table runners create a vibrant contrast against the rich dark woods. Tables are laid out with exquisite ceramics, jewellery, candles, vases, and photo-albums—in fact, anything that has caught Rebecca's eye during her travels can be found displayed along the shelves of the enchanting Cottage Boutique.

Inspired by a passion for art, travel, and film, Rebecca frequently travels across Asia, collecting intricate pieces and unique gift ideas. For three months each year, she trawls through the remote regions of China as well as Southeast Asia in search of antiques.

...sure to draw those looking for an experience that's a little off the beaten track.

products
ceramics • furniture • gifts • jewellery • textiles

features
antique furnishings • modern lifestyle products

nearby
Forbidden City • The Orchard • Tiananmen Square • Ritan Park

contact
4 North Ritan Road, Chaoyang District, Beijing 100020 •
telephone: +86.10.8561 1517 •
facsimile: +86.10 8561 1517 •
email: rebecca0929@yahoo.com •
website: www.cottage-china.com

Each piece is painstakingly shipped back and carefully restored to its former glory. A fervent supporter of local talent, Rebecca also constantly promotes up-and-coming artists by exhibiting their latest designs and works on the walls of her boutique. As such, a browse through the store's dizzying assortment of eclectic goods might yield contemporary one-off pieces created by talented designers from Beijing's avant-garde art scene.

Situated within a tiny artisan's enclave of galleries and picturesque cafés overlooking Ritan Park, the Cottage Boutique enjoys a charming ambience of calm and tranquillity. Just a short walk away from the mega malls of The Orchard and China World, the Cottage Boutique's artistic vibes, intimate atmosphere, and beautiful works are sure to draw those looking for an experience that's a little off the beaten track.

cottage warehouse

THIS PAGE: *Cottage Warehouse's ample space displays antiques to their best advantage.*

OPPOSITE (FROM LEFT): *Chinese furnishings and Southeast Asian details create an eclectic atmosphere; abstract paintings give the warehouse a modern touch.*

The opening of Cottage Warehouse was the fortuitous result of owner Rebecca Hsu's Cottage Boutique running out of space. Located in southeast Beijing's commercial warehouse district, Cottage Warehouse displays a diverse and stunning selection of antique Asian furniture and contemporary artworks, making the warehouse a not-to-be-missed destination for any homeowner.

Spread over 2,400 sq m (25,833 sq ft), the variety in this warehouse is remarkable. Housing an impressive range of Chinese antiques, visitors can be assured of finding a piece that will fit perfectly at home.

Cottage Warehouse's collection also extends to finds from Southeast Asia. For three months of the year, Rebecca travels throughout the region in search of unique pieces to bring back and restore.

Visitors to the warehouse are given informative guided tours through its extensive array of artefacts, while Rebecca and her helpful staff are on hand to provide invaluable advice on antique maintenance. For instance, a vase of flowers placed on an antique table adds moisture to an air-conditioned room, thus preventing the table from drying up.

...an inspirational mélange of traditional design and contemporary elegance...

products
Chinese and Southeast Asian antiques • contemporary artworks • modern designer furniture

features
bespoke service • regular art events and exhibitions

nearby
Ritan Park • Temple of Heaven

contact
4 North Ritan Road, Chaoyang District, Beijing 100020 •
telephone: +86.10.8561 1517 •
facsimile: +86.10.8561 1517 •
email: rebecca0929@yahoo.com •
website: www.cottage-china.com

Rebecca also has a passion for modern art, made evident by Cottage Warehouse's wide variety of abstract furnishings and artworks. From ancient Tibetan chests to avant-garde art, the Cottage Warehouse is an inspirational mélange of traditional design and contemporary elegance—a combination that would look great in any home.

Unsurprisingly, Cottage Warehouse is also a key outlet for some of Beijing's most experimental art installations. It doubles up as an exhibition space, hosting art and design events all year round. For art lovers, this is the perfect place to experience the best of old and new Chinese art in a setting that is, itself, unusual and evocative.

the village at sanlitun

Spread over an area of 53,000 sq m (570,487 sq ft), The Village at Sanlitun is set to re-invent the old neighbourhood of Sanlitun when it launches its first phase in the summer of 2008. Encompassing 19 building developments at the corner of Beijing's Gongti Beilu and Sanlitunlu, this all-in-one entertainment destination has exciting things in store, from designer boutiques and clubs, to cinemas and exhibitions. Combined with stunning contemporary architecture, The Village at Sanlitun will essentially be a fashionable, ultra modern hub that will have the world talking.

The commercial centre is regarded by many as a symbol of Sanlitun's rebirth. It is poised to be a 'funkier extension' of Beijing's central business district, injecting the area's nightlife with an added hip factor. The project's general manager says The Village at Sanlitun will become 'the cradle of rejuvenation of the entire Sanlitun area.'

THIS PAGE: **Modernity meets simplicity: two of The Village North's 'Diamond' buildings.**

OPPOSITE (FROM LEFT): **Alleyways in The Village South; The Maple Building in The Village South catches the afternoon sun.**

...an ultra modern hub that will have the world talking.

shopping
accessories • art and culture events • bars • cinemas • fine dining restaurants • high fashion stores • lifestyle shops

features
boutique hotel • open-plan leisure, culture and shopping community • multi-function hall with roof terrace

nearby
Sanlitun • embassy area • Workers' Stadium • central business district

contact
No.11 and No.19 Sanlitun Road, Chaoyang District, Beijing 100027 • telephone: +86.10.6536 0588 • website: www.thevillage.com.cn

The ambitious development consists of two parts. The south zone is the designated retail area covering a total floor area of 72,000 sq m (775,003 sq ft), in which 11 four-storey retail blocks will stand. A lofty multi-function hall—The Orange—with an expansive roof terrace shares the space. The north zone, slated to open six months after The Village South, will offer another seven four-storey retail blocks boasting international luxury labels such as Versace, Kosta Boda Orrefors, and Rolex. The Opposite House, an exclusive 99-room boutique hotel managed by the Swire Group, will also be situated on the grounds.

Size matters at The Village at Sanlitun, and the project will house China's largest Montblanc boutique and Asia's largest Puma store. Aiming to be at the forefront of cutting-edge fashion, it will also be home to the world's largest Adidas outlet, spanning 3,160 sq m (34,014 sq ft). A 1,700-seat, eight-screen cinema, along with more than 30 restaurants and bars in the vicinity will provide guests with a plethora of dining and entertainment options. The complex's 'no traffic' policy also provides visitors with a leisurely environment to shop and dine in. In a city notorious for being incredibly unfriendly to pedestrians, The Village at Sanlitun's shopping concept will undoubtedly come as a welcome surprise.

Designed by a team of architects from countries and cities as diverse as Britain, Hong Kong, New York and Japan, the shopping development will serve as a complementary counterpoint to the historical neighbourhood of Sanlitun, giving the area a well-deserved makeover. With its chic establishments and avant-garde surrounds, The Village at Sanlitun is set to herald China's new era—one that is cosmopolitan, forward-looking, and dynamic.

zenspa

THIS PAGE: *Vibrant reds and a calming water feature bring harmony to the ancient structure.*

OPPOSITE (FROM LEFT): *Indulgence at Zenspa; aromatherapy candles create a soothing atmosphere.*

Located in a *siheyuan* (traditional courtyard house), Zenspa is a sharp contrast to Beijing's frenetic lifestyle, providing a tranquil and luxurious retreat in the midst of China's bustling capital. Offering full-day treatments, Zenspa invites visitors to take time off and admire the beautiful, centuries-old architecture, while relaxing in the open courtyard or one of the spa's private treatment suites.

While the exterior retains all the original features such as curved tiled roofs, beautifully restored lattice screens and wooden columns in brilliant red, the interior is strikingly minimalist. Created by Match It's acclaimed founder and designer David Ng, Zenspa's layout incorporates elements of antique furniture, stones, and wooden planks to create a modern yet natural atmosphere. The

A tranquil and luxurious retreat in the midst of China's bustling capital...

Hong Kong-based designer uses his signature lacquer boxes in vivid colours to complement the rustic tones of the surrounding bare wood. With a contemporary tension pool, precise stone cladding, and customised furniture, the overall visual effect is simply stunning.

With its holistic approach to the physical and spiritual well-being of its guests, Zenspa has since received *SpaAsia*'s 'Best Spa National Category (China) Readers Choice Award' in 2007. The spa also has one of the widest selections of treatments in the city, and guests can choose from naturopathy, clinical aromatherapy, and Ayurvedic Shirodhara therapies, as well as Thai and Indonesian herbal massages. In addition, two saunas and a relaxation area are available for visitors to unwind in.

One of the most luxurious treatments offered at Zenspa is the four-handed massage, which has been likened to a choreographed dance with masseurs working in perfect unison to eliminate stress and tension. Also available are specially designed spa packages that begin with an invigorating scrub and wrap. The treatment ends with a thorough massage and a rejuvenating facial treatment—such as Zenspa's signature Burmese Thanaka facial—to add a glow to the body.

Guests are encouraged to enjoy Zenspa's soothing ambience upon the completion of their treatments so as to maintain their peaceful state of mind. A lounge area and a bar which serves healthy snacks and juices provide ideal surroundings for relaxation.

rooms
1 reflexology treatment room • 5 rooms • 4 suites

features
facials • lounge • massages • reflexology • snack bar • spa treatments

nearby
Beijing Amusement Park • Temple of Heaven Park • Ancient Observatory

contact
House 1, 8A Xiaowuji Road
Chaoyang District, Beijing 100023 •
telephone: +86.10.8731 2530 •
facsimile: +86.10.8731 2539 •
email: info@zenspa.com.cn •
website: www.zenspa.com.cn

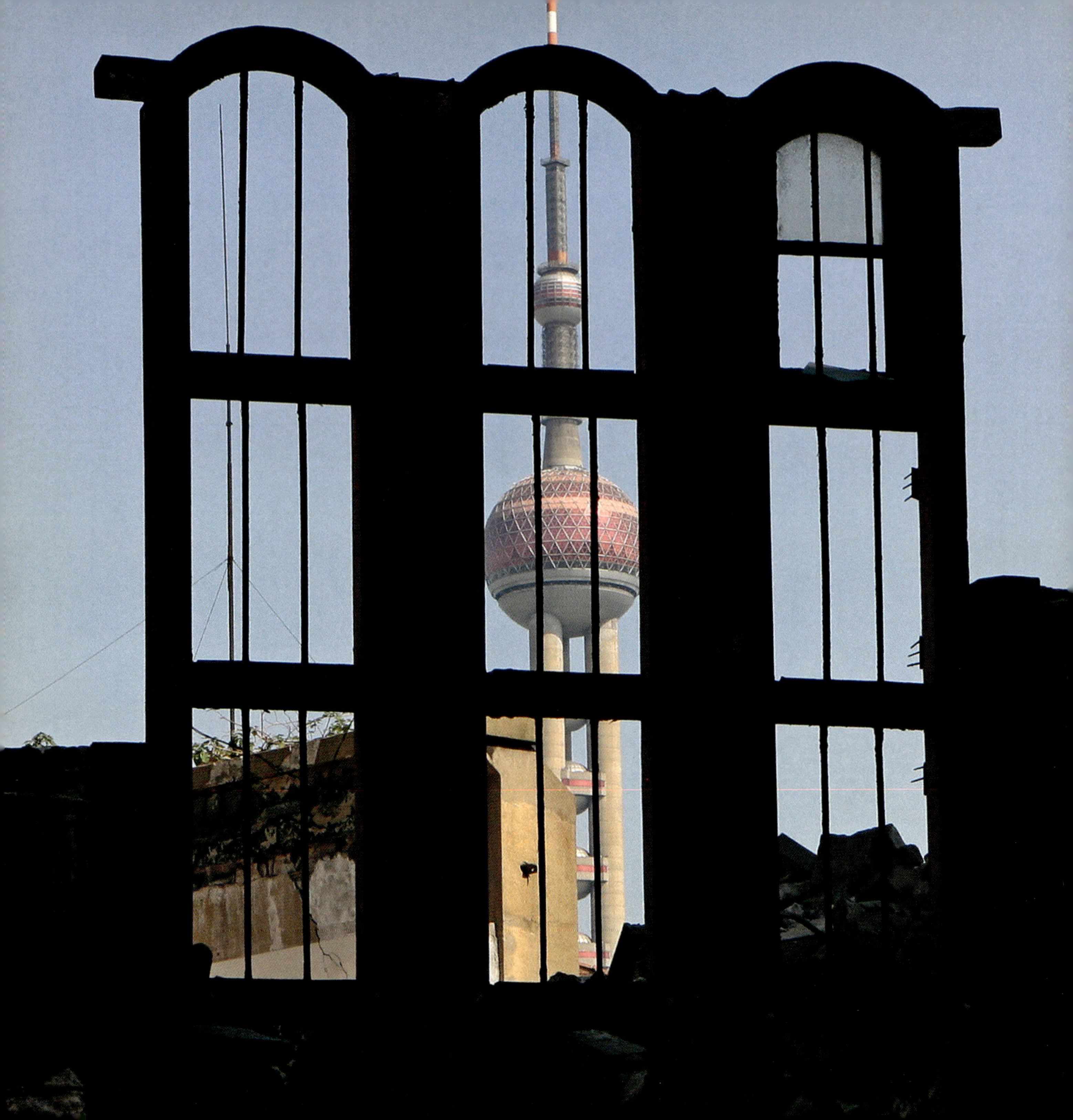

shanghai

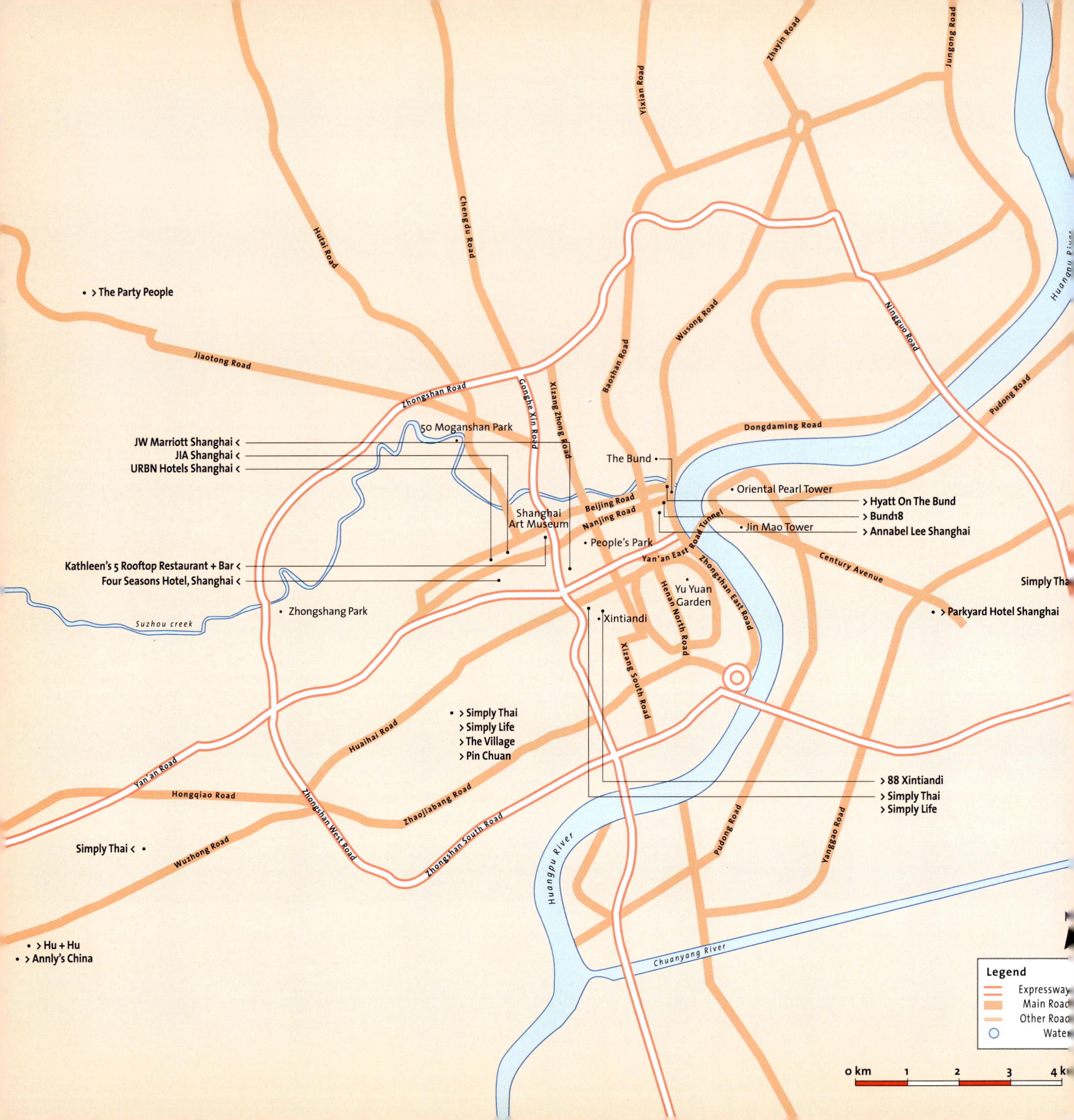

> The Party People
Jiaotong Road
Hutai Road
Chengdu Road
Yixian Road
Zhayin Road
Jungong Road
Huangpu River
Wusong Road
Baoshan Road
Ningguo Road
Zhongshan Road
Gonghe Xin Road
Xizang Zhong Road
50 Moganshan Park
JW Marriott Shanghai <
JIA Shanghai <
URBN Hotels Shanghai <
Dongdaming Road
Pudong Road
The Bund
Oriental Pearl Tower
> Hyatt On The Bund
> Bund18
> Annabel Lee Shanghai
Jin Mao Tower
Beijing Road
Nanjing Road
Shanghai Art Museum
People's Park
Yan'an East Road Tunnel
Century Avenue
Kathleen's 5 Rooftop Restaurant + Bar <
Four Seasons Hotel, Shanghai <
Zhongshan East Road
Yu Yuan Garden
Henan North Road
Simply Thai
> Parkyard Hotel Shanghai
Zhongshang Park
Suzhou creek
Xintiandi
Xizang South Road
> Simply Thai
> Simply Life
> The Village
> Pin Chuan
Huaihai Road
Yan'an Road
Hongqiao Road
Zhongshan West Road
Zhaojiabang Road
> 88 Xintiandi
> Simply Thai
> Simply Life
Simply Thai <
Wuzhong Road
Zhongshan South Road
Pudong Road
Yanggao Road
Huangpu River
> Hu + Hu
> Annly's China
Chuanyang River
Legend
Expressway
Main Road
Other Road
Water
0 km
1
2
3
4

a new world fusion city

Shanghai is one of the liveliest, busiest, and fastest-moving cities on earth. There is not another new millennium metropolis that has generated the same kind of buzz. Just the word—'Shanghai'—is instantly recognisable, immediately evocative.

talent magnet

Twenty-first century Shanghai is a giant magnet that attracts money and talent from around the globe. Each year, some US$10 billion in foreign investment flows into Shanghai, where it is soon injected into the city, ballooning the skyline with cutting-edge modern skyscrapers that spring up like mushrooms after an April shower. Swirled together, these ingredients—the amazing cash inflow and the global talent influx—have combined to create a new world 'fusion city' that is like no other place on earth.

On street level too, Shanghai is pushing the envelope. Every week, it seems, another new nightclub springs into existence, hipper and groovier than its month-old rivals. On the restaurant scene, it is the same thing: celebrity chefs, superstar interior designers, deep-pocketed financiers, the young and the restless—the magnet that is modern Shanghai has yanked them in.

Global talents aside, Shanghai also attracts migrants from all over China. Labourers are busy building the city, and so are earnest college students, young professionals, and managers-on-the-go, who add their own unique brand of ambition to this ever-pulsating, ever-changing city.

metropolis on the move

Shanghai's rapid evolution has been supercharged by a high-voltage jolt from the city government. Sensing history, the city fathers have launched a huge number of high-profile projects designed to lift the city out of its 40-year slumber, and launch it into the stratosphere.

This is a metropolis on the move: Pudong airport is tossing up two new terminals and laying down another runway for good measure. Five metro lines now criss-cross the city, with five more on the way, while high-speed rails will soon link the city to the rest of China. Meanwhile, a new cruise terminal is taking shape on the banks of the Huangpu River just north of the famous Bund.

These are all slated for completion by 2010 to coincide with the most ambitious scheme of all: Expo 2010. Shanghai is levelling more than 5 sq km (2 sq miles) of prime riverfront land,

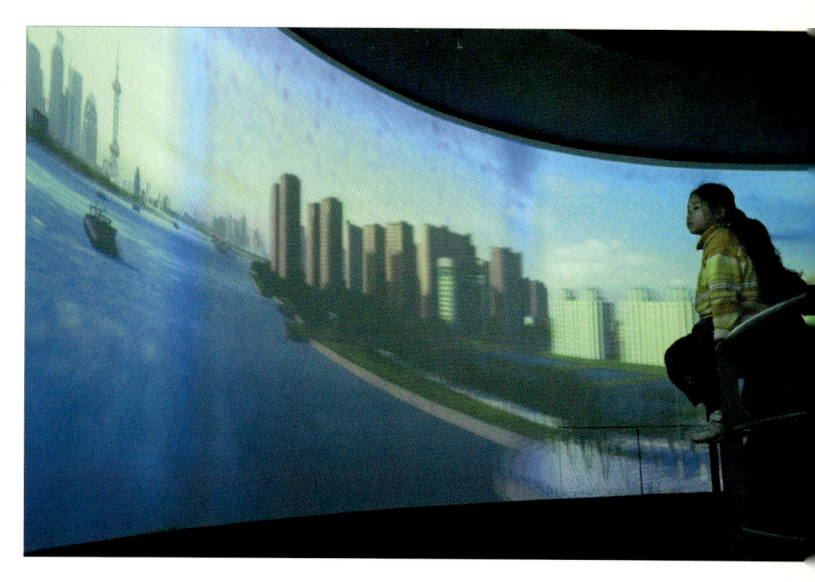

PAGE 76: *The Oriental Pearl Tower seen through the windows of a demolished historic building on the Bund.*

THIS PAGE (FROM TOP): *The Shanghai Urban Planning Exhibition Hall takes a look at Shanghai's past—and its future; 1933, an abattoir-turned-shopping mall, anchors the Hongkou district, Shanghai's trendiest new neighbourhood.*

sweeping away the rusty factories and shabby warehouses, to erect an unforgettable landmark exhibition that will sear the city into the global psyche. Even now, in a vast area on both sides of the Huangpu, just south of the iconic Bund, the bulldozers and cranes are incessantly in action.

Given the can-do spirit of the Shanghai city government, no one doubts that the deadlines of these infrastructural projects will be met. And when the expo opens for six months in the summer of 2010, it will be ready for the anticipated 70 million visitors.

yesterday once more

But Shanghai is not all about the brand-new. Far from the commercial streets of Nanjing Road, the busy construction sites of Pudong, and the ubiquitous transportation projects, most of the heavy lifting has already been done. Many parts of the old concessions and surrounding neighbourhoods, with their lane houses, London plane trees, and vaulting villas, are quiet and peaceful. They are as much a part of the fabric and identity of the city as the latest urban landmark.

The city had its salad days in an era of glorious architecture—the fabulous art deco years of the 1920s and 1930s. During those storied times, the world's finest architects—visionaries all—erected hundreds of stunning art deco classics in the city, from large hotels and industrial buildings to small apartments and offices. Those early 20th-century builders and architects knew what they were doing—the old buildings are classy and roomy, and they were built to last.

Today, many of these gentle giants and cosy confines have been lovingly renovated, and provide some of the classiest, calmest, and most beautiful buildings in Asia. When Shanghai boomed in the 1990s, would-be club owners and restaurateurs had stylish, ready-made spaces to renovate and move into, resulting in a welcome element of taste and style in the city's dining and partying venues. Visitors and residents alike can appreciate these graceful structures, and roaming the streets of the old concessions, to say nothing of the stately Bund, yields a treasure trove of venerable beauties.

city of tomorrow

This is the Shanghai of tomorrow: 21st-century bells and whistles, state-of-the-art restaurants with celebrity chefs, the latest and the greatest—a new Asian boomtown where the gold rush is still hot—but it is never without its stately welcoming retreats, peaceful old buildings, and calm quiet neighbourhoods. Nothing can beat this as a blueprint for the future.

THIS PAGE (FROM TOP): Nanjing East Road, one of the world's most famous pedestrianised thoroughfares, is one of the best places to people-watch in the city; attracted by the city's growing wealth and bottomless appetite for shopping, all the world's top luxury brands have set up shop in Shanghai.

OPPOSITE: Stately old colonial buildings gracing the Bund along the Huangpu River are nothing less than majestic.

...instantly recognisable, immediately evocative.

shanghai: dining out

Shanghai is a world-class dining emporium, a place where some of the world's top chefs unveil their latest culinary creations. Some of the ultra-chic eateries are on the Bund, others nestled inside the city's five-star luxury crash pads. Yet others are ensconced in delightful little out-of-the-way alleys, in old lane houses and mansions, and in lovingly renovated concession-era charmers.

chinese cuisine

The Shanghainese dining menu is replete with Chinese delights. Every type of Chinese cuisine is represented here, from sinfully rich Shanghainese dishes and spicy Sichuan delicacies that combine the signature hua jiao chilli with fresh natural ingredients for intoxicating tongue-tingling fusions, to mild and subtle Cantonese, fat, succulent Peking Duck, and hearty Xinjiang stews.

Lost Heaven Yunnan (38 Gaoyou Road) has a menu filled with exotic ethnic items such as rare local vegetables and mountain mushrooms, served in the signature Yunnan sour and spicy flavours with Burmese influences like milk and lemongrass. The décor is jaw-dropping: owner Robin Yin scoured his native Yunnan province for authentic artefacts, tapestries, paintings, and other decorations. Check out the back wall on the first floor—it is made entirely from Yunnan-style blocks of tea. **South Beauty 881** (881 Central Yan'an Road) is an elegant Sichuan eatery that consists of a classic, century-old mansion, and a brand-new single-storey restaurant. Both buildings sit on acres of plantation-style grounds, decorated with fishponds and shady trees. The signature dish is stone beef: pieces of spicy raw beef cooked at the table in a bowl of oil kept sizzling hot by red-hot rocks. Then there's **Xindalu–China Kitchen** (1/F, Hyatt on the Bund, 199 Huangpu Road) at the classy new Hyatt on the Bund, just north of Suzhou Creek, which serves the richest Peking Duck this side of heaven. Nobody leaves the wonderfully designed dining room hungry: the ducks waddle in, and the diners waddle back out. For luxurious fine dining, **Tan Wai Lou** (5/F, Bund18, 18 Zhongshan Dong Yi Road) epitomises Chinese haute cuisine.

Xintiandi is a key dining epicentre that features the greatest number of Shanghai's upscale eateries. One of the best is **SOAHC Restaurant & Tea Garden** (House 3, Lane 123, Xingye Road, South Block Xintiandi), which seamlessly blends shikumen (stone gate) architecture and contemporary style in a way that is unique and enchanting. SOAHC serves Huaiyang cuisine, a more delicate and refined cousin of Shanghainese; its speciality is an exceptional lion's head meatball with crabmeat that has a palate-tickling tanginess not often found in this tried-and-true dish.

international

Chinese food aside, Shanghai is fast becoming a Mecca of international cuisine, just as it was in its concession-era heyday. Celebrity chefs have flocked to Shanghai, adding their trademark spices and ingredients to the city's already-exotic swirl of

THIS PAGE (CLOCKWISE FROM TOP): *Sample Chinese haute cuisine in grand style at Bund18's Tan Wai Lou; Mesa Restaurant & Manifesto Lounge serves continental cuisine in modern Shanghai style; Issimo at JIA Shanghai combines designer plush with a comfortable homely feel.*
OPPOSITE: *Keep royal company when dining at the thoroughly modern Sens & Bund at Bund18.*

shanghai: dining out

flavours. Some of Shanghai's finest food is found in five-star hotels. Take the JW Marriott Shanghai, where **California Grill** (40/F, 399 Nanjing West Road) serves the fattest seafood appetiser platter in town, filled with an impossibly huge array of scallops, crab and lobster. Fat marbled sirloins and other continental cuisines are also on the menu. At the extravagant **Jade on 36** (36/F, Tower 2, Pudong Shangri-La Hotel, 33 Fucheng Road), a famous luxe hotel dining outpost, elegant fusion delights are served in a dining venue that has become a must-see. At **Shintaro** (2/F, Four Seasons Hotel, Shanghai, 500 Weihai Road), get an eyeful of the avant-garde art on the walls while dining on the equally artistic Japanese specialities.

For a hearty helping of genuine Shanghai chic, there is always the Bund. **M on the Bund** (7/F, 5 Zhongshan Dong Yi Road) serves classy but down-home continental food. It is honest-to-goodness meat and potatoes gussied up for the hipsters, but still recognisable as real food. The place is usually packed with happy people—a happiness that is greatly enhanced by a visit to the Glamour Bar downstairs. M on the Bund has company at the top from **Laris** (6/F, Three on the Bund, 3 Zhongshan Dong Yi Road) and **Sens & Bund** (6/F, Bund18, 18 Zhongshan Dong Yi Road), where the menus are continental, the wine lists are long, and the desserts to-die-for. But the Bund also boasts an eatery that won't lighten your wallet as much: **New Heights** (7/F, Three on the Bund, 3 Zhongshan Dong Yi Road). This top-floor favourite has a broad outdoor terrace that showcases the sweeping curve of the Bund, the boat-filled Huangpu River, and the eclectic architecture of Pudong. New Heights serves global diner food, including Thai red curry, burger and fries, five-spice duck breast, and bangers and mash—a perfect variety for such a cosmopolitan city.

Bund-area palaces aside, Shanghai has dozens of cosy cafés and restaurants in the narrow lanes and leafy streets of the old concessions. **A FuturePerfect** (House 16, Lane 351, Huashan Road) is a tiny gem tucked away in a quintessential Shanghai lilong, or lane. Its menu of modern continental cuisine is underscored by the best bread in town, while its tree-lined courtyard, complete with a concession-era villa as a backdrop, is the perfect setting for a flute of champagne under the summer stars. **Mesa Restaurant & Manifesto Lounge** (748 Julu Road) is another eatery that is all modern Shanghai, from its central location and sunny terrace to the beautiful black-clad wait-staff. The menu features oven-roasted sea bass, grilled veal medallions, snow-crab risotto, and other continental dishes.

For a good cause and a great Italian meal, head to **MoCA Caffé** (Gate 7. People's Park, 231 Nanjing West Road) on the top floor of the Museum of Contemporary Art. The restaurant supports the museum. Perched atop another institution, this time the Shanghai Art Museum, one finds the elegant **Kathleen's 5 Rooftop Restaurant & Bar** (5/F, 325 Nanjing West Road), recipient of rave reviews for its globally-inspired menu and fabulous panoramic views of downtown Shanghai.

THIS PAGE (CLOCKWISE FROM TOP LEFT): food, glorious food, from every corner of the world, is part of the Shanghai experience; admire Shintaro's avant-garde art collection while dining; eye-catching interiors characterise Shanghai's upscale eateries.
OPPOSITE (FROM LEFT): Dining at Kathleen's 5 Rooftop Restaurant & Bar is an uplifting experience; Xindalu–China Kitchen never fails to impress with its superb Peking Duck, served in sleek surroundings.

shanghai:diningout 85

shanghai's nightlife

When it comes to all-night entertainment, Shanghai has no rivals. A typical night out might start with a cold beer in a classy concession-era mansion, then move on to a Xintiandi nightspot for a fat martini, before a change of scene at a cosy lounge, and ending in a head-spinning, heart-throbbing dance club of whacky but superior design.

Shanghai's best pubs are within a few blocks of each other in the heart of the old French Concession. The biggest, brassiest, and most popular is the giant **Paulaner Brauhaus** (150 Fenyang Road), a brewery-restaurant with rows of Oktoberfest picnic tables that are invariably packed with happy drinkers. A trio of more traditional pubs lurks nearby: **O'Malley's Irish Pub** (42 Taojiang Road) is an Irish-themed joint with dark interiors, a nice courtyard, and happy guzzlers. Across the street is **Castle Oktober** (39 Taojiang Road), a brewpub located in a fine old villa, which cranks out a fine glass of hoppy, malty pilsner. Next door is **British Bulldog** (1 Wulumuqi South Road), another belly-up-to-the-bar venue that is cheerful and popular, with darts, pool table, pub trivia, and other tried-and-true beer-friendly features.

One of the city's must-see drinking venues is **Face Bar** (Ruijin Hotel Shanghai, Building 4, 118 Ruijin Er Road), an atmospheric opium-era watering hole located in an big old brick mansion on spacious grounds; outside, it's like sipping mint juleps on the veranda of a plantation house. A similar feeling of space exists at the marble bar at **Shintori** (803 Julu Road), a place that is cavernous but subtly lit, a welcome change from low-ceilinged restaurants in other crowded Asian capitals.

Most night-time trails lead eventually to **Xintiandi** (corner, Huangpi and Taicang streets), one of the liveliest late-night gathering spots in town. Every few steps will uncover either a nightclub with a live band, a classy cocktail joint, or a cosy little drinking den. Step into **TMSK** (Unit 2, House 11 Beili, Xintiandi Square, Lane 181, Taicang Road) for cocktails served in a unique setting decorated in dazzling liuli (coloured glass).

Other dedicated drinking zones include **Maoming Road**, between Fuxing and Yongjia roads, and **Tongren Road**, at the corner of Yanan. Both of these neighbourhoods boast a heady number of cocktail bars, mostly of the meet-and-greet variety.

If padded lounges are your thing, try **Manifesto Lounge** (748 Julu Road), one of the top watering holes in town; here, many a happy night has been whiled away to the sweet taste of mango martinis and lychee cosmopolitans. **Mint** (2/F, 333 Tongren Road), meanwhile, is a mega lounge that plays a variety of music from electronica to hip-hop. **Bar Rouge** (7/F, Bund18, 18 Zhongshan Dong Yi Road), the one-time queen of the new bars is a super-cool pad that has super-bad service and snotty patrons, but those are considered part of its charm, along with its juicy, spot-on cocktails and awesome views. For the mega-hip, **Attica** (11/F, 15 Zhongshan Dong Er Road) has elbowed aside Bar Rouge—it is really the same thing, but more so, with a throbbing heaving dance floor.

THIS PAGE (FROM TOP): *Designer food in designer settings at the top clubs; customers are enveloped by shimmering lights reflected off coloured glass known as 'liuli' at the lit bar of TMSK in Xintiandi; a DJ keeps the crowd on its feet until the wee hours of the morning.*
OPPOSITE: *Bar Rouge at Bund18 pulls in the city's movers and shakers.*

shanghai's nightlife 87

shanghai: a shopping sensation

For zealous shoppers—and who isn't one?—Shanghai is a moveable feast, a sumptuous buffet that offers everything from cheap-and-cheerful to ultra-luxe. The choices range from the top European brands to local items that can be found nowhere else. And very often, shopping in Shanghai means hobnobbing with battle-hardened local vendors and sharpening up those bargaining skills.

malls

If Shanghai were a Monopoly board, its Boardwalk, at the very peak of price and prestige, would be **Nanjing West Road**, especially near the intersection of Shanxi and Nanjing West roads. This is the land of luxury brands; name any famous European label and it will be sold in one of these fancy malls.

The parade of fashion marques in **Plaza 66** (1266 Nanjing West Road) seems never ending: it begins with a flagship **Mont Blanc** store on the ground floor, and continues like a set of classy models strutting down a designer catwalk. **Karl Lagerfeld** is here with a spacious emporium featuring his trademark shiny European couture, keeping fine company with the likes of **Tiffany**, **Chaumet**, **Fendi**, **Prada**, **Celine**, and **Christian Dior**.

Next door, **CITIC Square** (1168 Nanjing West Road) is anchored by a **Cartier** store, and features a selection of expensive, if ever-so-slightly more downstream, boutiques.

But there are few bargains to be had in these oxygen-thin upper ranges, because taxes boost the sticker prices of luxury goods in China more than 30%. Savvy shoppers know that fashion brands are cheaper in Hong Kong and elsewhere. Still, for window-shopping, the city can't be beaten.

Shanghai also has a heady trawl of upper-middlebrow shopping centres that serve daunting selections of clothing, handbags, man bags, fine writing instruments, luxury time pieces, and all the other baubles that may be carried, worn, placed on a finger or wrist or around a neck, or otherwise ostentatiously displayed. One of the most famous is **Super Brand Mall** (168 Lujiazui West Road), the biggest mall on the Pudong side of the river, and home to affordable brands like **H&M**, **Zara**, **Bossini**, **Nike 360**, and **Adidas**.

The Shanghai shopping smorgasbord doesn't end there—many more malls have landed like so many glass-and-metal flying saucers in select downtown neighbourhoods. These include **Cloud Nine** (1018 Changning Road) in the Zhongshan Park neigbourhood, **Raffles City** near People's Park (268 Xizang Central Road), and **Grand Gateway Mall** (1 Hongqiao Road), the queen of Xujiahui district, a neon-lit landmark that shines forth every night in a blaze of high-voltage incandescent glory.

shopping strips

Shanghai's second most upscale shopping zone is at the eastern end of **Huaihai Road**, near Chongqing Road. Here, Western and Asian brands sit side by side, along with a smattering of local products.

Japanese retailer **Uniqlo** (300 Huaihai Central Road) is one of these, with its selection of stylish outfits. Also on this strip are several outlets of **Three Gun**, a Chinese chain that sells mid-range silks and cottons.

The streets of Shanghai are filled with small boutiques, many of them offering local designer clothing, or even international brands, for a fraction of the usual price. These hidden gems yield themselves only to the most intrepid of shoppers, but the biggest cluster is on **Shanxi Road**, near the corner of Julu Road.

Shoppers in search of a genuine piece of art deco history should wander down to **Dongtai Road**, the city's famous antiques street. Along the main street are arrayed a variety of vendors selling inexpensive souvenirs, like old coins, Mao heads, watches, posters, birdcages, carvings, and such, but back from the main alleys are some genuine antiques. Most of these are lamps and fans that have been removed from old houses during the ongoing rebuilding of the city. There is also some furniture; again, careful bargaining and a keen eye are required.

markets

Beyond the upscale zones, Shanghai offers lots of unique shopping, which sometimes yields excellent bargains—and sometimes not! Shanghai markets are like one-of-a-kind hunting-and-gathering safaris.

Foremost among these was the famous but now departed Xiangyang Market, which disappeared in 2006. Happily, many of those vendors have

THIS PAGE (FROM TOP): High fashion and luxury brands lure Shanghai's young and trendy, who have more disposable income than ever before; chic Chinese-inspired style on display at homegrown designer boutique Annabel Lee Shanghai.
OPPOSITE: The pedestrian mall of Nanjing Road, Shanghai's premier shopping district.

shanghai:ashoppingsensation 89

shanghai: a shopping sensation

THIS PAGE (FROM TOP): Both local products and international brands find a ready market in Shanghai's cosmopolitan consumers; a colourful display of local food at a street market.
OPPOSITE (CLOCKWISE FROM TOP): Cyclists ride past on the street to Yu Yuan Garden, where all things Chinese can be purchased; candied apples sold on the Bund; a vendor weighs cherry tomatoes at a street market.

since re-grouped their bargain-happy stalls in scattered sections of town. The new **Xiangyang Market**, near the Science and Technology Museum in Pudong (Science and Technology subway station, Line 2) is a vast warren of stalls that specialises in fierce bargaining for goods claiming to be cashmere, wool, or 100% cotton, or North Face, Nike, Gucci, or other coveted brands. Some are, but most are not—let the buyer beware. This is a full-on meet-the-locals experience, but if you know your goods and your prices, and are prepared to negotiate like crazy, you can come away with a suitcase full of rare bargains.

Another collection of shops, also containing a few bargains that sparkle like diamonds among many lumps of coal, is the area around **Qipu Road,** near Henan Road. This zone features three big buildings with street-front shops that are replete with more clothes, shoes, handbags, toys, shorts and socks than you ever thought possible. Just don't assume that any of it is real. That way, if something IS real, it will be a pleasant surprise.

In a similar vein, there is the **Hongqiao International Pearl City** (3721 Hongmei Road). This sprawl of stores has, among many other items, plenty of Chinese-style goods of the silk slipper and designer chopstick variety. It also boasts a pearl emporium that specialises in freshwater pearls from the Yangtze Delta. As always, bargain hard.

The best place for cheap and cheerful 'China kitsch' souvenirs is **Yu Yuan Bazaar** (218 Anren Street), in the centre of Old Shanghai. This Ming Dynasty-era tourist attraction is surrounded by acres of shops selling an indescribable variety of Sinophilia, from canvas shoes, teapots and embroidered handbags to silk carpets and silk underwear–and everything else that the Middle Kingdom can produce for tourists. The sheer variety of silk is amazing, ranging from satin and damask to spun silk, raw silk, and cool, see-through silk of lavish softness.

There is a pattern to shopping in Yu Yuan Bazaar: typical souvenirs like fans, pearls, silk pajamas, terracotta warrior statues, and Mao memorabilia are lined up along the main streets, while tucked away deep inside the courtyards and buildings are hundreds of stalls selling goods, such as beaded necklaces, shopping bags of all shapes and sizes, wigs, yarn, women's purses, Chinese medicines, children's toys, jewellery, clothes, and so on. It is a hodge-podge of a place, but lots of fun and very rewarding.

The most 'local' shopping experience in Shanghai is **Fuyou Market** (457 Fangbang Road, corner of Fangbang Central and Henan South roads). During the week, it is an ordinary curio and bric-a-brac collection, but on weekends, it comes alive, as vendors from the countryside pour in with their wares, which can be anything from snuff bottles, old furniture, coins, and Buddhist statues to porcelain wares, baskets, and even 'dinosaur eggs'. The rural vendors are on the third and fourth floors, and on the sidewalks. Try to come before sunrise—the vendors do.

shanghai:ashoppingsensation 91

spas in shanghai

In just a few short years, the spa scene in Shanghai has surged onto the global consciousness as one of the world's foremost pampering hotspots. Many of the spas in Shanghai combine Western wellness techniques with ancient Chinese arts.

a five-star experience

At the luxury end of the spectrum sit the spas that are nestled in the classy confines of the five-star hotels. These include CHI, The Spa at Pudong Shangri-La; Mandara Spa at JW Marriott Hotel; and the Banyan Tree Spa Shanghai at The Westin Shanghai.

CHI, The Spa (Pudong Shangri-La, 33 Fucheng Road) is on the 6th floor of the Pudong Shangri-La's new Tower Two, and the entire floor, all 800 sq m (6,800 sq ft) of it, is dedicated to the spa. The elevators open into a calm, dark hallway, and the adjoining CHI lobby is filled with soft lights, soothing sounds, and sweet smells. The Aroma Vitality massage is an East-West combo that is part Japanese shiatsu and part Swedish. The décor is Tibetan, and so are some of the treatments, like the 20-minute Himalayan Water Therapy treatment.

Similarly, **Mandara Spa** (6/F, JW Marriott Hotel Shanghai, 399 Nanjing West Road) at the JW Marriott boasts private treatment rooms, adorned in the styles and colours of Asia. Its most sought-after treatment is called 'Taste of the Orient', which uses elements of Chinese culture, including fragrant five-spice powder, ginger, and jasmine. Its Mandara Massage combines five different styles from four Asian countries.

Banyan Tree Spa Shanghai (3/F, The Westin Shanghai, Bund Centre, 88 Henan Central Road) also incorporates time-honoured Asian herbs and ingredients in its extensive menu of treatments. The signature Royal Banyan treatment is a 3-hour indulgence that includes Thai acupressure therapy and the signature Banyan Massage.

small + personal

Shanghai is also filled with stand-alone spas, many of them situated in the delightfully peaceful lanes and alleys of the city.

One of the real gems is **Diva Life** (266 Ruijin Er Road), housed in a historical 1930s lane house a few steps down a classic alley. This charming spa feels like a classy, aging country home, and it offers treatments, wraps, scrubs, massages, and more, from around the world.

Another favourite is **Dragonfly** (20 Donghu Road), a Chinese spa chain that has 11 outlets throughout the city. Within its walls, blended stone-and-wood interiors mirror the designs of classic Chinese courtyard homes. Dragonfly offers excellent massages at affordable prices, and has a wide clientele. Try the lavender oil—it comes with rave reviews.

Finally, for the brave at heart, the city is filled with very local spas that offer authentic, time-honoured Chinese treatments such as cupping, acupuncture, and 'bruising' massage, in basic surroundings. Many people—Asians and Westerners alike—have emerged from these local treatments glowing with good health and filled with high praise for the practitioners.

THIS PAGE (FROM TOP): Diva Life encourages a meditative mood; enjoy relaxing treatments that combine Asian elements with Western techniques.
OPPOSITE (CLOCKWISE FROM TOP): The warm tones of the exotic décor and the soothing ambience of Mandara Spa (top and below right) create a calming retreat for the senses; Shanghai's spas offer a wide range of facilities, from luxury suites at hotel spas to comfortable treatment rooms at local day spas.

shanghai galleries + museums

Shanghai has a thriving art and museum scene that has been boosted by a sudden worldwide surge in Chinese art. Two broad art forms have emerged: one is traditional and has attracted a Chinese audience, the other is political pop-oriented and has attracted an overseas audience. Both are beautiful, but in money-happy Shanghai, neither form is a bargain. This has not stopped Shanghai from becoming a hotspot for showcasing contemporary art, particularly paintings, and the city is dotted with many superb art galleries.

Art is also a mainstay of Shanghai's numerous museums, sharing the spotlight with awe-inspiring ancient artefacts and equally eye-catching modern displays of technology. The top museums are all to be found in People's Square.

galleries

50 Moganshan Road has emerged as the city's premier gallery district. A stroll through this neighbourhood of remodelled warehouses will yield a treasure trove of galleries, some representing the city's best-known artists. This is where serious collectors, art students, investment-hunters—and those who just want to know what all the fuss is about—can get an eyeful of the latest cutting-edge art by Chinese painters, performance artists, photographers and sculptors.

Among the many galleries, **ShanghART** (Building 16 and 18) is one of the biggest and most well-known, having been instrumental in cultivating the art scene since it opened in 1996. **Art Scene** (2/F, Building 4) and **Eastlink Gallery** (5/F, Building 6) have also attracted faithful followings. In addition to representing some of the country's most exciting artists, they are known for their unconventional and sometimes controversial exhibitions.

museums

Shanghai Art Museum (325 Nanjing West Road) is housed in a stately stone structure that was once the Shanghai Race Club. Its eye-catching permanent collection includes modern Chinese oil paintings and pop art. The museum attracts big crowds, most of them Chinese and many of them young, who prowl the roomy galleries in search of entertainment and inspiration.

The **Museum of Contemporary Art**, or **MoCA** (Gate 7, People's Park, 231 Nanjing West Road), is a non-profit institution that is devoted to the arts. The museum was once a greenhouse and its glass walls remain intact, a set-up that allows a flood of daylight to illuminate the museum's high-ceilinged interior. The exhibits are mostly avant-garde, with a bias towards Chinese contemporary art.

Nearby is **Shanghai Museum** (201 Renmin Boulevard). With its state-of-the-art displays, detailed English signs, audio tours, and helpful staff, this is the undisputed queen of the local museums. Here, China's biggest collection of ancient art and artefacts is displayed in 11 cool, comfortable galleries.

The **Shanghai Science and Technology Museum Pudong** (2000 Century Avenue) is unique among

Shanghai museums. It is in Pudong, not Puxi, and is ultra-modern: it boasts high-tech modern exhibits in a buzzworthy building with a high 'wow' factor. The glass-and-steel behemoth has four theaters (two of which are Imax, and one an Iwerks), broad grounds, spouting fountains, vaulting skylight ceilings, and other 21st-century touches.

Meanwhile, out in the French Concession, the **Shanghai Museum of Arts and Crafts** (79 Fenyang Road) sits in a century-old, neoclassical mansion. With its high ornate ceilings, spacious lawns, stained-glass windows, marble staircases, and sculpted fishponds, the building itself is a special treat. But so is the little museum, which opened in 1960 as a workplace for craftsmen. Many of them are still here, tucked away in distant rooms, polishing their lacquers, carving their jades, and perfecting their papercuts.

THIS PAGE (FROM TOP): *The imposing Shanghai Museum by night; Shanghai's art and culture scene is filled with frequent exhibitions of both ancient (right and below) and contemporary (far right) works.*
OPPOSITE: *Shanghai is a showcase for both Chinese contemporary art and art from around the world.*

shanghaigalleries+museums 95

best views of shanghai

If you cannot take an eye-popping, awe-inspiring photograph in Shanghai, then put the camera away, because Shanghai is the most snap-worthy metropolis on earth. Point your lens in any direction and click away; chances are, it will capture something dramatic: a moment of rare beauty, a gaudy people-dwarfing skyscraper, a charming glimpse of 21st-century street life, or a beautiful old art deco building.

Photo-wise, everything starts on the **Bund** (Zhongshan East Road). On the west side are those iconic, stately buildings—the ones printed on postcards and mailed around the world. In the early morning, the rising sun gilds these statuesque, century-old wonders in a warm golden glow that spotlights the famous dome of the former **Hongkong and Shanghai Bank Building** (12 Zhongshan Dong Yi Road) and sparkles atop the clocktower of **Customs House** (9 Zhongshan Dong Yi Road). In the foreground, the citizens of Shanghai perform graceful taijiquan, providing the ideal frame for a fine souvenir snapshot.

On the other side of the river, in the evening's angled sunlight, the brand-new towers of **Pudong** blaze forth, and the glass windows of these gorgeous new monuments flash and spark with concentrated beams of reflected light. And those buildings come in all shapes and colours: pyramids, cylinders, blocks, and angled sculpted towers, while the river, too, becomes a stream of light, a dramatic backdrop for a postcard-perfect snap of the famous skyline.

For people shots, the **Bund Promenade**—the broad patio that fronts the river—provides great views on both sides. It is a 24/7 people-fest of kite flyers, taijiquan dancers, souvenir sellers, and tourists. The nearby **Nanjing East Road** pedestrian mall is a similar snap-fest, as the stream of humanity is surrounded by the eclectic buildings of the famous road.

This leads to **People's Park** (231 Nanjing West Road). Here, too, are iconic images galore. These range from the mega-modern, like the **Shanghai Museum** (201 Renmin Avenue), cleverly shaped to look like an ancient ding or bronze ceremonial vessel, to classy old beauties like the **Park Hotel** (170 Nanjing West Road) and the **Shanghai Art Museum** (325 Nanjing West Road).

People's Park is flanked by two terrific space-age towers: the **Shi Mao Building** (789 Nanjing East Road), home to Le Royal Méridien Shanghai, and **Tomorrow Square** (Nanjing West Road), home of the JW Marriott. If these don't make you yank the camera out of the bag, nothing will.

Nearby is the **French Concession**, a land of lane houses, mansions, and tree-lined streets that is home to myriad street-life scenes: cobblers fixing shoes, trays of steaming dumplings, wet markets surging with life forms human and otherwise, and the Shanghainese themselves, always quaint and camera-ready.

THIS PAGE (FROM TOP): *A vivid carpet of flowers fills People's Square; the Bund Sightseeing Tunnel is designed to dazzle; one of Shanghai's many charming parks and gardens.*
OPPOSITE: *A fabulous view of the Bund on the right and Pudong on the left flanking the Huangpu River; a modern sundial sculpture in Pudong expresses the melding of the old and the new in Shanghai.*

88 xintiandi

THIS PAGE: *Oriental screens create privacy for hotel guests.*
OPPOSITE (FROM LEFT): *Unwind in lush surroundings; open spaces with Chinese accents emphasise the serenity of 88 Xintiandi.*

Beyond the spectacular Taipingqiao Lake lies the cosy and exclusive 88 Xintiandi. The regal interior bespeaks Old World charm: a walk through the latticed grill gates brings one back to 1930s Shanghai, a realm of glitz and glamour often portrayed on the silver screen, where feminine figures in qi paos moved to hypnotic melodies.

The exoticism that has made Shanghai the 'Paris of the East' creates an alluring enclave in 88 Xintiandi, made all the more appealing when one considers Shanghai's continuous re-development and modernisation efforts. The Xintiandi precinct, within which this hotel is located, is the city's historical quarter. Immaculately preserved buildings embrace a plethora of galleries, boutiques, restaurants, and bars in the vicinity. As the glorious past thrives in the trendy present, visitors are immersed in a vibrancy that will paint their memories of Shanghai a rich, brilliant hue.

Within the hotel, soft lights and homely comforts imbue one with an intimate warmth that sets the tone for a luxurious stay. Elegance is best left simple and 88 Xintiandi has created a charming environment combining classical décor with an Old World feel. Wooden chests with ornate carvings and intricate oriental screens speak of exotic chinoiserie, while echoes of the French Concession abound in various forms—the exquisite chandelier gracing the lobby, the European architectural influence throughout the hotel, even the butler-style service that makes one feel like royalty.

Ensconced in stylishly appointed rooms, 88 Xintiandi guests can look out the large windows and be soothed by a spectacular lake view or take in the refreshing greenery from the nearby park. There are also rooms with views that span over the Chinese-style rooftops of the shikumen houses in Xintiandi.

...an ambience that is as sophisticated as it is calming.

All rooms are infused with Chinese and Southeast Asian elements, creating an ambience that is as sophisticated as it is calming. Full secretarial services, high-speed Internet access and an in-room fax machine ensure efficiency and convenience for business travellers working late. Personalised service is epitomised by the hotel's attentive staff, who are on hand to see to every need, even booking performance tickets on guests' behalf to ensure an unforgettable night out.

For a quiet evening in, spacious sitting rooms are outfitted with a flat-screen TV and DVD player to see to guests' entertainment. Nestled in custom-designed alcoves are luxurious beds that promise nothing less than sweet dreams.

Breakfast is served at the executive lounge, where guests can enjoy piping hot coffee, toast, and the morning sun streaming into the third-storey al fresco setting. For relaxation, head next door to the Alexander City Club, where there are gym facilities, a squash court, steam room, sauna, and an indoor swimming pool. With Shanghai's many noted dining destinations in mind, a couple of laps are just the thing to prepare for another gastronomical adventure.

This exclusive address has all the trappings of a chic, urban hotel, yet it reaches out to the weary traveller. As a home away from home, 88 Xintiandi's attention to personal comforts and high-living will assure visitors of a unique Shanghainese experience.

rooms
53

food
executive lounge: breakfast and afternoon tea

drink
executive lounge: evening cocktails

features
DVD player • flat-screen TV • indoor pool • gym • high-speed Internet access • open kitchen • spa • ticket bookings

business
computer and mobile phone rental • in-room fax machine • secretarial services

nearby
Shanghai International Exhibition Centre • Shanghai Museum • The Bund • Xintiandi

contact
380 Huang Pi Nan Road, Shanghai 200021 •
telephone: +86.21.5383 8833 •
facsimile: +86.21.5383 8877 •
email: inquiry@88xintiandi.com •
website: www.88xintiandi.com

four seasons hotel, shanghai

THIS PAGE: *Rain or shine, the indoor pool is ideal for a few refreshing laps.*
OPPOSITE (FROM TOP): *Warm colour tones give the rooms a cosy ambience; on the top floor of the hotel.*

Known as the 'Paris of the East', Shanghai is China's cultural hotspot, showcasing the country's finest restaurants and nightlife, amid modern architectural masterpieces and historical treasures. Coupled with the city's strengths as a regional financial and business capital, this explosive combination makes for an awe-inspiring destination.

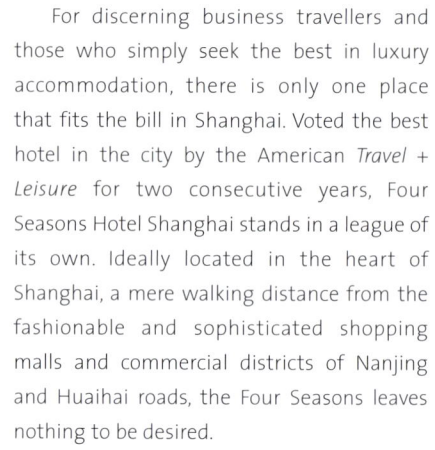

For discerning business travellers and those who simply seek the best in luxury accommodation, there is only one place that fits the bill in Shanghai. Voted the best hotel in the city by the American *Travel + Leisure* for two consecutive years, Four Seasons Hotel Shanghai stands in a league of its own. Ideally located in the heart of Shanghai, a mere walking distance from the fashionable and sophisticated shopping malls and commercial districts of Nanjing and Huaihai roads, the Four Seasons leaves nothing to be desired.

Housed in a sleek, new multi-storey building, the hotel is decorated in a classic, elegant style with charming oriental details. Guestrooms are bathed in a warm, golden light emanating from the shimmering beige and bronze fabrics, and the subtle light fixtures. Accented in the deep red and royal blue of ancient Chinese tradition, the rooms take on a sumptuous, regal quality. Yet, with DVD players, wireless high-speed Internet access, and data ports, among other modern conveniences, they combine opulence with practicality.

The spa and gym facilities at Four Seasons provide the ideal antidote to the bustling city outside—a place where guests can relax and unwind before another hectic day begins. Enjoy a cool dip in the 20-m (66-ft) indoor pool or a workout at the state-of-the-art cardio and weight training rooms. For the perfect end to the day,

...providing seamless service and personalised attention.

indulge in a traditional Chinese acupressure massage or select from one of many other pampering treatments available.

Superb Asian cuisine abounds at this stylish hotel. Master Chef Sam Yuen, who hails from Hong Kong, dazzles guests at the Si Ji Xuan restaurant, which offers classic Cantonese fare and exquisite dim sum. Alternatively, Shintaro is a Japanese bistro with an open kitchen concept that serves the freshest sushi and sashimi, apart from other specialities such as Japanese Green Tea Noodles with Shrimp Tempura and Teriyaki. Above all, an impressive avant-garde art collection adds to the sophisticated feel at Shintaro. Those looking for something a little more conventional can opt for international favourites at Café Studio or a feast at the Steak House. Round off the evening with a quiet drink at Jazz 37, which overlooks the city skyline and offers live music from some of Shanghai's most revered jazz musicians.

From a hotel package tailor-made just for women, to the hotel's impeccable butler service, Four Seasons Hotel Shanghai has truly thought of its guests' every possible need, providing seamless service and personalised attention.

rooms
360 rooms • 79 suites

food
Si Ji Xuan: Cantonese • Steak House: Western • Shintaro: Japanese • Café Studio: international

drink
Lobby Lounge • Jazz 37: bar

features
beauty salon • executive club lounge • fitness centre • high-speed Internet access • indoor pool • spa

business
ballroom • business centre • function rooms

nearby
Nanjing Road • Huaihai Road • People's Square • People's Park • Shanghai Grand Theatre • Shanghai Performance Arts Centre • Museum of Fine Arts • The Bund

contact
500 Weihai Road, 200041 Shanghai •
telephone: + 86.21.6256 8888 •
facsimile: + 86.21.6256 5678 •
email: reservations.shg@fourseasons.com •
website: www.fourseasons.com/shanghai

hyatt on the bund

THIS PAGE: *Rooms have front row seats to Shanghai's spectacular cityscape.*
OPPOSITE: *Hyatt on the Bund brings a minimalist garden into its lobby.*

Steeped in history and home to centuries-old architecture, the Bund is arguably Shanghai's most famous address. With the development of a new cruise ship dock and the World Expo site, the once-industrial northern part of the Bund is slowly re-emerging as a cultural and commercial centre. Hyatt on the Bund, one of the waterfront's newest and most impressive structures, is the latest addition to Hyatt International's Grand Hyatt brand in China, and a remarkable hotel in every sense.

Designed to give most rooms a stunning view of the historic Bund or Pudong's futuristic skyline, the hotel consists of two striking steel and glass towers, separated by a monumental atrium. Symbolised by its spectacular lobby, the scale of luxury at

...the scale of luxury at Hyatt on the Bund is, quite simply, awe-inspiring.

Hyatt on the Bund is, quite simply, awe-inspiring. Polished black granite floors coupled with rich woods in the expansive reception area make for a dramatic entrance. Overhead, a suspension bridge connects the East and West towers. Filled with natural light from the panelled glass roof and the floor-to-ceiling windows, the spectacular split-level lobby sets the tone for the hotel's impressive décor throughout.

No expense has been spared in creating the sumptuous rooms and suites of this impressive establishment, which are dressed in a soothing chocolate brown and beige palette. Contemporary in design, yet exuding warmth and cosiness, they are the perfect haven for rest and relaxation. Over-sized beds invite guests to lie back and take in the breathtaking views from the expansive windows, while a flat-screen, satellite TV provides the perfect excuse to laze around in the comfort of one's room the whole day.

Bathrooms can be opened up completely to create a studio-like space, or closed off for a more conventional set-up. Such versatility allows the stylish, marble-clad bathrooms—with rainfall showers and deep tubs—to be an integral part of the living space.

Every requirement of the business traveller has been carefully taken into consideration. High-speed Internet access, along with digital conference telephones and spacious work tables are a standard feature in all rooms. In addition, the Bund

THIS PAGE: *Enjoy a drink and relax in the hotel's contemporary, spacious lobby.*
OPPOSITE (FROM LEFT): *The exclusive Bund Club has its own dining area for guests; the hotel's azure pool beckons.*

Club features exclusive accommodation with unrivalled personalised service and privacy for an optimum working environment. Benefits include complimentary access to exclusive facilities and a conference room as well as refreshments throughout the day.

The business centre's facilities could not be more comprehensive. Offering translation and travel services, full administrative and secretarial assistance as well as cutting-edge audio-visual equipment, it is surely the closest anyone will get to having an office away from the office.

In a bustling, vibrant city such as Shanghai, it is not unusual for both tourists and those on business to arrive back at the hotel exhausted and in need of some serious pampering to get them back on their feet again. The Hyatt on the Bund has just the antidote in the form of the hotel's signature Yuan Spa.

The spacious Yuan Spa has 12 treatment rooms as well as whirlpools, cold plunge pools, steam rooms, and a sauna. Combining traditional Chinese wellness philosophies with European skincare treatments, Yuan Spa offers a wide array of massages, hydrotherapies, and bath rituals that promote serenity, vitality, and stability. With every comfort seen to, guests can while away the afternoon soothing the soul and rejuvenating the spirit.

In addition to the Yuan Spa, the fitness centre encompasses a 24-hour gym, indoor pool, and beauty salon, making it a facility for restoration and renewal to beat all others. With astonishing attention to detail, the creators of the gym have gone the extra mile to motivate guests during their workout: iPods loaded with playlists, equipment fitted with built-in fans, and personal screens with satellite channels are at the fingertips of those striving to burn a few extra calories.

Reflecting the grandeur and dynamism of the city in which it stands...

Dining at Hyatt on the Bund is an exciting journey through different cuisines, where guests can experience fine foods prepared to perfection in sophisticated, lively restaurants. The signature Vue Restaurant and Bar has a multi-level interior with panoramic views as a backdrop for its equally sensational international cuisine. Aroma brings together a casual, 'dining in the kitchen' concept, where several live cooking stations rustle up tasty favourites from teppanyaki and pasta to desserts, served hot off the pan for immediate enjoyment.

Clearly, no world-class hotel in Shanghai would be complete without an authentic Chinese restaurant, and Xindalu China Kitchen is just that. Regional specialities such as the legendary Peking Duck and claypot-baked Beggar's Chicken are unbeatable in this colourful setting. And what better way of recharging after a day of sightseeing than a comforting spot of tea accompanied by freshly baked pastries, cakes, and handmade chocolates at the Tea Room?

In the evening, look out from Vue Bar with a martini in hand to the bustling streets below. Reflecting the grandeur and dynamism of the city in which it stands, Hyatt on the Bund is truly the ideal destination for both business and leisure travellers seeking peerless service and luxury in an unbeatable location.

rooms
579 rooms • 52 suites

food
Aroma: international • Tea Room: European • Vue Restaurant: Western • Xindalu China Kitchen: Chinese

drink
Tea Room: tea salon • Vue Bar

features
Yuan Spa • 24-hour gym • hair salon • high-speed Internet access • indoor pool • satellite TV

business
business centre • conference facilities • limousine service • sercretarial services • translation services

nearby
The Bund • People's Square • Yu Yuan Garden

contact
199 Huangpu Road, Shanghai 200080 •
telephone: +86.21.6393 1234 •
facsimile: +86.21.6393 1313 •
email: info.shang@hyatt.com •
website: www.shanghai.bund.hyatt.com

jia shanghai

Twenty-first-century Shanghai is at the forefront of China's financial, commercial and cultural boom. The phenomenal rate of the city's progress has been widely compared to the speed of a lightning Maglev train. The rapidity of development is characterised by the way buildings seemingly disappear and appear overnight. The appearance of JIA Shanghai on the scene, however, is not so much an addition to the city's increasingly crowded landscape as it is a refurbishment of purpose, a re-imagining of ambition with flair.

Recreated from a renovated 1920s apartment building, JIA Shanghai opened its doors to the world in August 2007. The luxury establishment follows in the footsteps of JIA Hong Kong, the Philippe Stark designer hotel that sparked off a budding boutique trend in new Asia. As with Hong Kong, JIA's foray into Shanghai is an attempt to capture the paradox of the modern Asian city, to seek a stylish future while basking in familiar comforts—jia is, after all, Mandarin for 'home'.

To this end, the lobby feels as much like a contemporary art gallery as it does one's living room—the boundaries between furniture and objet d'art have been playfully smudged. Entering JIA Shanghai, guests are greeted by a stunning 'Cascade' installation. Set in a two-storey space, haute heritage birdcages are suspended from the ceiling above an undulating, contemporary Chinese, black lacquered sculpture. An idiosyncratic green velvet couch follows, encircling a black lacquered donut table illuminated by bare tungsten bulbs. The hotel's furnishings exude a tangible air of excitement throughout: dark chocolate walls and oak floors highlight

THIS PAGE (FROM TOP): Modern art and designer lighting in the lobby give JIA Shanghai an irreverent air; lushly designed rooms epitomise the boutique hotel's luxury lifestyle concept.

OPPOSITE (FROM LEFT): Issimo exemplifies the hotel's designer concept with its chic décor and quality cuisine; guests can relax in ultimate comfort and style.

...the perfect place for the stylish traveller to come home to.

the building's dramatic interior while giving it a rich, luxurious finish. If all this comes across as overwhelming at first, the lobby lounge with its cheerful red bamboo-inspired stools and lush sofas invites guests to take a moment and soak in the hotel's eclectic atmosphere.

Rooms range from cosy studios to sprawling penthouses. The balcony suite, in particular, offers a gorgeous art nouveau balcony overlooking the bustling intersection of Taixing and Nanjing roads—the latter being Shanghai's premier shopping street. Interiors are warm and alluring with dark timber-panelled walls and luxurious custom-designed rugs. Signature furnishings from Knoll, Minotto, Moroso, and Hans Wegner, and lighting by Flos and Artemide play up the designer lifestyle. To create that homely environment JIA Shanghai is famous for, rooms come complete with complimentary high-speed Internet access and Wi-Fi as well as a state-of-the-art home theatre system and extensive kitchen facilities.

In addition to its cutting-edge style, JIA Shanghai also prides itself on providing impeccable service laced with cheeky humour. Over New Year's Eve, guests returning from their revelry found a thoughtful gift waiting for them by their pillow: a pair of sunglasses and a pack of aspirin. With guests treated like beloved friends, the boutique establishment is likely to see many regular customers strolling through its doors.

The interior of Issimo—JIA Shanghai's restaurant and lounge—is rustic and cosy, and feels like a modern chalet with comfortable leather seating, logs for wood-burning ovens, and antler-shaped sculptures. Rustic furnishings are juxtaposed with contemporary pieces from noted designers. The menu, created by celebrity chef Salvatore Cuomo, features authentic home-style Italian cuisine cooked with passion, and includes award-winning pizzas baked in a wood-burning copper-clad oven specially imported from Naples. Issimo also features sensational cocktails and cool DJ music in its lounge.

With its designer lifestyle concept, dramatic artwork, and signature hospitality, JIA Shanghai is the perfect place for the stylish traveller to come home to.

rooms
39 studios • 14 suites • 2 penthouses

food
Issimo: authentic Italian

drink
Issimo: bar and lounge • lobby lounge

features
complimentary high-speed Internet and Wi-Fi access • flat-screen TV • home theatre system • kitchenette • Nintendo and Wii games available on request • techno gym

business
conference room • audio-visual facilities

nearby
Nanjing Road • People's Square • Shanghai Museum • The Bund

contact
931 West Nanjing Road,
Shanghai 200041, China
telephone: +86.21.6217 9000 •
facsimile: +86.21.6287 9001 •
email: info@jiashanghai.com •
website: www.jiashanghai.com

jw marriott shanghai

Since Shanghai shrugged off the heavy chains of market restrictions, it has transformed from a stagnant, sombre city into a dazzling dynamo of cultural and financial activity. The Shanghai of the 21st century is chic, cosmopolitan, and sophisticated; well up to meeting, and surpassing, the ever-changing tastes of international tourism. As one of Shanghai's most distinctive landmarks, the JW Marriott Hotel Shanghai towers 60 storeys above street level. A shining symbol of Shanghai's new-found vibrancy, the striking complex is living testament to the city's rapid development and vast economic wealth.

Located in Puxi—the heart of Shanghai's commercial and shopping district—JW Marriott Hotel Shanghai forms part of the massive Tomorrow Square compound, combining easy access to the city's finest dining and cultural attractions with the lush greenery of People´s Park. Those with time on their hands can visit the Museum of Fine Arts, or take a leisurely boat ride down the Huangpu River to view the Bund's many architectural treasures, all of which are also within walking distance from the hotel.

The interior of JW Marriott Hotel Shanghai is as impressive as the establishment that houses it; no expense has been spared in

THIS PAGE (FROM TOP): A heated indoor pool allows swimming throughout the seasons; stylish booths at Wan Hao Chinese Restaurant create an intimate dining atmosphere.

OPPOSITE (FROM TOP): Opulent furnishings bring luxury to another level; the ultra-chic champagne bar at JW's Lounge.

A shining symbol of Shanghai's new-found vibrancy...

creating an atmosphere of luxury and elegance. With 360-degree views of Shanghai's skyline, the sightseeing continues long after guests return to their rooms.

Shanghai's high-octane pace might prove to be overwhelming, but guests can look forward to a quiet, soothing environment to relax in at the end of the day. The rooms at the JW Marriott Hotel Shanghai are specially designed with this in mind, featuring a classic modern décor with natural wood veneers, silk-textured wallpapers, and fabrics accented with motifs that bring traditional Chinese chambers to mind.

Those having to work after-hours can do so in absolute comfort, with all the necessary hi-tech accessories at hand. Similarly, the 24-hour business centre provides full secretarial services, while function and meeting rooms, complete with state-of-the-art equipment, allow conferences and meetings to be conducted according to one's specifications.

Should the city start taking its toll on the business traveller or even the most enthusiastic tourist, the two-storey health club, inclusive of a 24-hour gym, indoor and outdoor pools, and jacuzzis, invites the weary to refresh and recharge. Indulgent guests can adjourn to the Mandara Spa with its wide selection of body massages, baths, and scrubs, while bookworms looking for a private reprieve can pick up any of the 1,500 bilingual titles at the hotel's library on the 60th floor.

Dining at the JW Marriott Hotel Shanghai is bound to be a memorable experience. The flagship Wan Hao Chinese Restaurant showcases exquisite traditional Cantonese cuisine alongside regional specialities in a contemporary, relaxed atmosphere, while JW´s California Grill is a scintillating mix of Californian and Asian styles that dazzle both the eye and the palate. The trademark Marriott Café serves international fare throughout the day, and afternoon tea at the Lobby Lounge is an event in itself with over 40 teas to choose from. For evening cocktails and champagne, JW's Lounge is ideal to unwind in and watch the city light up for the night.

With its exceptional amenities, impeccable service, and world-class dining all within a privileged location, visitors need look no further than the JW Marriott Hotel Shanghai for a delightful, memorable stay.

rooms
342 rooms • 255 serviced apartments

food
JW's California Grill: Californian-Asian • Lobby Lounge: afternoon tea • Marriott Café: international • Wan Hao Chinese Restaurant: Cantonese and Shanghainese

drink
JW's Lounge: bar

features
24 hour health club • high-speed Internet access • indoor and outdoor pools • library • satellite TV • spa

business
24 hour business centre • ballroom • executive boardroom • meeting rooms

nearby
The Bund • People's Park • People´s Square • Xintiandi

contact
399 Nanjing West Road, Shanghai 200003 • telephone: +86.21.5359 4969 • facsimile: +86.21.6375 5988 • email: mhrs.shajw.reservations@marriotthotels.com • website: www.marriotthotels.com/shajw

parkyard hotel shanghai

Traditionally, Puxi has been the heartbeat of Shanghai, located on the west side of the winding Huangpu River. Across in Pudong, however, things are beginning to liven up. Regarded as China's financial and commercial hub, Pudong's rapid modernisation has updated Shanghai's old-fashioned image by giving it a stunning, futuristic skyline.

Home to commercial developments and towering skyscrapers, this recently developed economic centre has acquired a new landmark: the Parkyard Hotel Shanghai. Launched in early 2007, its graceful surroundings have given Pudong's architectural landscape a breath of fresh air. Consisting of five low-rise buildings encircled by two beautifully manicured gardens, guests at the Parkyard are able to enjoy its lush grounds while sipping cocktails at the lounge. A tranquil ambience permeates the 26,500-sq-m (285,244-sq-ft) compound, creating an ideal escape from the bustling city outside.

The art deco influence reminiscent of Shanghai's colonial past is very much alive in the establishment's interior décor and furnishings. Guests are not the only ones who have come to appreciate the Parkyard's unique architecure: the hotel's emphasis on aesthetics earned it a bronze medal at the Asia-Pacific Interior Design Awards in 2007.

With the New Shanghai Expo Centre and Zhangjiang Hi-Tech Park nearby, the Parkyard is an ideal base for business travellers. Taking in the sights and sounds of Shanghai is also a breeze, with the Zhangjiang metro station and the revolutionary Maglev train station just a short stroll away.

THIS PAGE: *Clean lines enhance the calm ambience of the rooms.*

OPPOSITE (CLOCKWISE FROM LEFT): *The indoor pool looks out to the hotel's gardens; take in the fresh air while enjoying a meal al fresco; indulge in a refreshing spa session at the Parkyard.*

...everything that 21st-century China embraces: modernity, sophistication, and the future.

Guestrooms are decorated with earth tones and wooden accents, exuding a simple elegance that makes one feel at ease. Crisp white sheets and a goose-down duvet beckon with the promise of a good night's sleep, while wireless Internet access enables guests to maintain contact with the office and home easily. The urban oasis that is the Parkyard is fully appreciated when one pulls aside the curtains to reveal the lovely gardens below.

Priding itself on being a first-rate business hotel, the Parkyard features a fully-equipped business centre to make work trips a pleasure. Function rooms outfitted with the latest audio-visual equipment ensure the smooth execution of any seminar or conference. Business travellers may also want to consider the suites on the executive floor, which come with extra touches such as complimentary massages to refresh both the mind and body.

Massages are not the only activity to be enjoyed at the Parkyard's spa. Saunas and steam baths relax the mind, while the nearby indoor pool and comprehensive fitness centre invite guests to work up a healthy sweat.

For dining options, the Woodside Café's open kitchen concept is a definite crowd-pleaser. Serving innovative Asian fusion cuisine buffet style and à la carte, the café promises a memorable dining affair. A drink at the lobby lounge is an ideal way to unwind after a hectic day, offering a soothing mix of live music and professionally mixed cocktails. For those on the go, the Parkyard Station with its selection of oven-baked pastries and delicious sandwiches is the place to stop for a quick bite before heading out.

The Parkyard Hotel Shanghai represents everything that 21st-century China embraces: modernity, sophistication, and the future.

rooms
241 rooms • 59 suites

food
Woodside Café: Asian fusion •
Parkyard Station: pastries and sandwiches

drink
Lobby Lounge

features
fitness centre • indoor pool • satellite TV •
spa • wireless Internet access

business
ballroom • business centre • function rooms

nearby
New Shanghai Expo Centre •
Zhangjiang Hi-Tech Park

contact
699 Bi Bo Road, Zhangjiang
Hi-Tech Park, Shanghai 201203 •
telephone: +86.21.6162 1168 •
facsimile:+86.21.6162 1169 •
email: service@sh.parkyard.net •
website: www.parkyard.com

urbn hotels shanghai

THIS PAGE: *The rooms' minimalist, zen-like layout creates an inviting ambience for guests to relax in.*

OPPOSITE (FROM LEFT): *URBN Hotels Shanghai provides a pleasant respite from the bustling city; the private rooftop garden of the penthouse offers an excellent view of the city.*

The partnership of Jules Kwan and Scott Barrack is known for turning old buildings into niche redevelopments. Their flair for creating exciting modern living spaces is once more shown in the chic URBN Hotels Shanghai.

Situated near Shanghai's former French Concession, the luxury establishment resulted from the artful restoration of a 1970s factory. It is a tasteful mix of modern design and art deco touches, echoing the architecture of its surrounding streets. The eco-conscious abode is also China's first carbon neutral hotel, setting the benchmark for future projects.

URBN Hotels Shanghai's environment-friendly approach is evident with its renovation of an existing structure, use of recycled or

Bringing together the best of Asian culture with the latest in eco-chic...

locally-sourced bricks, tiles and hardwoods, as well as the installation of passive solar shades and water-based air conditioners. These fixtures reduce the hotel's carbon emissions, while providing all the modern comforts expected of a boutique hotel. Such renewable energy sources are designed to co-exist seamlessly with the hotel's artistic décor, allowing guests to focus on enjoying the experience of a green holiday.

Guestrooms are designed with a sleek, contemporary look in mind, softened by wood floors and rustic silks, which give the room a soothing ambience. A plush wrap around sofa in each room invites guests to put their feet up, while the lush platform bed forms the centrepiece. With an array of custom-designed bath products available, the stand-alone bathtub will be hard to resist, while in-room fitness kits, i-pod docking stations, and even special intimacy kits are provided to give rooms a personal touch.

The trendy Jiaozhou Road location is a vibrant hub of activity. The business, and entertainment district of Nanjing Road is just a short stroll away, while the former French Concession is a charming quarter to explore.

For an even more up close and personal introduction to the local culture, guests can choose from the hotel's extensive range of classes, ranging from basic Mandarin lessons to Chinese cooking workshops.

Bringing together the best of Asian culture and the latest in eco-chic, URBN Hotels Shanghai aims to give guests the ultimate in Chinese hospitality.

rooms
1 courtyard suite • 2 penthouses • 23 rooms

food
Room Twenty Eight: Western fusion

drink
Room Twenty Eight: lounge • URBN private bar

features
Chinese culture classes • flatscreen TV • high-speed Internet access • in-room fitness kits • in-room massage services • private courtyard garden • walking and bike tours

business
prestige car service • mobile phone rental • private function room • secretarial services • translation services

nearby
former French Concession • Nanjing Road • People's Square

contact
183 Jiaozhou Road, Shanghai 200040 •
telephone: +86.21.5153 4600 •
facsimile: +86.21.5153 4610 •
email: info@urbnhotels.com •
website: www.urbnhotels.com

kathleen's 5 rooftop restaurant + bar

THIS PAGE (FROM TOP): *Kathleen's 5 offers an impressive range of wines to go with its delectable cuisine; the classic interior exudes an Old World charm.*

OPPOSITE (FROM TOP): *Enjoy fine dining and the spectacular views at the same time; look forward to an array of innovative international fare.*

If a hard day's shopping or hectic schedule generates the desire for a restorative sundowner or a first-class meal in exceptional surroundings, keep this name in mind. Kathleen's 5 Rooftop Restaurant and Bar serves its inimitable style of international cuisine from a spectacular location on the fifth floor and rooftop of Shanghai's historic Museum of Art building. Whether as a backdrop for an intimate tête-à-tête or a venue for a private function, this Shanghai institution's prime location and gourmet menu are just waiting to impress.

Overlooked by the city's famous clock tower, the 360-degree views of downtown Shanghai from this glass-walled wonder are incomparable. The People's Square teems with activity below, while the skyline features the unmistakable silhouettes of the Grand Theatre and the art deco-inspired Park Hotel. In the middle of this visual cacophony lies a peaceful bamboo garden, a haven of calm in the centre of Shanghai's social and commercial hub.

Serenely surveying all of this is Kathleen Lau's stylishly lit Rooftop Restaurant. Born in Canton and educated in New York, Kathleen is something of a local institution herself, being a columnist on contemporary Shanghai life and the writer of an authoritative city guide. But it is Kathleen's 5 for which she is most renowned, as countless rave reviews in *Bon Appétit*, *Shanghai Tatler*, and *French Cosmopolitan* prove. A culinary magnet for the city's cultured and sophisticated crowd, it is a well-sited venue for coffee, cocktails, and innovative à la carte dining all year round.

...blends confident modernism with nostalgic tradition.

Kathleen's talented chef produces an ever changing menu. Starters include Chilled Cucumber Soup with Oyster, Radish and Caviar, and Beef Tartar with Quail's Egg, Black Truffle and Potato Wafer. For something different from the usual Chinese rice and noodle dishes, savour the unique Lobster and Fish Mousse Cannelloni, a succulent rack of Australian Lamb with Rosemary Jus, or the tasty Saffron and Mascarpone Risotto. Don't forget to save space for the divine K5 dessert tasting plate. Capable of turning your attention away from the stunning view, its seasonal selection of bite-sized desserts might include the delectable chocolate fondant and mousse with pistachio and praline ice cream, and the coconut passion fruit bavarois.

Reflecting its menu, the restaurant's interior design blends confident modernism with nostalgic tradition. The original indoor dining room retains much of its historical character, its sweeping arches and columns vestiges of the building's rich past as the British Racing Club. Yet on the rooftop's open-air terraces and striking, weather-proof glass corridors, the ambience is a stylish one with crisp white tablecloths striking a stark contrast with the restaurant's innovative multi-hued lighting.

Kathleen's 5 provides delicious globally-inspired cuisine in a sleek setting at one of Shanghai's most enviable vantage points. Seek out this exceptional dining and visual experience as the panoramic highlight of a trip to China.

seats
455

food
international

drink
cocktails • extensive wine list

features
dining room • wedding receptions • private events

business
conference facilities

nearby
Shanghai's Grand Stage • Urban Planning Exhibition Centre • People's Square

contact
5th Floor, Shanghai Art Museum, 325 Nanjing Xi Road, 200003 Shanghai •
telephone: +86.21.6327 2221 •
facsimile: +86.21.6327 0004 •
email: info@kathleens5.com •
website: www.kathleens5.com.cn

simply the group

There is one name synonymous with the finest of entertaining, dining, and retail experiences, and that is 'Simply'. Acclaimed by the press, Simply The Group encompasses five lifestyle brand concepts ranging from unique home furnishings and signature restaurants to a boutique shopping village. Each component blends Asian traditions with contemporary sophistication, an appealing combination that reflects the cosmopolitan vibe of Shanghai.

Simply Thai is the group's flagship and most recognisable property. Acknowledged widely as China's first authentic Thai restaurant, the original outlet was opened in 1999 in the

...synonymous with the finest of entertaining, dining, and retail experiences...

French Concession and now reigns supreme, having been named the 'Best Restaurant' in its respective category for five consecutive years by *That's Shanghai*. As rave reviews continued to flood in from *Shanghai Tatler* and the *Zagat Guide*, the second Simply Thai opened its doors among the shikumen houses of Xintiandi, offering a bar and lounge area as well as a function room. Two more branches followed, in the enclaves of Hong Mei in the Gubei district and Jin Qiao in Pudong.

As testimony to its authenticity, the *Shanghai Daily* reported that 'even the Thai royals dine at Simply Thai when visiting Shanghai'. This is no surprise, for its inimitable regional dishes—each served with stylistic innovation and professionalism—are as delicately flavoured and exquisitely prepared as in any gourmet restaurant within Thailand itself. Be it tom yum seafood soup, green curry or mushrooms sautéed with chilli, any craving for Thai food will be rewarded at this leading dining establishment.

The consistency and quality of all four Simply Thai outlets are strictly maintained as preparations are made in its central kitchen located outside the city centre. This world-class facility also manages Simply the Group's other restaurants as well as its catering arm.

With The Party People, Simply The Group has extended its philosophy of impeccable service and freshly prepared cuisine to the sphere of private and corporate entertainment. As Shanghai joins New York and London as a playground of the international elite, this premium catering service is primed to lend a

OPPOSITE: *Begin the evening with a delicious meal at Simply Thai.*

THIS PAGE (FROM TOP): *Indoors (left) or al fresco (right), Simply Thai offers guests an inviting dining atmosphere; Thai cuisine at its best.*

shanghai/restaurants 117

THIS PAGE (ANTICLOCKWISE FROM BOTTOM):
Simply Life's intricate tableware make excellent gifts; no event is complete without The Party People's stellar catering service; Simply Life redefines contemporary Chinese style.
OPPOSITE: *Vibrant colours and prints abound at Simply Life.*

sophisticated touch to any themed ball, corporate launch, wedding, or gala event. With an extensive menu of over 100 dishes to choose from, The Party People is sure to make any event a smashing success. It already counts Shanghai's 'It list' among its clientele.

The newest addition to the Simply family is Pin Chuan, a charming restaurant serving authentic Sichuan cuisine in the heart of the French Concession. Situated in a grand mansion reminiscent of 1930s Shanghai, the dining ambience is one of subtle elegance. With master chefs hailing from Chengdu, the capital of Sichuan province, Pin Chuan will satisfy any cravings for the aromatic spicy food that Sichuan cuisine is so famous for.

To add a beautiful touch to one's home, pay a visit to one of the Simply Life stores. Each outlet is a contemporary treasure trove brimming with every conceivable luxury for the modern home. Innovative Chinese designs abound inside, seen in the textured fabrics of handbags and silk photo albums swathed in shades of fuchsia, tangerine, and cyan. To grace the dinner table are cutting-edge glassware designs and eye-catching tableware collections. For an exotic Chinese ambience in the bedroom, choose from a dazzling array of colourful silk cushions and deliciously scented and sculpted candles. From local brands such as Asianera, Dragonworld, Jooi, and Simply Life's own house label to world renowned names such as Alessi, Ronsendahl, and Riedel, there is bound to be something that will capture one's fancy.

Simply Life burst onto the home fashion scene in 2000, and soon established itself as Shanghai's leading home design store. As the city's appetite for home-grown talent and international products grew, the lifestyle boutique expanded to include an outlet on Madang Road, in the chic retail hub of Xintiandi.

If one is looking for a unique shopping experience, head to The Village on leafy Dong Ping Road. Situated on the site of the esteemed Soong clan's former family chapel—the Soong sisters incidentally married China's most influential men of their era—The Village is a magnet for all things interesting and original.

In old Shanghai, it was said that the British Concession could teach one about business, but it was in the French Concession where

...a magnet for all things interesting and original.

one would be taught how to live. The Village, with its eclectic mix of shops, a French bakery, tea salon, and spa continues that tradition. A delightful haven where shopping is a true pleasure, a leisurely stroll among The Village's charming boutiques and eateries is but another opportunity to see and be seen at the eclectic core of Dong Ping's buzzing social life.

This diverse cluster of carefully selected shops is designed to pamper and indulge. Its impressive portfolio includes the Village Retreat. Managed by Simply The Group, the day spa's selection of rejuvenating treatments uses only products from Decléor Paris. Facials, massages, and body treatments take place in an aromatic atmosphere, encouraging spa-goers to throw off the stresses of the day and relax in comfort. The Village Retreat's combination of soothing aromas and exquisite oils promises an experience that will restore both body and soul.

Whether seeking intricate silver jewellery, Asian-inspired fashions, or luxurious leather goods from any of The Village's boutiques, The Village epitomises Simply The Group's vision of cosmopolitan Shanghainese lifestyle—a delightul mix of the old and the new.

Luxury living is incomplete without Simply the Group. With its collection of concept stores and fine dining restaurants scattered across the city, the lifestyle brand is slowly, but surely redefining Shanghai's image as a fashionable, classy metropolis for all to admire.

shopping
Simply Life: bags • fabrics • glass and tableware • home accessories and gifts

food
Simply Thai: classic Thai • Pin Chuan: Sichuan

drink
Simply Thai (Xintiandi): bar

features
The Village: spa retreat and boutiques •
The Party People: catering services

nearby
Dong Ping Road • French Concession • Xintiandi

contact
Simply Thai (French Concession): 5C Dong Ping Road, Shanghai 200031 • telephone: +86.21.6445 9551 •
Simply Thai (Xintiandi): corner of Madang Road and Xing Ye Road, Shanghai 200021 • telephone: +86.21.6326 2088 •
Simply Thai (Hong Mei): 28 Hong Mei Road, Lane 3338, Shanghai 200021 • telephone: +86.21.6465 8955 •
Simply Thai (Jin Qiao): Jin Qiao Pudong, Green Sports and Leisure Centre, Shanghai 200021 • telephone: +86.21.5030 1690 •

Pin Chuan: French Concession, 47 Tao Jiang Road, Shanghai 200031 • telephone:+86.21.6437 9361

Simply Life flagship store: 159 Madang Road, Shanghai 200021 • telephone: +86.21.6326 2088 •
Simply Life: 9 Dong Ping Road, Shanghai 200021 telephone: +86.21.34060509

The Village: 6 Dong Ping Road, Shanghai 200031 telephone:+86.21.6466 5123

The Party People: 3 Future Island, level 1, Sui De Road, Shanghai 200333 • telephone: +86.21.5477 0998

general facsimile: +86.21.6431 6334 •
email: goodtimes@simplythegroup.com •
website: www.simplythegroup.com

annabel lee shanghai

Annabel Lee Shanghai is a luxurious yet unpretentious home accessories boutique where eye-catching displays ripple with the finest Chinese silks, linen and embroidery. Proudly worn by fashionable high society and clued-in cosmopolitan travellers, a lustrous silk creation from Annabel Lee Shanghai's latest collection is eminently elegant and chic, completing every woman's wardrobe.

Situated on a quiet lane along Shanghai's vibrant and rejuvenated waterfront, Annabel Lee Shanghai's flagship store showcases the Peony Embroidery Cashmere Shawl, a must-have accessory in vibrant shades of azure or crushed crimson. The peony is China's national flower, renowned for its beauty and historically associated with wealth and prosperity; as an upscale gift or a bit of self-indulgence, the peony shawl is imbued with subtle cultural significance. With its intricate, double-sided embroidery, each of these unique creations absorbs one of Annabel Lee Shanghai's skilled craftspeople for an entire month, reinforcing the store's dedication to quality craftsmanship.

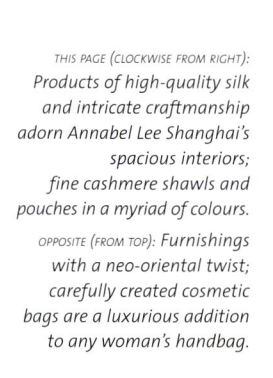

THIS PAGE (CLOCKWISE FROM RIGHT): Products of high-quality silk and intricate craftmanship adorn Annabel Lee Shanghai's spacious interiors; fine cashmere shawls and pouches in a myriad of colours.

OPPOSITE (FROM TOP): Furnishings with a neo-oriental twist; carefully created cosmetic bags are a luxurious addition to any woman's handbag.

...eminently elegant and chic, completing every woman's wardrobe.

Annabel Lee Shanghai also offers soft cashmere covers and throws, which are as adaptable as their colourways and textures are varied. Drape them casually over a bed for a stylish touch, or display their fine designs on a feature wall. Better yet, give them a more functional lease of life, as a blanket while enjoying a cosy afternoon nap, perhaps.

To add a show-stopping centrepiece to any room or for an enviably chic gift, Annabel Lee Shanghai also carries a prestigious range of products including silk handbags, dressing gowns, cushion covers, and unique tableware. These are all handmade by passionate, traditionally-skilled people based throughout China, each bringing a distinctive touch of their region and an individual flair to their work. The embroidery from Jiangsu province is particularly sought after.

The materials, aesthetic innovation, and techniques incorporated into these iconic products have all been inspired by China's rich cultural and artistic legacy. Each original creation succeeds in revealing to discerning shoppers along the Bund and beyond just what contemporary Chinese creativity has to offer the fashion world, wrapped up with a little timeless tradition for good measure.

These high-quality silk and embroidered treasures radiate quality, and are guaranteed to surpass the expectations of even the most demanding client. The gowns, drapes, and vivid patterns elaborate the flashes of inspiration from young designers both at home and abroad, exemplifying how China has caught the imagination and influenced the artistic currents of creatives internationally.

On the theme of inspiration, the exclusive boutique actually derives its name from an Edgar Allen Poe poem, concerning a very graceful, beautiful woman. This is fitting, for, like the poem, Annabel Lee Shanghai is graceful, artistic, and unforgettable.

In additional to its flagship store along the Bund, Annabel Lee Shanghai has another boutique situated in the popular shopping and socialising district of Xintiandi. Original, stylish, and functional, the works of art from Annabel Lee Shanghai not only make life more beautiful, living itself becomes a more stylish and colour-infused experience.

products
dressing gowns and housecoats • handbags and purses • home accessories • shawls and scarves • tableware

features
hand-made embroidery • silk and cashmere products

nearby
The Bund • Xintiandi

contact
Bund flagship store, No. 1, Lane 8, Zhongshan Dong Yi Lu (The Bund), Shanghai 200002 • telephone: +86.21.6445 8218

Xintiandi store, Unit 3, House 3, North Block, Xintiandi, Lane 181, Taicang Road, Shanghai 200021 • telephone: +86.21.6320 0045

general facsimile: +86.21.6323 0093 • email: press@annabel-lee.com • website: www.annabel-lee.com

annly's china

THIS PAGE: *Each artefact finds a place to shine in Annly's showroom.*

OPPOSITE (FROM TOP): *Annly's dramatic centrepieces are bound to light up any room; an old side table has been given a new lease of life.*

Breathing new life into old furniture is what Annly Chan does with a magical flourish. The founder and owner of Annly's China finds great pleasure in restoring antiques and endowing them with a modern flavour. It is precisely this that draws customers to her U-shaped office and showroom, where they are greeted personally by Annly herself.

'I delight in uncovering the true essence and beauty of each treasure that enters my showroom', she says. Indeed, Annly's renowned showroom holds countless precious pieces. To ensure their authenticity, antiques are carefully documented. This allows Annly and her staff to have an in-depth understanding of each piece, and the knowledgeable answers they offer underscore the passion Annly and her team have for each restored artefact.

Born in China, Annly graduated from the Taiwan National Art Academy and migrated to the US with her family shortly after. During a short visit to mainland China in 1986, Annly felt an instant connection to her homeland. Finding herself deeply intrigued by its rich culture and traditions, Annly decided to make Shanghai her new home.

Like all new residents in Shanghai, Annly found herself with an empty apartment to fill. Rummaging through the local markets for suitable fittings, she discovered an innate talent for turning discarded furniture into beautifully refurbished pieces. Before long, Annly set up her first antique warehouse in Wu Zhong Road, amassing a collection of antiques and artefacts from across China. Her ability to give forgotten pieces a new veneer of sophistication soon led to the development of an international client base.

In 2003, Annly's antique warehouse moved to its present location off Zhongchun Road, near Hong Qiao Airport. The new space now houses a gallery with an interesting collection of Chinese art, complementing the wealth of Annly's restored antiques. Today, the dynamic lady continues to oversee every detail of her business: talented craftsmen and artists are engaged to restore her extensive inventory

...restoring antiques and endowing them with a modern flavour.

products
custom-restored Chinese antiques • sculptures • paintings

features
art gallery • showrooms • tea room

nearby
Hong Qiao Airport

contact
No. 68, Lane 7611, Zhong Chun Road, Shanghai 201101 •
telephone: +86.21.6406 0242 •
facsimile: +86.21. 6405 7322 •
email: annlyschina@gmail.com •
website: www.annlychina.com

of high-quality products, while international designers and artists have been invited to create contemporary furnishings and artwork for the home. However, working closely with customers remains a top priority. Guided by the principles of 'authenticity, simplicity, and elegance', Annly says she is only satisfied when her customers are satisfied.

From Shanxi to Fujian, Annly scours the Chinese countryside for authentic pieces. Once restored to their former glory, additional fixtures are added to give each antique a modern-day functionality. This is done in accordance with customers' individual wishes. For instance, a wedding armoire could be transformed into a TV console, while a spinning wheel could be reconfigured as a side table—the possibilities are endless.

Smaller accessories are equally pleasing and range from stone Buddhas and beautiful porcelain bowls to rod iron lanterns. Like everything else in Annly's China, these skillfully restored pieces will undoubtedly add charm and character to any living space.

shanghai/shops 123

bund18

The architecturally iconic riverfront of Shanghai's Bund is one of China's most striking cityscapes. A mile-long strip of cultural heritage lining the banks of the Huangpu River, the Bund looks out to Pudong's skyline, Shanghai's glittering, 21st-century financial centre.

Bund18 is its most prestigious address. This stunning neoclassical construction received the UNESCO Asia-Pacific Heritage Award in 2006 after two years of careful restoration. As Shanghai's classiest and most fashionable high-end retail centre, Bund18 is home to world-class luxury brands and some of the most stylish bars in town. Without a doubt, Bund18 is Shanghai's most impressive post-millennium lifestyle and retail complex, and its beautifully restored, 80-year-old wrought iron gates have well and truly reopened for business.

Standing proudly on the thriving waterfront, this regal six-storey treasure is brimming with designer boutiques from Gabbiani and Ermenegildo Zegna to the exquisite jewellery and watches of Boucheron, Patek Philippe, and A. Lange & Söhne. With Bund18, the Bund has regained the glory of its halcyon days, worlds away from the 'funereal piers' as depicted by J. G. Ballard in his novel *Empire of the Sun*, and immortalised by Steven Spielberg in his film of the same name.

THIS PAGE (FROM TOP): *High fashion goes hand in hand with Bund18's elegant surroundings; Bund18's restored exterior.*

OPPOSITE: *Have a drink and relax in the lofty atrium.*

...Shanghai's most impressive post-millennium lifestyle and retail complex...

These chic establishments are clustered within Bund18's new, dramatic interior, in which awe-inspiring columns stretch upwards from the restored original mosaic floor, past traditional stone-carved fireplaces, to the 7-m- (23-ft-) high atrium above. This respect for the craftsmanship and integrity of the building singles Bund18 out from other commercial ventures along the river.

Art lovers may have already caught wind of Bund18's Creative Centre, the city's most sought-after arts event space. This sprawling space makes its home on the fourth floor, playing host to a changing series of exhibitions and launches in collaboration with some of the world's greatest names in art and design— London's Victoria and Albert Museum, couture house Dior as well as local artists Zhou Tiehai and Zhang Peili.

Lounge18 is the newest addition to this glamorous complex. By night, this bustling venue for design aficionados offers an extensive variety of art exhibitions ranging from painting and sculpture to interactive media installations. By day, the lounge is a hub for creative talent, where specially invited artists, writers, and celebrities chair lively forums and open lectures.

YOUNIK is a living testament to Bund18's continuous support for Shanghai's creative industries. Unfazed by the abundance of international brand names nearby, this vibrant concept store showcases the products of up-and-coming designers, jewellers, and

THIS PAGE: *Bund18's immaculately restored interiors.*

OPPOSITE (FROM LEFT): *Lounge18's inviting atmosphere ensures that conversation continues long into the night; the expansive exhibition spaces of Bund18's Creative Centre.*

artists from the burgeoning local creative scene. With Shanghainese soft sculpture designer Lin Ya-Li as a prime example, shoppers can look forward to avant-garde creations ranging from clothes to home accessories in this edgy boutique. Also constantly spotted are fashionable socialites and celebrities strolling through the long list of stores, making a visit to Bund18 a star-studded experience.

After a day's worth of intensive shopping, indulge in a meal or a cool drink at one of Bund18's excellent restaurants. In the atrium, the boutique Sibilla Café awaits those looking for some light refreshments or its signature paninis. The fifth floor is home to the exclusive Chinese restaurant Tan Wai Lou. Enjoy master chef Zhi-Hai Tou's innovative mix of traditional regional and Cantonese cuisines. Diners also have the option of taking their meal in a private dining room. Sens & Bund resides one level up, a contemporary French restaurant managed by three-star Michelin chefs Jacques and Laurent Pourcel. For a nocturnal pick-me-up, the elite Bar Rouge has an interior as glowing and dramatic as the Pudong skyline which it overlooks from an expansive open terrace.

A walk down the Bund is akin to flipping through the pages of a glossy history book, passing former banks, trading houses, embassies, and the iconic Masonic and Shanghai clubs. Each building has seen its share of secrets, intrigue, and high-powered decisions being made through the years. With gothic, baroque, neoclassical, renaissance, and art deco styles interestingly juxtaposed side by side, the Bund gives one the opportunity to wander through a veritable exhibition of world architectural styles.

Bund18 was originally constructed in 1923 by the British firm Palmer and Turner, and was the former headquarters for the Chartered Bank of India, Australia and China. In 2003,

...one of Shanghai's most exclusive dining and entertainment destinations...

with Kokaistudios' Filippo Gabbiani heading the project, an expert team of architects and engineers were called upon to begin Bund18's extensive facelift. With a wealth of archival material and specialised cleaning tools on hand, the restoration team spent two years deliberating over every detail to ensure that the building was faithfully restored. All of Bund18's modern additions have been carefully added in a bid to preserve the original design of the stately establishment.

Keeping Bund18's rich heritage in mind, the building's exterior was cleaned with toothbrushes so as to avoid the use of any damaging processes or chemicals. Such sterling efforts were rewarded on the global stage when the restoration project won the distinguished UNESCO Asia-Pacific Award for Culture and Heritage Conservation in 2006. The rejuvenated historical landmark now stands as one of Shanghai's most exclusive dining and entertainment destinations, housing the flagship stores of some of the world's most coveted luxury brands.

Bund18 has gained a new lease of life, setting the stage for future generations to appreciate fine dining, the arts, and an exceptional retail experience. With its long history, modern design, and superb location, Bund18 successfully balances the commercial needs of the present with the intrinsic value of the past. Without a doubt, it is the essential way to experience the new and old aspects of multi-faceted Shanghai.

shopping
A. Lange & Söhne • Boucheron • Cartier • Ermenegildo Zegna • Gabbiani • Lilyrose • Patek Philippe • S.T. Dupont • YOUNIK • Ulysse Nardin • Vertu

food
Sens & Bund Restaurant: French • Sibilla Café: Italian • Tan Wai Lou Chinese Restaurant: Cantonese and regional

drink
Bar Rouge • Lounge18

features
boutiques • events and art space • restaurants • UNESCO Asia-Pacific Distinction Award for Cultural Heritage Conservation

nearby
The Bund • Pudong

contact
18 Zhongshan East Road, Shanghai 200002 •
telephone: +86.21.6323 8099 •
facsimile: +86.21.6323 3099 •
email: info@bund18.com •
website: www.bund18.com

hu + hu

Mention 'Hu & Hu', and locals will point you in the direction of one of Shanghai's most respected antique shops. This bright and airy treasure trove is filled with striking centrepieces from bygone eras, waiting to adorn chic city apartments and rustic pieds-à-terre. Hu & Hu's eclectic interiors and unique, highly collectible pieces promise to tell visitors the real story of old China.

The two Hus in question are sisters-in-law Lin and Marybelle. These two affable ladies are famed for their 'no bargaining' policy, which comes as something of a relief for those uncomfortable with haggling, a commonly expected Asian practice. Their attention to detail and their friendliness has not gone unnoticed, with *Fodor's* praising Hu & Hu for its excellent personalised service.

The first port of call for art historians or those seeking decorative yet functional items for the home, Hu & Hu is popular with Shanghai's cosmopolitan crowd and clued-up travellers. Its product range boasts a vast geographical and chronological span, including such items as the wash basins of former Shandong landlords, and the personal wine cabinet of a Fujian merchant.

Hu & Hu's impressive portfolio ranges from small, delicate items such as hand-carved jewellery boxes to larger pieces of

THIS PAGE (FROM TOP): A colourful antique cabinet will spice up any living space; browse through Hu & Hu's extensive collection of antiques.

OPPOSITE (CLOCKWISE FROM TOP LEFT): Regardless of size, each piece is carefully refurbished to its original brilliance; a skilfully restored portrait.

...unique, highly collectible pieces promise to tell visitors the real story of old China.

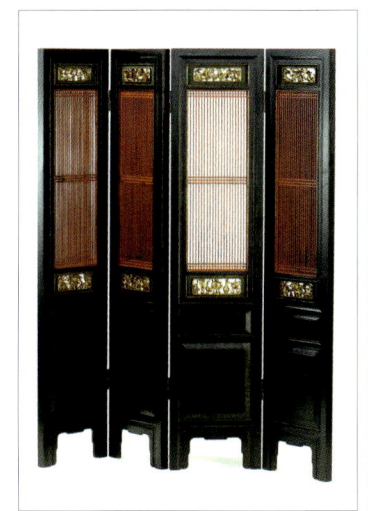

products
carvings • wooden home accessories • paintings • restored antique furniture •

features
custom resoration • international shipping services

nearby
Hong Qiao Airport

contact
Cao Bao Road, Alley 1885, No. 8, Shanghai 201101 •
telephone: +86.21.3431 1212 •
facsimile: +86.21.5486 2160 •
email: hu-hu@online.sh.cn •
website: www.hu-hu.com

furniture and exquisite, wooden artefacts. Items can either be chosen in a beautifully finished, 'ready-to-go' showroom state, or selected for customised restoration according to personal taste. With an extensive selection to explore and hand-pick from, a visit to Hu & Hu is bound to turn into an exciting journey through China's history.

From mountainous Tibet to the old Imperial capital of Beijing, Hu & Hu's antiques are sourced from thousands of villages across China. At any time, a visit to the Hu & Hu warehouse can turn up an Anhui farmer's wedding bed, an intricate 'Chinese rococo' table from Sichuan, or a beautifully lacquered cabinet from Zhejiang province. For the home, Hu & Hu's must-have list of accessories includes willow twig baskets, wooden trays, sideboards, and wall carvings.

While rummaging through historical pieces at Hu & Hu, discover how the classic lines of its antique furniture integrate into contemporary life: a granite bowl originally used for pounding rice becomes a flower vase, while an altar table is transformed into a computer stand. Adding rich oriental accents to modern homes and offices, Hu & Hu customises every object with a meticulous eye, preserving the integrity of each piece for future generations.

Historically, Chinese furniture has been appreciated for its exceptional craftsmanship—not a single nail is used. These same skills are painstakingly replicated by Hu & Hu's talented craftsmen, allowing forgotten antiques to find their way to new homes. So make a trip down to Hu & Hu and bring a piece of Chinese history into the 21st century.

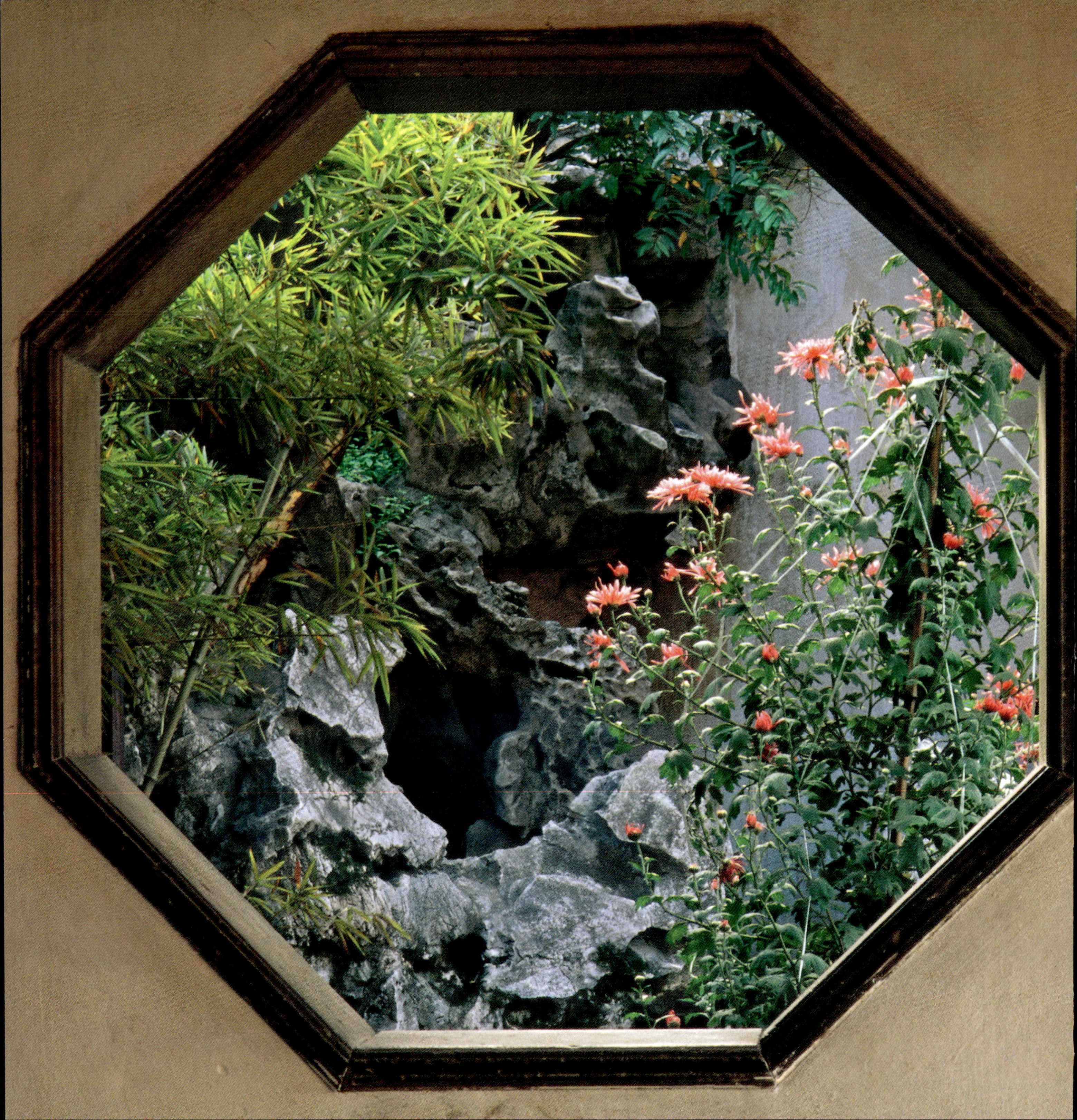

suzhou+nanjing

Jiangsu

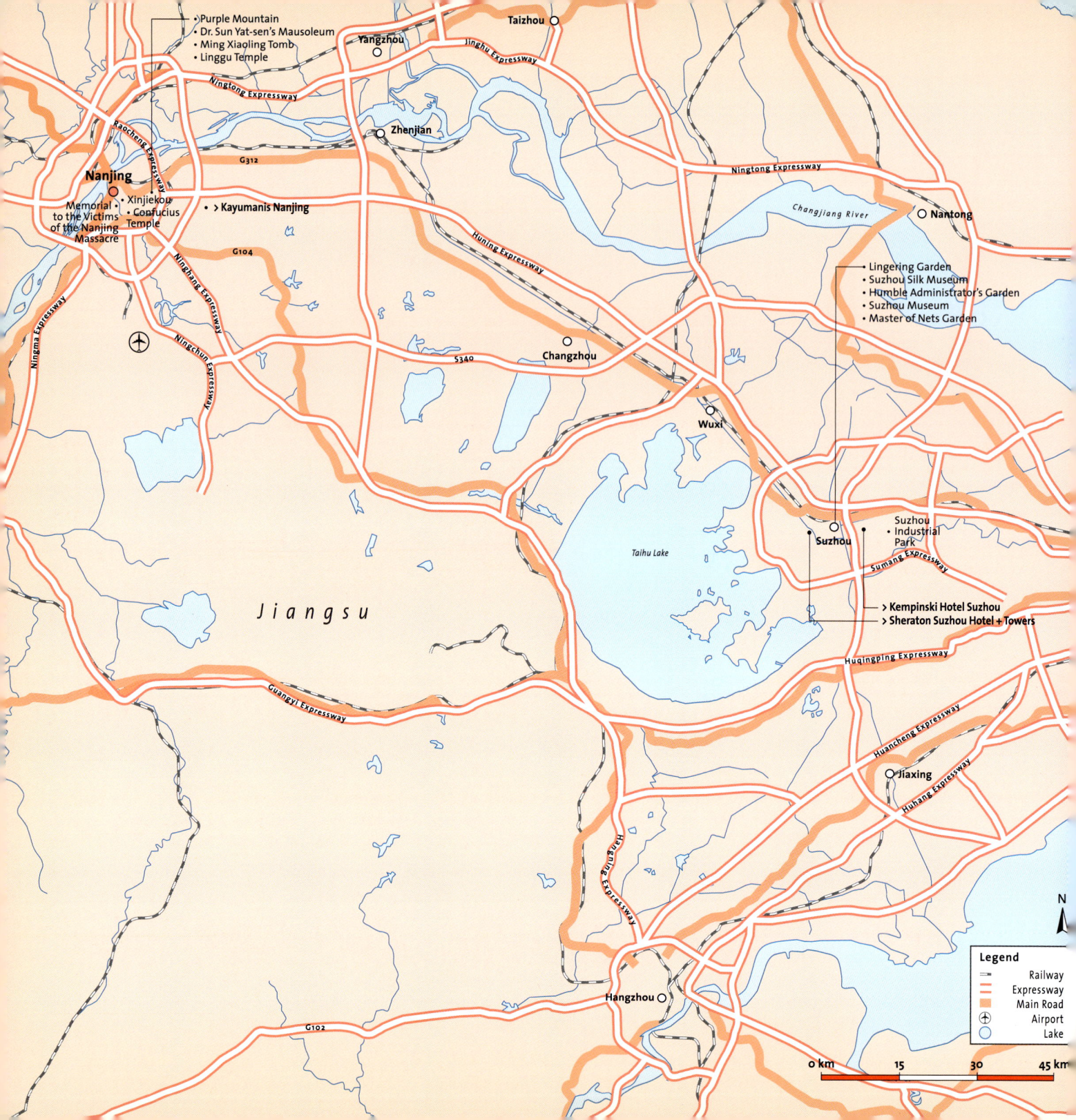

- Purple Mountain
- Dr. Sun Yat-sen's Mausoleum
- Ming Xiaoling Tomb
- Linggu Temple

Taizhou
Yangzhou
Zhenjian
Nanjing
- Memorial to the Victims of the Nanjing Massacre
- Xinjiekou
- Confucius Temple
> Kayumanis Nanjing

Nantong
Changjiang River

- Lingering Garden
- Suzhou Silk Museum
- Humble Administrator's Garden
- Suzhou Museum
- Master of Nets Garden

Changzhou
Wuxi
Suzhou
Suzhou Industrial Park
> Kempinski Hotel Suzhou
> Sheraton Suzhou Hotel + Towers

Taihu Lake

Jiaxing
Hangzhou

Expressways: Raocheng, Ningtong, Jinghu, Ningma, Ningxiang, Ningchun, Huning, Sumang, Huqingping, Huancheng, Huhang, Hanghu, Guangyi

Roads: G312, G104, S340, G102

Legend
- Railway
- Expressway
- Main Road
- Airport
- Lake

0 km — 15 — 30 — 45 km

a tale of two cities

Jiangsu is one of China's richest provinces. It is situated along the eastern coast of China, with the Yellow Sea to the east and the country's longest river, the Yangtze, to the south.

suzhou: 'venice of the east'

Historically, the Jiangsu region was dotted with flourishing riverside towns, the most famous being Suzhou. The maze of canals and arched bridges prompted Marco Polo to dub Suzhou the 'Venice of the East'. In his book *The Travels of Marco Polo*, the 13th-century explorer praised the city for its unsurpassed luxury and refinement. The town's economy thrived from the Tang (618–907) and Song (960–1279) dynasties onwards. The area became so well known that in the Chinese language, ancient expressions emerged such as 'Heaven above, Suzhou and Hangzhou below' and 'The harvests of Suzhou and Huzhou can feed the nation'. The city's golden age dawned in the 10th century, when the opening of the Grand Canal linked the flourishing Yangtze Delta with Beijing in the north. The growth of commerce and industry continued into the Ming (1368–1644) and Qing (1644–1911) dynasties and led to Suzhou's emergence as one of China's major cultural centres. The city was known for its superior silk, which was coveted by Chinese royalty and European buyers. Suzhou is also responsible for what is today considered the quintessential Chinese garden. Merchants and rich officials would commission gardens that reflected the Chinese aesthetic of taming natural elements. The large rocks found in these gardens are known as 'tortured' rocks, so named because they were submerged for years in nearby *Tai Hu*, or Lake Tai, to achieve a twisted, pockmarked effect.

But ancient Suzhou is quickly being swept up in China's galloping economy. These days, locals would probably point to the Fendi and Armani stores on Renmin Road as hallmarks of the city's luxury. And among the traditional Chinese gardens, all under the protection of UNESCO, modern glass buildings and a sleek new train station are being built. Still, the architecture and lifestyle that once elevated this riverside town to the highest levels of artistic fame during the Ming and Qing dynasties remain, and they are worthy of a leisurely exploration.

PAGE 130: *Enjoy a moment of peaceful contemplation at one of Suzhou's UNESCO-protected Chinese gardens.*

THIS PAGE (FROM TOP): *Rickshaws, tourists, and residents mingle on Suzhou's traditional streets; a Jiangsu woman embroidering by hand.*

suzhou+nanjing 133

THIS PAGE (FROM TOP): Snow blankets the traditional rooftops of the Nanjing Folklore Museum; sellers maintain the age-old craftsmanship that made Jiangsu products a treasure to merchants in ancient China.

OPPOSITE: Nanjing's modern train station welcomes wheelers and dealers swooping in to ride the city's economic wave.

nanjing: capital city

Up the river from Suzhou is Nanjing, the capital of Jiangsu and a city that has had starring roles in Chinese history. In Chinese, Nanjing is known as 'an ancient capital of 10 dynasties', though some report that Nanjing saw the rise and fall of only eight dynasties. Significantly, Nanjing (which means 'Southern Capital') was the nation's capital in the early years of China's golden age (Ming dynasty, 1368–1644) and again in the early years of the Republic of China, from 1911 to 1937.

The Ming Emperor Zhu Yuanzhang made Nanjing the capital of China in 1368, and it would remain so through the height of the Ming dynasty's glory and to its violent end. By the mid-1600s, falling tax revenues led to failures to pay the army promptly, which in turn led to desertions. Silver from the West weighed heavily on the Chinese economy, and harsh weather and poor state supervision led to undernourishment. All these elements resulted in the overthrow of the Ming dynasty by the Manchus, tribesmen from China's northern frontiers.

Almost 300 years later, Nanjing would become the nation's capital once more. It was in Nanjing that revolutionary leader Dr Sun Yat-sen, acting as provisional president, established a new republic when the last Qing emperor, Emperor Pu Yi, abdicated in 1912. It was the lifelong desire of Dr Sun, popularly known as 'The Father of the Revolution', 'The Father of the Republic', and even 'The Father of Modern China', to overthrow the Qing dynasty and modernise China along Western lines. The Revolutionary Alliance wanted the leader of China to govern from Nanjing, marking a symbolic step toward the formation of a civilian regime. Unfortunately for Dr Sun, his republican dreams would be ruined by criticism and party infighting, and he would be driven into exile once more the following year. Dr Sun's historical footprint in Nanjing is marked by an impressive memorial and mausoleum on Purple Mountain.

Over two decades after Dr Sun's revolutionary success (and failure), Nanjing would witness yet another historical event, though one much more sombre. In 1937, the city was the site of one of history's most brutal massacres, which is frankly documented by Chinese-American historian Iris Chang in her book *The Rape of Nanking*. The massacre is commemorated in a haunting memorial in the southwestern part of town.

Today, Nanjing is an important industrial and commercial city. Many visitors first step foot in the city via its new, modern train station, while the international airport sees double-digit annual increases in passenger traffic. Nanjing is also a major base for China's technology and outsourcing industries. The end result is a city dotted with proud vestiges of a turbulent past, and glossy new skyscrapers marking a modern future.

Jiangsu is one of China's richest provinces...

suzhou + nanjing: dining out

Jiangsu cuisine, sometimes called Huaiying cuisine, is one of the eight major cuisines of China. As the province is located on the Yangtze's delta, fresh fish and other seafood feature prominently. While some regional foods of China are known for their heavy sauces or gut-wrenching spiciness, Jiangsu's dishes are celebrated for their light and mellow taste. Presentation is a source of pride and particular emphasis is placed on carving.

suzhou

Guanqian Street is a large pedestrian street where one can find a mix of modern-day international eateries, such as McDonald's, Kentucky Fried Chicken, and Starbucks, standing alongside centuries-old traditional Chinese restaurants.

The most popular of these enduring establishments is the 200-year-old **Songhe Lou** (141 Guanqian Street). The restaurant has a muted atmosphere, with maroon drapes embroidered, aptly enough, with gold Chinese longevity symbols lining the walls. Songhe Lou prides itself on its version of songshu guiyu (squirrel-shaped Mandarin fish), a speciality of Jiangsu province. The dish consists of a meticulously carved, deep-fried carp served piping hot in a sweet and sour sauce.

Down the lane is **Deyue Lou** (43 Taijian Alley, Guanqian Street), which is twice as old as Songhe Lou. The secret to its longevity must surely be its tasty honey-glazed braised pork.

Jitang Mian Guan (1 Hanzhong Road) is named after its house speciality: chicken noodle soup. Its recipe produces a thick, savoury broth with scrambled egg, hand-rolled noodles, and diced scallions.

For fine dining, the Sheraton Suzhou Hotel & Towers has several options, among them the **Garden Brasserie** (Sheraton Suzhou Hotel & Towers, 259 Xin Shi Road), which overlooks the property's private landscaped garden, and offers both buffet-style and à la carte Chinese and Western dishes, and the elegant **Celestial Court** (Sheraton Suzhou Hotel & Towers, 259 Xin Shi Road), which specialises in Cantonese cuisine and other local dishes.

nanjing

A stone's throw from downtown Nanjing is **1912** (corner of Taiping Bei Road and Changjiang Street), a dining and nightlife area designed with grey brick and traditional rooftops. Head to the northeast corner to dine in style at **Bellagio** (Building A1, 52 Taiping North Road), furnished with plush blue seats and beaded curtains. Bellagio is best known for its shaved ice desserts, either served as a tall, fluffy mound of ice shavings (bingshan, or ice mountain) or blended like a smoothie (bingsha, or ice sand).

Nearby, **South Beauty** (Building 17, 8 Changjiang Hou Street) serves Sichuan fare in minimalist East-meets-West décor. Its version of the classic kung pao chicken is loaded with spicy Sichuan peppercorns.

Local tourists know to book at least a day in advance to dine at **Guibin Lou** (12 Chao Ku Street), a restaurant serving traditional Nanjing food in a lively street near the Confucian Temple. Deep-fried quail and shredded carrot pancakes are the house specialities.

Jinying Dajiulou (3–4/F, Jianhua Building, 56 Shigu Road) is popular with locals. They serve shuangse tudouni, the Chinese version of mashed potatoes with a dash of colour added for flair.

For an intimate French dining experience, head to the cosy environs of **Le 5 Sens** (52–1 Hankou Road), run by French expatriate Michael Martin. His menu is dotted with sumptuous classics such as coq au vin and quiche Lorraine.

And if one opts to spend a day on Purple Mountain, stock up on snacks at **Skyways Bakery and Deli** (10 Taipingmen Street), which serves fresh, homemade bread, and excellent pastries.

THIS PAGE (CLOCKWISE FROM TOP LEFT): A chef demonstrates his skills at preparing fresh hand-made noodles; go where the locals go for a taste of the flavourful Huaiying cuisine; dining is an art in the upscale establishments.
OPPOSITE: The elegant Celestial Court at the Sheraton Suzhou Hotel & Towers serves Cantonese classics in a refined setting.

suzhou + nanjing: a shopping sensation

Jiangsu is known for its unrivalled silk production. Historically, Suzhou was the centre of silk production during the Tang (618–907) and Song (960–1279) dynasties, and during the Ming (1368–1644) and Qing (1644–1911) dynasties, Suzhou's weavers were responsible for providing high-grade silk to the royal families. Buyers from as far away as Europe coveted the silk fabrics produced in this humble city. Ancient China's silk monopoly was so tightly guarded that exporting a live silk-spinning worm was once punishable by death. Today, Suzhou's silk companies and weaving mills offer luxurious, handmade products. Silk bedding and duvet covers are the favoured indulgences.

As for Nanjing, the city has gone upscale and international, in keeping with a more cosmopolitan outlook. For retail therapy in familiar surroundings, there is an impressive range of international flagship stores to choose from. But for a shopping experience among the locals, be sure to make a trip to one of the city's bustling night markets.

suzhou

The newly renovated **Suzhou Museum** (204 Dong Bei Street) has an excellent museum shop stocked with high-quality art and artefacts. The store features Suzhou handicrafts such as finely stitched silk paintings, embroidered silkware, ornate wooden lattice frames, and ethnic silverware. Outside the museum, **Dong Bei Street** has a number of small shops selling Chinese bric-a-brac. Be sure to bargain hard. For an interesting walk through Suzhou's silk history, visit the **Suzhou Silk Museum** (2001 Renmin Road). A modern look at Suzhou's silk industry is offered at the nearby **Suzhou Kaidi Silk Co.** (1965 Renmin Road), which provides English-language tours that end in a showroom stocked with everything silk. The **Dong Wu Silk Weaving Mill** (782 Binhe Road) is another stop for silk aficionados. It is the only grade-one state enterprise in China's silk industry and is almost 100 years old.

nanjing

Xinjiekou (intersection of Zhongshan and Huaqiao roads) is where you will find international brands and large department stores in Nanjing. The newest addition is the six-storey **Deji Plaza** (18 Zhongshan Road). The first floor is where high-end luxury names such as **Lanvin** and **Louis Vuitton** have set up flagship stores.

A popular local night market located on **Hunan Road** (between Zhongshan Bei and Zhongyang roads) is where locals go to peruse outdoor stalls selling a mix of flashy bags, accessories, and clothing. For a lively atmosphere, head to the area around the **Confucian Temple** (Jiankang Road), where the pedestrianised street is filled with Chinese retailers and street vendors selling everything from polo shirts to Ming dynasty hats. The area is bustling at all hours, but it is most lively at night, when all the neon signs lend their festive colours to the skyline.

THIS PAGE (CLOCKWISE FROM TOP): *Rolls of silk being dried at a workshop; Mao memorabilia on display at a street market in Nanjing; colourful silk threads hang from a market stall; a vibrant design of goldfish embroidered on a silk cloth.* OPPOSITE: *Huge displays of international luxury brands have become a part of the local landscape in Nanjing.*

suzhou+nanjing:ashoppingsensation 139

best views of suzhou + nanjing

With picturesque rock gardens and arched bridges, Suzhou offers a bevy of photo opportunities. Plan a visit to the Suzhou Museum's central garden for a modernist twist on the city's traditional charms.

In Nanjing, the vast number of cultural attractions on Purple Mountain will satisfy even the most avid photographer.

suzhou

Photo opportunities abound in Suzhou. Start at the **Humble Administrator's Garden** (178 Dong Bei Street), which is anything but humble. The vast garden covers 5.3 hectares (13 acres) and houses a maze of connected pools and islands. It was built for an imperial bureaucrat in the early 16th century and includes pavilions for viewing the moon and composing poetry.

Step into the future at the **Suzhou Museum** (204 Dong Bei Street), which reopened in the form of a striking new building in October 2006. Its new design is courtesy of I. M. Pei, a China-born American architect probably best known for designing the glass pyramid at the entrance to the Louvre Museum in Paris, France. Head to the museum's central garden in the early afternoon, when the stunning work of minimalist design touched with traditional Chinese architecture is bathed in sunlight. The garden has a fish pond surrounded by angular rocks against a stark white background, a bamboo forest, and a glass and steel pavilion.

At the **Master of Nets Garden** (11 Kuojiatou Alley), head through the back door of the main entrance and turn around to photograph intricate carvings of traditional Chinese courtyard life, found on the wooden door frame. The Hall for Keeping the Spring, in the northwest corner of the garden, was the model for the Ming Furniture Room in the Metropolitan Museum of Art in New York.

In the northern part of town, **Lingering Garden** (338 Liuyuan Road) has a huge central pond, best shot through the crevices of the garden's rock formations.

nanjing

Nanjing's **Purple Mountain** (Zhongshan National Park) is dotted with no fewer than 85 attractions. The highlight is **Dr Sun Yat-sen's Mausoleum**, a stark white building topped with a blue tiled roof best shot from one of the 392 steps that lead to the mausoleum. Turn around to get a beautiful shot of the mountain forests and the city below.

Just a trolley ride away lies the **Mingxiao Ling Tomb**. Proceed to the back of the tomb for beautiful photos of the its weathered, grey stone. Especially evocative is a pair of old trees whose roots have cracked through the stone pavement flanking the entrance.

On the other side of the mountain is **Linggu Temple**. On a clear day, head to the top of the temple for a bird's eye view of the surrounding mountain and the city. From the temple, follow the signs to **Guiling Stone House**. The crumbled remains of what was once the villa of a Kuomintang officer make for an eerily beautiful picture.

For a more urban, and festive, neon-lit atmosphere, head downtown to the **Confucian Temple** (Jiankang Road), where one can photograph oversized statues of the stately philosopher and his loyal students. This is also the perfect time to snap away at the eclectic mix of modern shoppers on the buzzing streets just outside the temple.

In contrast, at the southwestern end of town, the chilling **Memorial to the Victims of the Nanjing Massacre** (418 Shuiximen Street) is located on an execution and mass burial site, which was used during the Japanese invasion. The memorial's modern architecture is at once abstract and brutally frank. It is thought-provoking and certainly worth a visit.

THIS PAGE (FROM TOP): *A dramatic sculpture reaches out to passers-by at the Memorial to the Victims of the Nanjing Massacre; the gleaming blue tiles of the roof of Dr Sun Yat-sen's Mausoleum stand out against the backdrop of Purple Mountain.*
OPPOSITE: *A picturesque view of a Chinese junk on the river at sunset.*

bestviewsofsuzhou+nanjing

kayumanis nanjing

THIS PAGE (FROM TOP): *Relax and luxuriate in one of the open-air hot springs; the villas' tranquil surroundings make it ideal for a peaceful retreat.*
OPPOSITE (FROM TOP): *Kayumanis Nanjing mixes traditional furnishings with modern décor; this East-West fusion extends to its style of cuisine as well.*

The glorious capital during the Ming Dynasty, Nanjing remains a picturesque symbol of traditional Chinese life. Encircled by a dramatic mountainscape, this burgeoning destination is surrounded by the Yangtze River in the eastern province of Jiangsu. Nanjing has an extraordinary cultural legacy as well as a myriad of natural resources, from mineral-enriched hot springs to charming lakes. For the discerning traveller, it is also home to Kayumanis Nanjing, a spacious and luxuriously appointed private villa complex.

Indonesia's Kayumanis group introduced their unparalleled levels of personalised service and seamless luxury to Nanjing in the summer of 2007. Since then, these intimate and romantic villas have earned several accolades. Set among a watercolour of ancient willow trees and vibrant tropical gardens, each of the 21 beautifully appointed villas provides an exclusive hideaway for honeymooning couples, executives on a break, and intrepid independent travellers.

The one- and two-bedroom villas are artfully arranged around a private swimming pool, with natural hot springs in which to relax. With five-star standards of luxury, each individual property offers up to 700 sq m (7,535 sq ft) of absolute comfort, convenience and space, complete with the services of a discreet private butler.

The villas have been sensitively designed to reflect traditional Chinese values, and the superb natural environment in which they blend. Each is thoughtfully equipped with a gourmet kitchen, and an integrated living and

...the ideal stopover for the historian, as well as the sophisticated traveller.

dining area with satellite TV, high-speed Internet access, and entertainment system. For an exotic alternative to the gleaming, air-conditioned bathroom, there is an impressive outdoor shower room with a deep, expansive bath—perfect for guests to indulge in an aromatic bath beneath the star-filled skies.

Kayumanis Nanjing's pampered guests are treated to a complimentary massage upon arrival. This exclusive resort also boasts its own cutting-edge spa. With three double-treatment rooms and a generously proportioned sauna and jacuzzi, this wellness retreat provides an extensive menu of rejuvenating massage and spa treatments based on age-old wisdom and healing Chinese herbs—perfect as a follow-up to a walking or cycling tour of Nanjing's many attractions.

For a pleasurable evening, head to nine, the hotel's signature restaurant, which seats up to 40 guests in stylish comfort. Serving a mouth-watering array of Asian- and Western-influenced cuisine, its skilled chefs also create unique dishes for those with special dietary requirements. Afterwards, adjourn to the cosy atmosphere of the bar or lounge for a digestif. Discover the classic vintages in the extensive wine cellar, or have a quiet read from the selection of books available in every villa.

Nanjing is a microcosm of China, representing the peaceful co-existence of Old World charm alongside contemporary culture and convenience. With cultural riches right at the doorstep—from the Ming tombs to bustling Suzhou—Kayumanis Nanjing is the ideal stopover for the historian, as well as the sophisticated traveller.

rooms
21 villas

food
nine: contemporary Asian and Western

drink
bar • lounge • wine cellar

features
butler service • fully-equipped kitchens • high-speed Internet access • jacuzzi • minibar • open-air hot springs • private outdoor pool • sauna • spa • sundeck with loungers

business
courier services • faxing • laptop facilities • limousine service

nearby
biking • nature walks • Presidential Palace • Ming tombs • Confucius Temple • Suzhou

contact
Sizhuang Village, Tangshan Town, Nanjing 211131 •
telephone: +86.25.8410 7777 •
facsimile: +86.25.8410 2666 •
email: nanjing@kayumanis.com •
website: www.kayumanis.com

kempinski hotel suzhou

The established Kempinski brand of luxury hotels first took hold in Europe in 1897. It has since made its way around the world to the Middle East, Africa, South America, and, in recent years, Asia. In China, the Kempinski Hotel Suzhou is the latest in a string of Kempinski hotels located in Beijing, Shenyang, Wuxi, and other cities.

Nestled within the China-Singapore Suzhou Industrial Park (SIP), the Kempinski Hotel Suzhou is an exceptionally designed building complete with extensive facilities. The spectacular new five-star hotel is set against the picturesque Jinji and Dushu lakes, and overlooks the 27-hole Jinji Lake International Golf Club, allowing it to offer its urban pleasures within a refreshingly lush setting.

One may find the existence of a hotel in an industrial park something of an anomaly. However, it was precisely with the SIP's vast development in mind that the Kempinski Hotel Suzhou was built to cater to the comfort of business travellers. Not only is the hotel just a short 15-minute trip to many of the world's top 500 companies, its prime location within the Jinji Lake area underscores Kempinski Hotel Suzhou's commitment to supporting the development of business, tourism, and urban ecological design in the SIP.

To ensure that the needs of business travellers are fully met, the hotel boasts a 24-hour, fully-equipped business centre that provides secretarial services to make

...urban pleasures within a refreshingly lush setting.

work trips a hassle-free experience. Eight meeting and conference rooms ranging from 120 to 170 sq m (1,292 to 1,830 sq ft) come complete with comprehensive audio-visual facilities, catering to conferences and seminars of all sizes. The hotel is also Wi-Fi enabled, allowing business executives to stay connected throughout its premises.

Despite its focus on business travellers, the proceedings at the Kempinski Hotel Suzhou are never 'strictly business'. Leisure-seekers will find just cause to spend a suitably indulgent weekend in this luxurious abode. Airy and spacious guestrooms measuring 48 sq m (517 sq ft) and above come with plush, contemporary furnishings, expansive marble bathrooms, and 40-inch flat-screen TVs with satellite channels. The majority of the rooms commands a breathtaking view of Dushu Lake, Jinji Lake or the adjacent golf course.

To fully experience the Kempinski brand of hospitality, guests can choose from a variety of suites and executive floor rooms. Privileges include private check-in and express check-out, exclusive access to the executive lounge, which serves complimentary breakfast, afternoon tea, and evening cocktails, and, subject to availability, late check-out and complimentary use of the executive floor.

The Kempinski Hotel Suzhou has an extensive range of dining options. Fine dining establishments include Wang Hu Ge Chinese Restaurant, which serves exquisite Cantonese and Huai Yang cuisine, Seasons—an all-day dining restaurant—which offers a wide variety of delectable international fare, and a Japanese speciality restaurant. The Lobby Lounge or the Panorama Cigar and Wine Bar is the ideal place to unwind after a long day, where the considerable list of Old and New World wines is served against a stunning view.

To kick-start the evening, head to world-famous German microbrewery Paulaner Bräuhaus. Here, guests can wash down a Bavarian *brotzeitbrettl* with a pint of freshly brewed Munich lager to the vibes of live music. Guests can choose to sit indoors or on the restaurant's patio overlooking the garden and Dushu Lake.

OPPOSITE: *The Kempinski Hotel Suzhou is a magnificent sight in the evening.*
THIS PAGE: *Elegantly appointed rooms offer stunning views and luxurious amenities.*

THIS PAGE: *Savour an exquisite meal at Wan Hu Ge Chinese Restaurant.*

OPPOSITE (FROM LEFT): *Prepare for an intimate spa experience; Kempinski Hotel Suzhou's Japanese speciality restaurant offers authentic creations and panoramic views of the area.*

While the above would satisfy most, the Kempinski Hotel Suzhou has two other unique offerings to place it in a class of its own. The first, found next to the main hotel, is a 6,000-sq-m (64,583-sq-ft), state-of-the-art health and recreation centre with fitness and sports facilities under one roof. Guests looking for an intensive workout can head to the fitness centre and indoor tennis and squash courts. For water babies, the 50-m (164-ft) indoor pool, framed by ornamental columns, potted plants, and lively fountains, is perfect for a lazy afternoon at any time of the year. Guests will need little encouragement to head to the spa with its selection of refreshing mind and body treatments, steam rooms, saunas, and jacuzzis.

The Grand Ballroom is the hotel's other unique feature. 15 m (49 ft) in height and unobstructed by pillars, the ballroom seats

...front row seats to one of China's techno-development hotspots.

up to 1,500 persons for a banquet. Guaranteed to dazzle, the ballroom is adorned with 24 intricate chandeliers specially imported from the Czech Republic. The hotel's experienced events management team is also always on hand to assist in throwing even the most outrageously glitzy and glamorous parties.

For relaxation of a different kind, guests can escape to the natural haven of the freshwater Dushu Lake and the hotel's serene surroundings, perfect for a stroll at any time of the day. Alternatively, visit the famous Jinji Lake, just five minutes away by car. The 7.4-sq-m (80-sq-ft) lake, combined with 10 sq m (108 sq ft) of its surrounding environs, has been transformed from rural farmland into China's largest municipal park. Lush forests and wading pools are artfully landscaped around an amphitheatre, aquarium, a yacht dock, manicured gardens, and open plazas. To make the most of these features, the hotel conducts lakeside activities to ensure that guests fully enjoy their sojourn by the lake.

With many more exciting projects in store for the SIP, a room at the Kempinski Hotel Suzhou will mean front row seats to one of China's techno-development hotspots. Pampered by the best of modern luxuries in a beautiful, verdant setting, guests at this exclusive establishment will find their needs taken care of in the most refined way.

Be it for business or leisure, look no further than the Kempinski Hotel Suzhou for a truly memorable experience.

rooms
381 rooms • 75 suites • 2 penthouse suites

food
Paulaner Bräuhaus: German • Seasons: international • Wang Hu Ge Chinese Restaurant: Chinese • Japanese speciality restaurant

drink
Panorama Cigar and Wine Bar • Paulaner Bräuhaus: German microbrewery • The Lounge

features
executive lounge • fitness centre • high-speed Internet access • indoor pool • indoor squash and tennis courts • satellite TV • spa

business
24-hour business centre • ballroom • conference facilities • meeting rooms • secretarial services

nearby
27-hole Jinji Lake International Golf Club • Dushu Lake • Jinji Lake

contact
168 Guobin Road, Suzhou Industrial Park, Suzhou, Jiangsu Province 215021 •
telephone: +86.512.6289 7888 •
facsimile: +86.512.6289 7866 •
email: info.suzhou@kempinski.com •
website: www.kempinski-suzhou.com

sheraton suzhou hotel + towers

THIS PAGE (FROM TOP): Admire Sheraton Suzhou Hotel & Towers' classical Chinese style while lounging by the pool; cosy hotel rooms make guests feel at ease.
OPPOSITE (FROM LEFT): The hotel is enchanting in the evening; dining al fresco in the hotel's immaculate gardens.

For a delightful detour en route to or from Shanghai, look no further than the exquisite garden city of Suzhou. Just an hour from the big city, Suzhou is famous for its natural beauty, rich heritage, and splendid history. Filled with classical architecture and numerous hypnotic landscapes—of which nine ornamental gardens are UNESCO world heritage sites—a stay at the magnificent Sheraton Suzhou Hotel & Towers will make the sojourn to Suzhou truly worthwhile.

Allegedly named by Venetian explorer Marco Polo, Suzhou is fondly known as the 'Venice of the East' for it abounds with picturesque canals, historical silk markets, and intricate gardens. With colourful gardens and a placid lagoon, the Sheraton Suzhou Hotel & Towers is a convenient escape from nearby commercial districts such as the China-Singapore Suzhou Industrial Park. A microcosm of Suzhou's picture-perfect environment, the stately Sheraton is an essential stopover for the discerning cultural or business traveller to the region.

The Sheraton Suzhou Hotel & Towers boasts a selection of impeccably finished rooms and suites. Deluxe rooms combine splendid furnishings and richly coloured décor with every modern convenience available. In addition to high-speed Internet access, in-room fax machines and satellite TV, all rooms offer luxurious bedding, spacious baths, and oriental-style furniture, creating an intimate and inviting atmosphere.

The junior suites are ideal for extended stays, with well-equipped kitchens for private dining in a comfortable home-away-from-home environment. Executives availing themselves of the Sheraton's superb conference facilities will appreciate the added indulgence that the Tower Rooms provide: the host of additional benefits include private check-in, butler service, deluxe amenities and access to the exclusive Towers Lounge.

The Sheraton's wining and dining venues are designed to appeal to all moods and culinary preferences. For a traditional English tea or professionally mixed cocktail, the relaxing Garden Lounge is the place to be, while The Delicatessen and Bakery offers a tempting selection of treats—guests are shamelessly enticed by the aromas of freshly baked gourmet cakes and pastries.

As night descends, the casual Garden Brasserie commands an unparalleled view of the hotel's expertly manicured Chinese gardens, while offering innovative Western and Asian dishes in a buffet setting or à la carte. Carefully prepared Chinese delicacies in the form of signature Cantonese and Suzhou creations can be enjoyed in The Celestial Court's several private dining rooms. Finally, adjourn to the Pagoda Lounge to relax as live traditional Chinese music serenades guests through the night.

To melt away the previous evening's excesses, devote an afternoon to the health and fitness centre. The tennis courts and

...a must for guests looking for a classically-inspired Chinese experience.

fully-equipped gym will put one's physique through its paces before the soothing steam and sauna rooms work their blissful magic. Guests will have the option of soaking in the Roman-style heated indoor pool or reclining by the infinity-edge outdoor alternative.

For an unforgettable location that combines fine dining, corporate excellence, and leisure opportunities under one exquisitely crafted roof, the Sheraton Suzhou Hotel & Towers is a must for guests looking for a classically-inspired Chinese experience.

rooms
358 rooms • 28 suites

food
The Celestial Court: Cantonese and Suzhou • The Delicatessen and Bakery: pastries • Garden Brasserie: Western and Asian • Garden Lounge: afternoon tea

drink
Garden Lounge • Pagoda Lounge

features
butler service • fitness centre • high-speed Internet access • indoor and outdoor pools • massage services • pantry • satellite TV • sauna and steam rooms • tennis courts • Towers Lounge

business
ballroom • boardrooms • business centre • conference facilities

nearby
Suzhou Gardens • Suzhou Museum • Suzhou Old City

contact
259 Xin Shi Road, Suzhou, Jiangsu 215007 •
telephone: +86.512.6510 3388 •
facsimile: +86.512.6510 0888 •
email: sheraton.suzhou@sheraton.com •
website: www.sheraton.com/suzhou

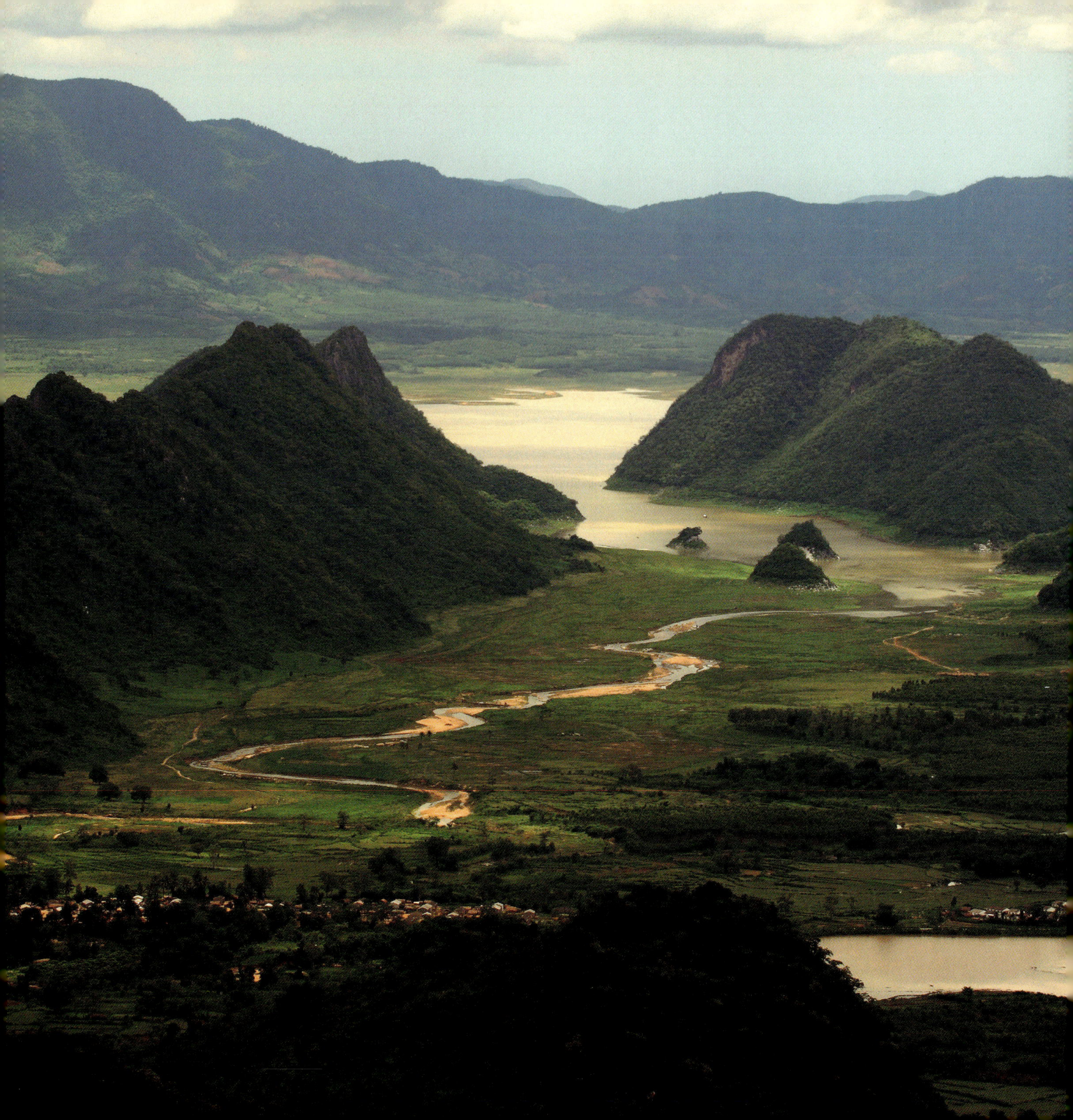

hainan

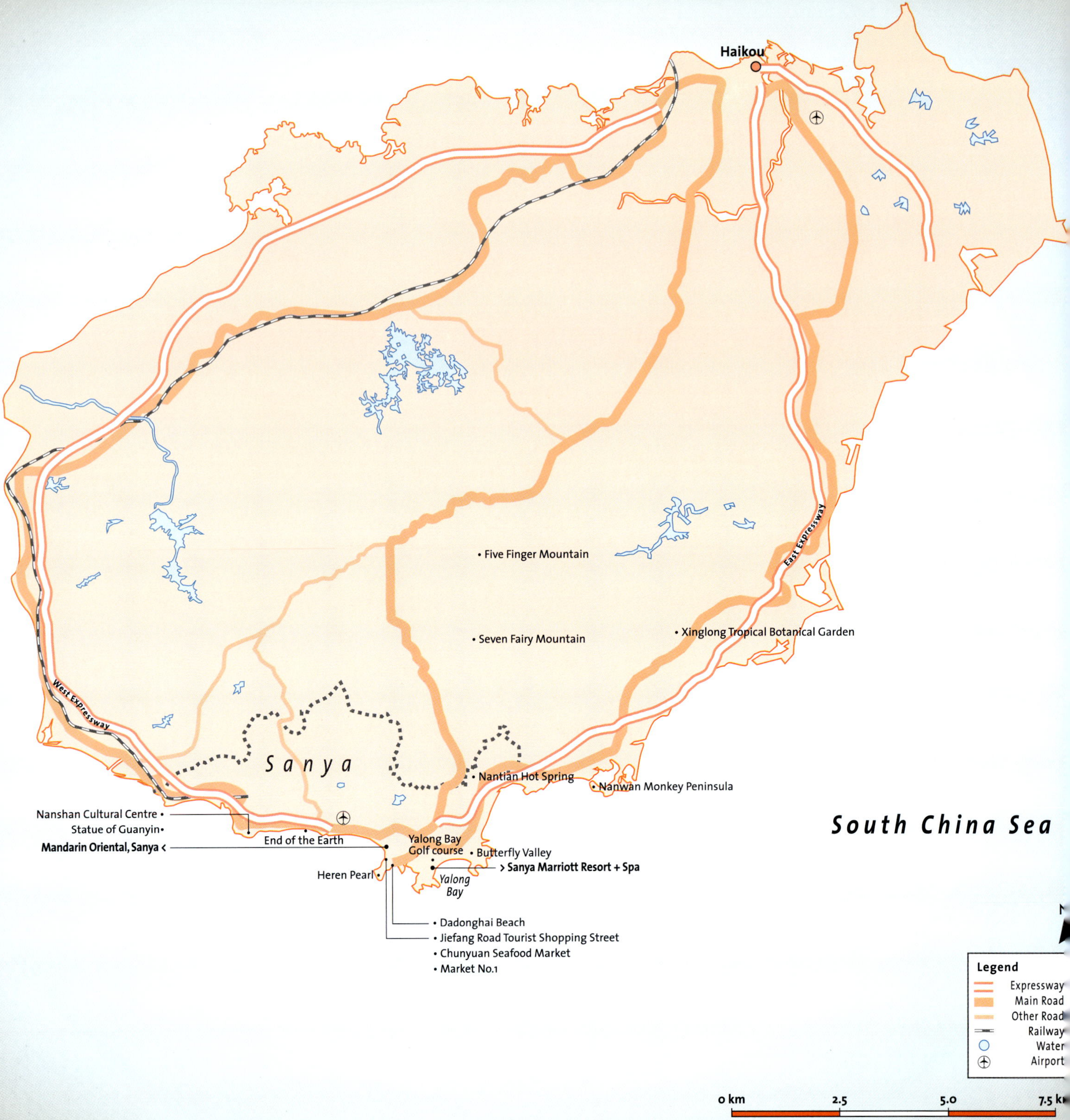
Haikou
East Expressway
West Expressway
Five Finger Mountain
Seven Fairy Mountain
Xinglong Tropical Botanical Garden
Sanya
Nantian Hot Spring
Nanwan Monkey Peninsula
South China Sea
Nanshan Cultural Centre
Statue of Guanyin
Mandarin Oriental, Sanya
End of the Earth
Yalong Bay Golf course
Butterfly Valley
Sanya Marriott Resort + Spa
Yalong Bay
Heren Pearl
Dadonghai Beach
Jiefang Road Tourist Shopping Street
Chunyuan Seafood Market
Market No.1
Legend
Expressway
Main Road
Other Road
Railway
Water
Airport
0 km
2.5
5.0
7.5 k

the 'tail of the dragon'

Ancient records dubbed the island of Hainan the 'tail of the dragon', the last unexplored frontier of China. Its remote location made it a perfect place to exile renegades, such as the Song dynasty poet Su Dongpo, who was banished in the 11th century for his radical writings and beliefs. Jayaatu Khan was also exiled here during the Yuan dynasty, only to return to the mainland and eventually rule as emperor from 1329 to 1332.

tied to history

Charlie Soong (1863–1918) is arguably the island's most famous historical figure. Hainan-born, Soong was the first international student at Trinity College (present-day Duke University) and later graduated from Vanderbilt University in the US. He returned to China to be a missionary but eventually became one of the nation's most successful businessmen. He would become closely tied to the nation's politics both through his support of the Tongmenhui led by the revolutionary leader Dr Sun Yat-sen and through his children, who would each play a significant role in the history of 20th-century China. His daughters were the famous Soong sisters: Ai-ling was the wife of H.H. Kung, once the richest man in China and Premier of the Republic of China from 1938 to 1939; Ch'ing-ling, the wife of Dr Sun, and May-ling, a.k.a. 'Madame Chiang Kai-shek', the wife of the Nationalist leader. It was during the political upheaval of the 1920s and 1930s that Hainan made history as Communists and Nationalist Party forces battled for control of the island.

Hainan's history is also, to some extent, the history of its ethnic minorities and their enduring folk art and culture. The official ethnic groups of Hainan are the Han, Li, Miao, and Hui. With such a multi-ethnic society, it is no wonder the island celebrates a number of local festivals. Sanyuesan (literally 'Three Month Three') is held on the third day of the third month of the lunar calendar, usually early March on the Western calendar. During Sanyuesan, the Li and Miao hold traditional wedding and ancestor-worship ceremonies. A more modern festival occurs during the first 10 days of April, when the island hosts the Hainan International Coconut Festival. Expect to see quirky coconut lamps and plenty of street-side coconut tastings during this celebration.

hainan today

Hainan has found itself in the international spotlight a few times in recent years, although not always for the best reasons. In 2001, for example, the island became the focal point of diplomatic tension between China and the US when a US Navy EP-3 Aries II made an emergency landing on

PAGE 150: *Stunning mountains and lush rainforests in Hainan's interior offer the perfect urban escape.*

THIS PAGE (FROM TOP): *Hainan was known as the 'tail of the dragon' in ancient China; the colourful traditional ethnic costume of the Li.*

Hainan after a collision with a Chinese fighter jet (the island is home to several important People's Liberation Army Navy air bases), a matter that has yet to be resolved. More recently, Zhang Huimin, an eight-year-old girl, ran from Sanya—a seaside town at the southern tip of the island—to Beijing to showcase her Olympic potential for the 2008 Beijing Olympic Games. Zhang's father, who followed her on a bicycle, was accused of abuse by both domestic and international media; the pint-sized athlete had covered 3,500 km (2,175 miles)—the equivalent of about 82 marathons—in 55 days!

Political intrigue and extreme athletics aside, Hainan is today known first and foremost as a popular Chinese tourist destination, luring visitors with tropical temperatures ranging from 22°C (72°F) to 26°C (79°F) and boasting about 12 hours of daylight every day, all year. The destination of choice is Sanya, China's very own Hawaii-like getaway. Five years ago, there were only a handful of mid-range hotels; today, popular names from Crowne Plaza to Sheraton to Ritz-Carlton are cropping up along the area's white-sand beaches.

holiday capital

With average January temperatures of 28°C (82°F), Sanya is China's holiday capital. It is located at the southern tip of Hainan Island and looks out over the South China Sea. A population of 450,000 means the city is also pleasantly un-crowded, a rarity in China. More than 20 different nationalities inhabit Sanya, though like the rest of China, Putonghua, or Mandarin, is the common language. Perched at the southernmost end of Sanya, one stretch of beach has earned the moniker of the 'End of the Earth' or Tianya Haijiao.

The city hosts a number of events each year. Arguably its most notorious event, however, is the International Wedding Festival held at the End of the Earth, which entails a mass outdoor wedding celebration that takes place every November. Hundreds of couples from around China, and occasionally from around the world, gather by the beach to vow their eternal devotion to each other, travelling to the end of the earth to prove their love will last to the end of time.

Sanya is still a delightful destination even if one is not a nuptial-seeking couple. It is a perfect place to escape from China's muggy skies and the stressful tempo of city life. With quality dining options and a bevy of international five-star hotels moving in, Sanya is on track to becoming a world-class holiday destination.

THIS PAGE: *Hainan's tropical climate makes it a destination unlike any other in China.*

OPPOSITE: *The twinkling lights of international five-star hotels mark Sanya's cityscape.*

...a popular Chinese tourist destination, luring visitors with tropical temperatures...

hainan: dining out

With the explosion of five-star hotels and international visitors, Sanya has developed a robust international dining scene. One can find here everything from pizza to sushi. The food of choice, naturally, is seafood, and at least one evening spent dining on fresh fish or lobster is in order when visiting Sanya.

seafood

Chunyuan Seafood Square (Hexi Road, near City Park) is a huge outdoor area filled with hundreds of tables and plenty of seafood vendors. Prices, offered by the *jin*—roughly 0.5 kg (1.1 lb)—are written on white boards placed behind the vendors. Diners may choose to have their order steamed, served in a hot pot or fried. Off the tourist track is **Feipo Seafood Restaurant** (Shengli Road), where one can pull up a stool and dine with the locals. **Sampan Seafood Restaurant** (Gloria Resort Sanya) bills itself as a Cantonese restaurant but serves a variety of dishes from all over the mainland. Try the generously portioned salmon sashimi.

For an upscale dining experience at one of the international resorts lining Yalong Bay on the eastern side of the city, try **.IZE** (Hilton Sanya Resort & Spa) for its premium seafood and fine wine. Sit indoors and watch colourful ocean life float around the central aquarium, or head to the patio to listen to ocean waves while dining. **Dongjiao Palm Tree Seafood Restaurant** (109 Yuya Avenue) is another upscale seafood restaurant. Traditional folk dance performances accompany evening meals.

chinese cuisine

Chinese Restaurant (Mangrove Tree Resort) offers Chongsan, Hakka and Shunde cuisine. The menu features casserole, dim sum and Chinese barbeque options. For Hainanese food, try **Liguo Restaurant** (Hexi Road), which offers a wide range of local dishes. On weekends, bring a big appetite to **Osmanthus Restaurant** (Resort Golden Palm) for its seafood barbeque buffet. This restaurant also specialises in local Hainanese dishes.

asian cuisine

At **Indochine** (1/F, Building A, Sanya Marriott Resort & Spa), a seat next to the dramatic open kitchen affords mouthwatering views of the authentic French-Vietnamese fare on offer. The restaurant's mustard-yellow walls and dark wood furniture create a cosy atmosphere. For vegetarian fare, try **Spice Garden** (Sheraton Sanya), which offers a good number of healthy choices. Combine a trip to the Nanshan Cultural Centre with a meal at **Yuan Qi Lou** (Nanshan Cultural Tourism Zone). This is perhaps the only completely vegetarian restaurant in the area.

international

Versailles Restaurant (Hexi Road) offers a mélange of Asian and Western options. The first floor has a cabaret feel, complete with a central grand piano, while the second level is reminiscent of an outdoor French bistro with a dash of tropical colour added, courtesy of a few aquariums. If it's pizza one craves, head to **Roma Pizzeria** (1 Haiyun Road), by far the best pizza joint in town.

THIS PAGE (CLOCKWISE FROM TOP LEFT): Enjoy authentic French-Vietnamese cuisine (top left and top right) in the warm glow of Indochine (below) at the Sanya Marriott Resort & Spa.
OPPOSITE: Fine views accompany the fresh seafood served at the Hilton's .IZE restaurant on Yalong Bay.

hainan's great outdoors

Many visitors define outdoor activity in Sanya as lying perfectly still on a lounge chair and having service staff deliver coconut drinks. For those who are a bit more inclined towards movement, Hainan offers plenty of water-related activities and a few respectable golf courses.

sporting action

Golf is a popular sport for resort visitors and there are several courses around Sanya. The best option is **Yalong Bay Golf Club** (Yalong Bay National Resort District), designed by American Robert Trent Jones II. It has repeatedly ranked amongst China's top 10 golf courses. The Robert McFarland-designed **Sun Valley Sanya Golf Resort** (Yalong Bay National Resort District) is another popular option. Sun Valley's 340,000-sq-km (131,275-sq-mile) course overlooks the Yalong Bay Basin. The 27 holes of championship-level golf come with China's only par

6 (828 yards!) at the 18th hole. For a lighter round on the green, **Kangle Garden HNA Resort** (Xinglong Town, Wanning) offers an 18-hole course.

For another kind of ball game, the Chinese women's Olympic volleyball team is in residence at Sanya Bay until the 2008 Olympics. As a result, volleyball courts are found on most beaches and a professional facility with multiple courts is being set up beachside on Sanya Bay.

sea sports

The bays and tropical waters of Sanya offer pleasant opportunities for scuba-diving. Natural coral reefs and tropical fish live in the clear waters, with visibility at depths of 16 m to 20 m (52 ft to 66 ft). Popular dive spots include Mei Ren Reef Island, Wild Pig, Xi Pai and West islands. Organise a scuba trip with **Sanya PADI Diving** (Crowne Plaza Hotel Sanya) for a day of exploration.

Surfing has recently taken off on Hainan's east coast. **Sanya Surf Club** (Room 8219, 2/F, Yindu Hotel, 8 Huyuan Road), offering services in English and several other languages, arranges day trips from Sanya. Other popular water sports and water-related activities in the area include snorkelling, jet-skiing, underwater sea walking, underwater sightseeing boats, and speedboats, wave runners, and sailboats. Parasailing is another popular activity, one to be tried on breezy days, of course. All these activities can be enjoyed at various locations around the island and can be organised through activity centres at major hotels.

hot springs

Natural hot springs are a pleasant way to soothe muscles tired out by golfing excursions or water sports. The **Pearl River Nantian Hot Spring Resort** (Tengqiao Expressway Entrance) is a quick 20-minute drive from Yalong Bay and a convenient tourist choice. The base of **Seven Fairies Mountain** (Baoting National Rainforest Park) hosts about 20 hot springs with an average temperature of 70°C (158°F)—the hottest spring registers at 94°C (201°F). The area (along with **Five Finger Mountain**) is also a popular trekking spot.

THIS PAGE (FROM TOP): Sanya has several good golf courses for those who fancy a round on the green; enjoy a day of sea sports or laze on the beach at one of Sanya's bays, then head to one of the dining establishments nearby when the sun goes down.

OPPOSITE: Take advantage of Hainan's tropical climate with a boat trip around Sanya's bays and neighbouring islands; go snorkelling or scuba-diving among coral reefs and the colourful tropical fish that inhabit them.

best views of hainan

THIS PAGE: *A glorious tropical sunset on the shores of Sanya.*

OPPOSITE (FROM TOP): *The large stone sculpture at the entrance to Luhuitou Park is based on a romantic legend upon which the area is named; Chinese characters carved upon the rocks at the 'End of the Earth'; a Li minority village deep in the verdant interior of Hainan Island.*

Sanya is overflowing with picturesque natural scenery, punctuated every now and then by humbling human-made structures. Even a basic point-and-shoot will capture beautiful images of China's tropical paradise.

One of Sanya's most imposing sights is its **statue of Guanyin** (Buddhism's Goddess of Mercy), which, standing at 108 m (354 ft), can be photographed during the plane ride into town. For a closer view, head to the **Nanshan Cultural Centre** (Nanshan Cultural Tourist Area), which also houses several Buddhist temples and offers views of the sea.

Upon arrival in Sanya, most Chinese tourists make a beeline for the **End of the Earth** (Tianya Haijiao Tourist District). The largest rocks on the beach have been inscribed with the Chinese characters of the name of this tourist destination—the perfect backdrop for capturing a memento, on camera, of a visit here.

More tropical views await at the popular **Sanya Bay**, **Dadonghai Bay**, and **Yalong Bay**, where brilliant blue skies, white sandy beaches, swaying green coconut groves, and the clear waters of the South China Sea guarantee vibrant photographs.

For a brush with nature, take advantage of the cooler morning air with an early trip to **Butterfly Valley** (Yalong Bay International Tourist Area), where over 100 species of butterflies flutter amongst the flora. Children will enjoy a trip to **Nanwan Monkey Peninsula** (Nanwan Hou Dao Tourist District, Xincun Town), also known as Monkey Island. The island is covered in forest and fruit trees. Try wandering off the beaten path to encounter these primates in a more natural habitat. A visit to **Luhuitou Park** (Luhuitou Peninsula), which sits atop a hill, affords wonderful panoramic views of the sea, mountains, and downtown Sanya.

Alternatively, go beyond Sanya's boundaries to visit some of Hainan's parks and nature reserves for a view of its verdant interiors. **Xinglong Tropical Botanical Garden** (Xinglong Redai Zhi Bo Yuan, Wanning) is just an hour's drive from Sanya. Built in the mid-1950s, it was the first of its kind in China. The vast park hosts over 1,200 tropical plants from 40 different countries and regions. Walking tours take visitors past cacao, coffee, pepper, and vanilla plants, and tropical fruits such as coconut and durian. To capture charming vistas in lush natural surroundings, arrange for a day trip to **Five Finger Mountain** (Shui Man Xiang). The mountain range has five peaks—the highest stands at 1,867 m (6,125 ft)—and is dotted with villages of ethnic minority communities, banana farms, and waterfalls.

bestviewsofhainan 161

mandarin oriental, sanya

THIS PAGE (FROM TOP): *Indulge in the resort's spa facilities; Hainanese accents give luxurious rooms a local touch.*
OPPOSITE (FROM LEFT): *Getting in the mood for a holiday; breathtaking seaviews from every angle.*

There are few resorts that offer expansive views of the South China sea from every room, suite, and villa—and this is just one of many things that makes Mandarin Oriental, Sanya special. Spread over 12 hectares (30 acres) of private beachfront on Coral Bay, and just 20 minutes from Sanya Phoenix International Airport, the resort's location is unparalleled.

Mandarin Oriental, Sanya boasts 297 elegantly appointed rooms, most with direct access to the resort's private beach. Guests can also choose from the Pavilion rooms—complete with a private plunge pool or gazebo, as well as any of the 15 private villas and 19 suites scattered throughout the compound. For that extra touch of exclusivity, each of the resort's villas comes with its own lap pool, garden, relaxation pavillion, in-room spa services, and access to The Cliff, a lounge serving complimentary breakfast, snacks, and cocktails.

Rooms are decorated along the lines of contemporary Asian architecture, with a distinct Hainanese flavour. Coconut-weave headboards complement the room's warm décor and crisp bedlinen, accentuating the relaxed, tropical atmosphere that Hainan Island is famous for. Floor-to-ceiling windows bring in the sea breeze while providing a mesmerising view of the beach. Modern amenities such as plasma TVs, high-speed Internet access, and Nespresso machines provide the requisite urban conveniences.

At the sprawling 3,200-sq-m (34,445-sq-ft) spa village, guests will be spoilt for choice with the wide variety of massages, facials, heat- and hydrotherapies offered. Sessions are carried out in any of the 18 treatment suites, each furnished with steam and rain showers, and an outdoor bathtub. Eight couple suites and two VIP villas are also available for even greater luxury. Reserved especially for VIP villa guests, the spa's 'secret garden' features outdoor treatment areas and a private bathing house. To keep in line with the resort's focus on well-being, a qualified traditional Chinese medicine doctor is on hand to offer personal consultations and Chinese-inspired therapies.

Naturally, dining options abound at this exquisite resort, with 11 restaurants and bars. This includes Yi Yang, which

...expansive views of the sea at every turn...

serves classic Cantonese cuisine. Diners can look forward to fresh dim sum for lunch and traditional Chinese favourites in the evening.

With a direct view of the ocean, Fresh serves the finest seafood on the island. Its unique wood and coconut fire grill, and Southeast Asian and French cooking styles make this beachfront grill perfect for intimate dinners and informal gatherings. Expect signature dishes such as Gratinated Lobster with Mustard Shell Cream and Singapore-style Pepper Crabs, as well as an extensive wine list to complement the meal. Wave offers creations inspired by American and Mexican cuisine, while the sunken Pool Bar, located in one of the resort's three infinity-edged pools, will be a treat for guests.

To end the evening on a high note, head to MO Blues, the resort's jazz bar. Choose from a large selection of single malt whiskies and savour the sultry sounds of internationally-renowned jazz performers and musicians. Cigar connoisseurs will be delighted to chill out at the bar's cigar divan. This walk-in humidor harbours some of the world's finest cigars, along with a range of Middle Eastern shishas. For a personal touch, a professional cigar roller is on hand to assist guests who prefer their cigars made to order.

With its idyllic surroundings, faultless service, and comprehensive facilities, a stay at Mandarin Oriental, Sanya would be nothing short of heavenly.

rooms
176 rooms • 87 pavilion rooms • 15 pool villas • 19 suites

food
Fresh: Southeast Asian & Provençal • Mee & Mian: noodle bar • Pavillion: international • Wave: American & Mexican • Yi Yang: Cantonese

drink
Breeze: lounge • Cha: tea house • MO Blues: jazz bar, cigar divan, and wine cellar • Pool Bar • Sunset Bar

features
The Cliff executive lounge • fitness centre • infinity-edged pools • golf simulator • high-speed Internet access • pirate theme kids' club • private beach with coral reef • private check-in in guestrooms • satellite TV • spa village • tennis courts • water sports

business
ballroom • business centre • complimentary mobile phone rental • function rooms • MICE facilities and services • secretarial services • translation services

nearby
Dadonghai • Sanya Phoenix International Airport

contact
12 Yuhai Road, Sanya City 572000, Hainan Province, China •
telephone: +86.898.8820 9999 •
facsimile: +86.898.8820 9393 •
email: mosan-reservations@mohg.com •
website: www.mandarinoriental.com/sanya

sanya marriott resort + spa

At the southernmost tip of Hainan Island—otherwise known as China's tropical paradise—is the pristine Yalong Bay, where the sprawling compound of Sanya Marriott Resort & Spa lies. Home to the best beachfront views the crescent-shaped bay has to offer, the Sanya Marriott is the perfect place to explore one of Hainan Island's most scenic spots.

To keep in line with the bay's impressive reputation for mesmerising views, the resort has pulled out all the stops when it comes to indulgence and luxury. Guestrooms feature ocean, garden or mountain views, while a wide array of facilities and activities are in place to keep holiday-makers satisfied.

Guests can lap up the sunshine in the two-tiered lagoon pool or soak in the outdoor heated whirlpool for an extra dose of heat therapy, where relaxed muscles herald the start of the holiday. For those intending to get the perfect tan, outdoor activities such as parasailing, scuba diving and jet-skiing promise a radiant, sun-kissed complexion before leaving for home.

The Quan spa is another highlight not to be missed. Combining science and ancient beauty practices, the spa uses water that has had its structure improved by specially designed crystalline vivifiers, mechanisms that use created energy fields to infuse water with

THIS PAGE (FROM TOP): *The pool looks out to the pristine beaches of Yalong Bay; cheerful colours reflect the resort's tropical environment.*

OPPOSITE (FROM TOP): *Intimate dining at Indochine; Quan Spa's soothing interiors.*

...the perfect place to enjoy one of Hainan Island's most scenic spots.

more energy. Not found elsewhere in China, this qi water is not only healthier to drink and bathe in, but also improves metabolism and blood circulation. For an invigorating qi water experience, the Vichy showers and baths come highly recommended, while tropical themed Quan body treatments, complete with traditional Chinese beauty rituals, keep the mind and body well pampered.

Although the Sanya Marriott is an idyllic retreat, it also caters to business travellers. With a fully equipped business centre and a host of multilingual staff nearby to assist, business-minded guests can work hassle-free in the comfort of the shade. Such attention to service and detail has earned the hotel *Travel Weekly's* prestigious Asia Industry Award for 'Best MICE Facility and Service Hotel 2007', among other accolades.

Dining in the Sanya Marriott Resort & Spa can be a wonderful adventure. Sip on a tropical fruit frappé at the Sea Breeze Pool Bar & Grill, chill out at the laid-back Deep Blue beach bar, or visit the View Lounge for drinks and live music. Indochine is a must for a sumptuous French-Vietnamese meal with a vast wine list to match its lively Asian flavours, while the best of Cantonese and regional dishes can be found at Wan Hao Chinese Restaurant. Last but not least, Marriott Café's international buffet keeps diners spoilt for choice, and like the resort itself, keeps guests coming back for seconds.

rooms
431 rooms • 25 suites

food
Indochine: French-Vietnamese • Sea Breeze Pool Bar & Grill: light meals • Marriott Café: international • Wan Hao Chinese Restaurant: Cantonese and regional

drink
Deep Blue: beach bar • Sea Breeze Pool Bar & Grill • View Lounge

features
Quan Spa • beach lawn • fitness centre • high-speed Internet access and wi-fi • outdoor pools • putting green • satellite TV • sauna and steam room • sea sports • tennis courts

business
ballroom • boardroom • business centre • meeting rooms

nearby
Dadonghai • Yalong Bay • Sanya Bay

contact
Yalong Bay National Resort District, Sanya, Hainan 572000 •
telephone: +86.898.8856 8888 •
facsimile: +86.898.8856 7111 •
email: sanyaresort@marriotthotels.com •
website: www.marriott.com/SYXMC

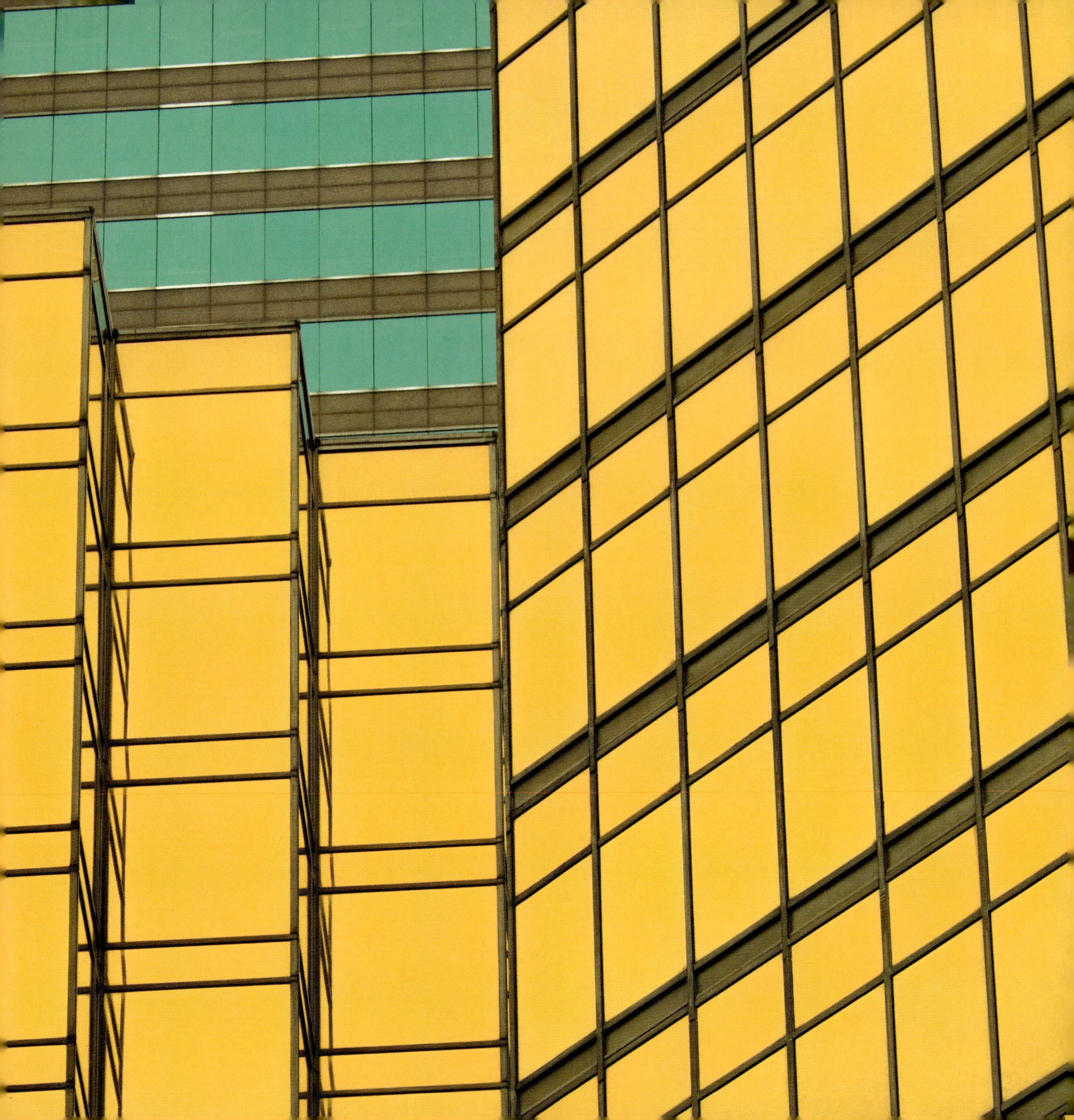

hongkong

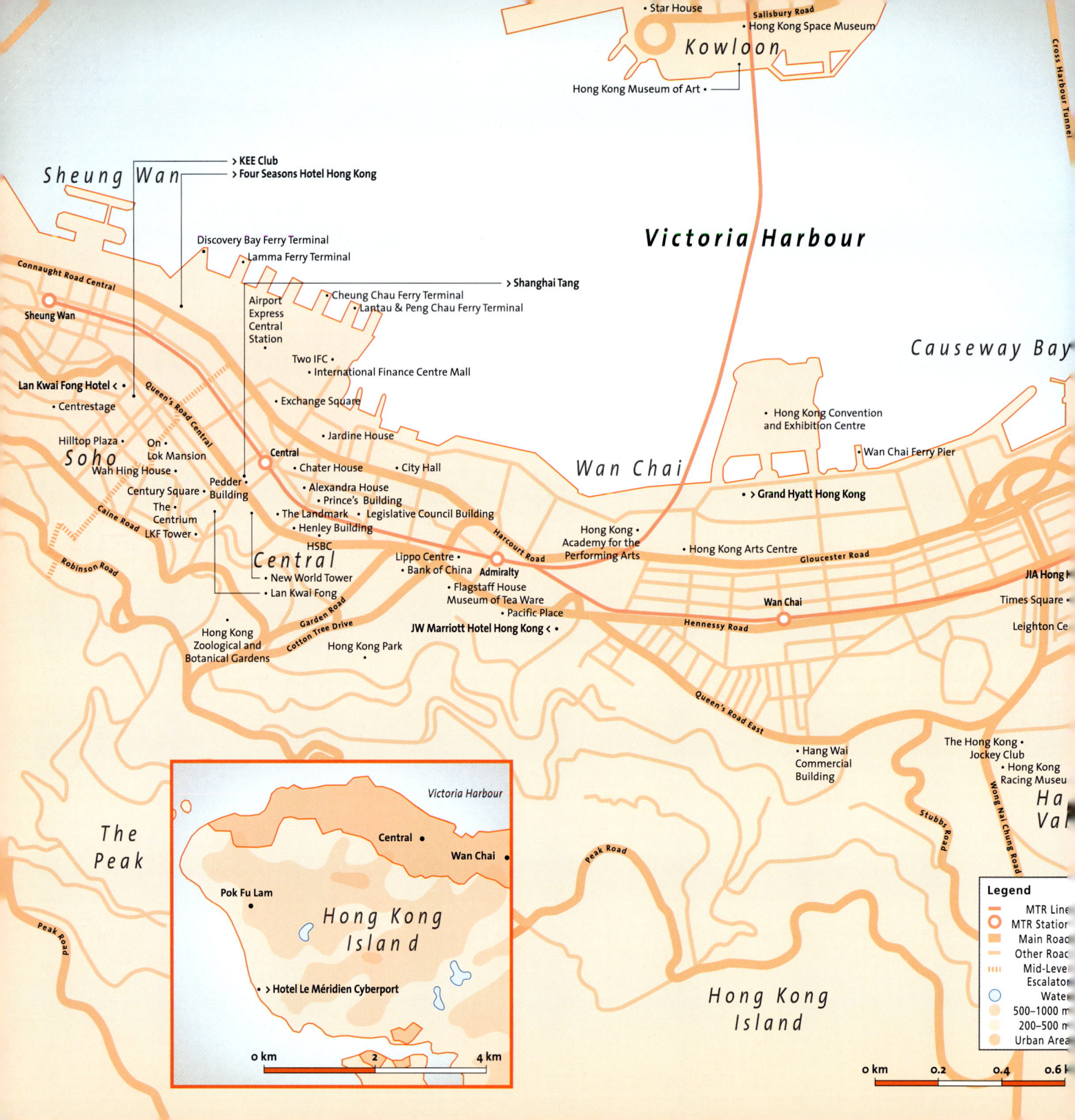

Kowloon
- Star House
- Salisbury Road
- Hong Kong Space Museum
- Hong Kong Museum of Art

Victoria Harbour

Cross Harbour Tunnel

Sheung Wan
- › KEE Club
- › Four Seasons Hotel Hong Kong
- Discovery Bay Ferry Terminal
- Lamma Ferry Terminal
- Cheung Chau Ferry Terminal
- › Shanghai Tang
- Lantau & Peng Chau Ferry Terminal
- Airport Express Central Station
- Connaught Road Central
- Sheung Wan
- Two IFC
- International Finance Centre Mall
- Exchange Square

Causeway Bay
- Hong Kong Convention and Exhibition Centre
- Wan Chai Ferry Pier

Soho / Central
- Lan Kwai Fong Hotel ‹
- Centrestage
- Hilltop Plaza
- On Lok Mansion
- Wah Hing House
- Century Square
- The Centrium
- LKF Tower
- Queen's Road Central
- Pedder Building
- Jardine House
- Chater House
- City Hall
- Alexandra House
- Prince's Building
- The Landmark
- Legislative Council Building
- Henley Building
- HSBC
- New World Tower
- Lan Kwai Fong
- Lippo Centre
- Bank of China
- Admiralty
- Flagstaff House Museum of Tea Ware
- Pacific Place
- JW Marriott Hotel Hong Kong ‹
- Hong Kong Academy for the Performing Arts
- Hong Kong Arts Centre
- › Grand Hyatt Hong Kong
- Harcourt Road
- Gloucester Road
- Wan Chai
- Hennessy Road
- Times Square
- Leighton Ce
- JIA Hong K

Wan Chai

Caine Road
Robinson Road
Garden Road
Cotton Tree Drive
Hong Kong Zoological and Botanical Gardens
Hong Kong Park

Queen's Road East
- Hang Wai Commercial Building
- The Hong Kong Jockey Club
- Hong Kong Racing Museu
- Stubbs Road
- Wong Nai Chung Road
- Ha Val

Inset: Hong Kong Island
- Victoria Harbour
- The Peak
- Pok Fu Lam
- Central
- Wan Chai
- Hong Kong Island
- › Hotel Le Méridien Cyberport
- Peak Road

0 km — 2 — 4 km

Legend
- MTR Line
- MTR Station
- Main Road
- Other Road
- Mid-Level Escalator
- Water
- 500–1000 m
- 200–500 m
- Urban Area

0 km   0.2   0.4   0.6

cosmopolitan culture

Beyond the clichéd postcard images—the bustling markets, neon-filled streets, and gleaming architectural wonders shooting into the sky—there is much more to the thrilling, captivating city of Hong Kong than meets the eye. Look past the obvious, and you'll find an exhilarating metropolis with a rich history, cosmopolitan culture, and surprises around every corner.

a varied life

Accounts of the modern history of Hong Kong often begin with its establishment as a British colony. But long before China ceded Hong Kong Island to the British in 1842 and Kowloon in 1862, and before the British signed their 99-year lease of the New Territories in 1898, Hong Kong had had a varied life of its own. Indeed, the earliest settlements on this former British colony are said to date back to Neolithic times, and the people of Southern China settled here around 100 BCE. The territory was ruled by Imperial China for some two millennia until the 1800s when the European colonial powers were actively gaining footholds in Asia. It was not much developed, but it was known for its natural harbour—and for being a notorious pirates' hideaway.

Despite few natural resources and a tiny population, Hong Kong has remarkably adapted, persevered and grown into a glamorous cosmopolitan city, a triumph of the market-led, laissez-faire economy. It has not been an easy journey: Hong Kong has persisted through several wars, disease outbreaks, political overhauls, and countless scandals. Probably the most significant milestone in the territory's contemporary history was its return to China on July 1, 1997. Despite being inextricably tied to mainland China by geography, history, and even economy, the little territory—less than 1,100 sq km (425 sq miles) in size and barely 1,104 sq km (426 sq miles) to China's southeast—has remained defiantly independent in spirit. About 7 million people live, work, and play in Hong Kong; 95 per cent of the population is Chinese, but diverse cultures have contributed to the unique fabric of Hong Kong. The largest expatriate communities are from the Philippines, Indonesia, and the US, with significant numbers also from South Asia.

giving nature space

Across the territory, which includes Hong Kong Island, the Kowloon Peninsula, the New Territories, and 262 outlying islands, there are approximately 6,350 people per sq km (18,176 per sq mile). It therefore comes as quite a surprise to many that, for such a densely populated land, about two-thirds of Hong Kong remains undeveloped—even, at times, impossible to develop,

PAGE 166: *A detail of one of Hong Kong's many modern, downtown high-rises.*

THIS PAGE (FROM TOP): *The dizzy pace of city life is captured in this image of Hong Kong taxis speeding by in their distinctive red-and-white livery; Hong Kong's young and trendy hang out at one of the numerous cafés in the chic SoHo district.*

thanks to its rugged terrain and government protection. It is apt that Hong Kong's symbol, the Bauhinia flower, comes from nature. Hong Kong is much greener than one might expect. About 40 per cent of the total land area is protected by the government from being cleared for development. The battle between conservation and lightning-speed urbanisation continues, but intrepid nature enthusiasts, runners, hikers, surfers, and active weekenders still have numerous reservoirs, hills, coastlines, marshes, and woodlands in which to play. In total, there are 23 country parks, 15 'special' areas, and 733 km (455 miles) of coastline with pretty, white-sand beaches. A sub-tropical climate that rarely goes below 10°C (50°F) in winter or above 31°C (88°F) in summer makes for many pleasant months of outdoor activities.

vibrant city

The territory's lush terrain is one of Hong Kong's attractions, but it is usually the urban image of the leading financial centre and the glitz and glamour of a bustling metropolis that first pops into one's mind. Hong Kong's high standard of living proves that this is not just a popular perception—Hong Kong is one of the most expensive cities on the planet.

The people of Hong Kong are, however, an impressively ambitious and entrepreneurial breed, adaptable by necessity and both driven and spoiled by decades of success. Hong Kongers have developed and maintained the sixth largest foreign exchange market, the seventh largest stock market, and the freest economy in the world, a position it has held for many years. In 2007, Forbes listed a whopping 28 Hong Kong residents on its 'World's Billionaires' list (thanks, in part, to Hong Kong having some of the lowest taxes in the world). Even the less affluent here show an admirable determination to succeed and learn. Highly educated, many locals speak both official languages, Cantonese and English, English being the lingua franca of business and government. Mandarin is a common third language, while a fascination with travel has encouraged many to learn other languages.

A Confucian sense of duty lies at the heart of life in this exciting city, where multiple generations often live and eat together. It is easy to overlook the inherent sense of family in a culture that outwardly loves to acquire and spend money. In terms of purchasing power per capita, Hong Kong people rank among the highest in Asia, as evidenced by the city's rich shopping, dining, and entertainment offerings. Here, however, conspicuous consumption is not a vice; it is a hard-won right for a resilient people who have adapted to challenging and changing circumstances through the ages to make Hong Kong the vibrant city it is today.

THIS PAGE (FROM TOP): *Hong Kong's neon-scape promises the intrepid traveller an exciting night on the town; Hong Kong is one of the world's most expensive cities, but its citizens know how to live the high life.*
OPPOSITE: *The territory's famous waterfront by night.*

...a rich history, cosmopolitan culture, and surprises around every corner.

hong kong: dining out

Hong Kong approaches food with the giddy excitement of a child on Christmas morning. Except, here, it is a daily occurrence. Food is such an important concept in the social psyche that 'nei sik jor fan mei?' ('Have you eaten?') is a perfectly acceptable substitute for hello, or 'nei hou ma?' ('How are you?').

In a society where entertaining at home is not very popular because most homes are too small to accommodate larger numbers of people, dining out plays a significant role in the culture. The intrepid visitor will be delighted to find, then, that from streetside dai pai dong stalls to swish temples of haute cuisine, Hong Kong offers almost every culinary style to tempt even the most discerning foodie.

chinese cuisine

The fresh, clean, and sophisticated flavours of Cantonese cuisine dominate in Hong Kong, but countless other restaurants allow diners to indulge in the spiciness of Sichuan, the sweetness of Shanghai, or the intensity of Beijing.

The exclusive members-only **China Club** (13/F, Old Bank of China Building, Bank Street, Central) takes its nostalgic elegance from old Shanghai but also features one of the best contemporary Chinese art collections around. This fashionable setting is the backdrop for Cantonese classics served by the equally impeccable waitstaff.

The **Aqua** group of restaurants (www.aqua.com.hk) offers unique dining experiences—from the antique furniture, Chinese motifs, and spicy Sichuan cuisine of **Shui Hu Ju** (G/F, 68 Peel Street, Central), to the sleek design, amazing harbour views, and Northern Chinese signature dishes of **Hutong** (28/F, One Peking Road, Tsim Sha Tsui). At **Aqua Luna**, dinner is served in dramatic style on board an authentic handcrafted Chinese junk with blazing red sails while cruising the harbour.

Cantonese restaurants in hotels have also made a name for themselves, including **Lung King Heen** (Four Seasons Hotel Hong Kong, 8 Finance Street, Central) and **Spring Moon** (The Peninsula Hong Kong, Salisbury Road, Tsim Sha Tsui).

Yung Kee (32–40 Wellington Street, Central) is an institution, famous for its Cantonese roast meats, including the not-to-be missed roasted goose and delicious char siu (barbecued pork). **Fook Lam Moon** (35–45 Johnston Road, Wanchai), although set in an unfashionable area of Wanchai, attracts the rich and famous for its traditional Cantonese food—as evidenced by each Mercedes Benz and uniformed chauffeur perennially waiting outside.

Of all the Cantonese specialities, dim sum ('touching the heart') is perhaps the most popular and yum cha ('drinking tea') is an important social ritual. **Luk Yu Tea House** (24–26 Stanley Street, Central) has offered the authentic teahouse experience since it opened in 1933. The best seats are often occupied by high profile regulars. **Maxim's Palace** (2/F, Low Block, City Hall, Connaught Road, Central) serves up traditional favourites in a quintessential dim sum environment, complete with bamboo baskets full of dumplings delivered via roaming pushcarts. A quieter option is the cute **Dim Sum** (63 Sing Woo Road, Happy Valley), where deluxe versions of classic dumplings are served well into the night, far beyond the usual dim sum hours of about 10 am to 3 pm.

Not to be outdone by other cities, Hong Kong has its own celebrity chefs. Jacky Yu of **Xi Yan** (3/F, 83 Wanchai Road, Wanchai) is a pioneer of the 'private dining' trend, where spaces feel more like a home than a restaurant, and the delectable menu ensures the freshest of ingredients and the most intricate of preparations. Based on Cantonese cuisine, Xi Yan opened in 2000 and was followed by other innovative Yu concepts and even a TV show.

THIS PAGE (FROM TOP): *Hong Kong offers a world of cuisines. Chinese (top) and Japanese (right) are just two of a myriad; revellers can start the night right with a drink at the stylish bar of Hutong before moving on to dinner.*
OPPOSITE: *Expect views and décor that are as sumptuous as the cuisine at Hong Kong's top eateries.*

hong kong: dining out

asian cuisine

It is notoriously difficult to secure a reservation at Nobu Matsuhisa's restaurants in New York and London, and it has been no different at Hong Kong's **Nobu** since it opened at the InterContinental Hong Kong (18 Salisbury Road, Tsim Sha Tsui). The city's passion for dining has also drawn other renowned names, such as **Zuma** (5–6/F, The Landmark, 15 Queen's Road, Central), based on the trendy London restaurant that specialises in the informal Japanese izakaya style of dining. The city's most stylish congregate in the cosy upstairs bar/lounge before heading down to dinner in the main restaurant or terrace on temperate evenings.

international

With its reputation as a food capital, it should come as no surprise that Hong Kong has attracted a number of acclaimed international chefs. **L'Atelier de Joel Robuchon** (4/F, The Landmark, 15 Queen's Road, Central) is a cosy red-and-black affair featuring an open kitchen encircled by seating around a bar, and private rooms. It offers a menu of classics in tapas-style portions and an excellent wine list. At **Spoon** (InterContinental Hong Kong, 18 Salisbury Road, Tsim Sha Tsui), the modern, innovative cuisine of Alain Ducasse is prepared to perfection with enviable views of the harbour. **Pierre** (Mandarin Oriental Hong Kong, 5 Connaught Road, Central) goes by a single name, but those in the know recognise it as 3-Michelin-star Chef Pierre Gagnaire's dramatic restaurant where the sights of the city through oversized windows are upstaged only by the seductive, complex dishes. The **Mandarin Grill + Bar** (1/F, Mandarin Oriental Hong Kong, 5 Connaught Road, Central) is a cosy favourite of old-timers and newcomers alike.

Other beacons of exquisite contemporary fine dining include the charming, long-standing **M at the Fringe** (1/F, South Block, 2 Lower Albert Road, Central), and the glamorously sensual **OPIA** (JIA Hong Kong, 1–5 Irving Street, Causeway Bay). At **Ingredients** (23–29 Wing Fung Street, Wanchai), with its oyster bar and rooftop patio, the emphasis is on tantalising the senses. Meanwhile, an exemplary French meal awaits at **Caprice**, the stylish signature restaurant of the Four Seasons Hotel Hong Kong (8 Finance Street, Central).

Owner and wine lover Frank Sun welcomes guests to the intimate **Tribute** (G/F, 13 Elgin Street, Central) boutique restaurant, where Western dishes featuring a mix of influences are the order of the day. At **Chez Patrick** (8–9 Sun Street, Wanchai), Chef Patrick Goubier has re-created a Paris apartment as the perfect setting for fine French dining. His popular foie gras is, of course, on the menu. For a more casual meal in a European brasserie setting, **Press Room** (108 Hollywood Road, Central) and its neighbouring café, **Classified**, are top of the line choices.

While Italian restaurants have existed in Hong Kong for decades, it was only in the recent past that fresh deliveries from Italy allowed for the true fare to be served consistently. True gourmands know which day of the week **Da Domenico** (G/F, Sunning Plaza, 10 Hysan Avenue, Causeway Bay) has its mozzarella flown in. **Gaia** (G/F, Grand Millennium Plaza, 181 Queen's Road, Central) never disappoints with its excellent food, sumptuous décor, and attentive service. For a taste of Rome, there is **Cinecittá** (9 Star Street, Wanchai), complete with old Vespas parked at its door.

For a contemporary al fresco setting, try **Top Deck** (Top Floor, Jumbo Floating Restaurant, Shum Wan Pier Drive, Wong Chuk Hang, Aberdeen), which is located on the highest level of the famous Jumbo Floating Restaurant. Stop by for a drink and enjoy the view before tucking into Asian favourites from its extensive menu. For dining by the sea, sample Mediterranean fare at **Cococabana**, (UG/F, Beach Building, Island Road, Deep Water Bay), one of the best restaurants set on the beach.

And lest we forget that all-important fourth meal of the day, Hong Kong reminds us of that colonial legacy—the High Tea—with grand, tiered presentations of tea, scones, crumpets, and more daily at **The Lobby** (The Peninsula Hong Kong, Salisbury Road, Tsim Sha Tsui), and **The Clipper Lounge** (Mandarin Oriental Hong Kong, 5 Connaught Road, Central).

For a sweet ending, there are decadent desserts to please every palate—from chocolate indulgence at sweet little **Chocolux** (57 Peel Street, Central), to the all-natural, seasonal Italian-style ice cream of **XTC Gelato** (Shop B, 45 Cochrane Street, Central), to traditional Asian desserts by **Xi Yan Sweets** (G/F, 8 Wing Fung Street, Wanchai), another of celebrity chef Jacky Yu's success stories.

THIS PAGE (FROM TOP): Detailed attention to presentation adds to the pleasure of dining in Hong Kong's world-class restaurants; the cosy and friendly ambience of the Mandarin Grill and Bar.

OPPOSITE (CLOCKWISE FROM TOP LEFT): The strikingly modern décor of L'Atelier de Joel Robuchon; the dramatic setting at Pierre is upstaged only by its stellar menu.

hong kong's nightlife

Hong Kong works hard and plays even harder. Long days at the office give way to nights out on the town. Shops, markets and spas obligingly stay open until 10 pm or later. Tickets to performances and films sell out to full houses. And every night, chic bars and hip nightclubs are hopping with activity.

Private clubs are de rigeur, attracting the privileged social set and the tycoons, as well as visiting celebrities. (The concierge at top hotels can arrange access for guests.) Stylish and exclusive, **KEE Club** (6/F, 32 Wellington Street, Central) is a hidden gem in an unassuming building just steps away from frenetic Lan Kwai Fong. It features different areas for fine dining, cocktails, and dancing. Replicating its London predecessor, **M1NT** (108 Hollywood Road, Central) is distinguished by its 'shareholder' memberships and a controversial tank filled with baby sharks. Members are allowed entry by fingerprint ID. Hip lounge **Halo** (LG/F, 10–12 Stanley Street, Central) takes it to the next level with face recognition technology embedded in its mysterious sliding doors at the entrance. Once inside, it's the Flirtini cocktails and truffle oil French fries that keep them coming back. Cool, young Hong Kongers head to **Volar** (Basement, 38–44 D'Aguilar Street, Central), a place of regular local celebrity sightings, where even club members are forced to wait on the street when the small club invariably fills up. Playing pool may seem rather common, but at **Racks** (7/F, 2–8 Wellington Street), it is a private member affair.

At other hot Hong Kong clubs, the question is not so much 'Are you a member?' but 'Are you on the list?' The hanging birdcages and elegant red lanterns of **dragon i** (UG/F, The Centrium, 60 Wyndham Street, Central) appeal to the aesthetes, but it is the models who draw in the Belvedere-ordering moguls and bankers in droves. Regular guest DJs from around the world, designer décor, and a pleasant outdoor area make this one of the most popular nightlife hotspots. The fashion crew also mingles with the business executive set at the mellow **Armani Bar** (2/F, Chater House, 11 Chater Road, Central), housed near a constellation of stores by Giorgio Armani.

Live music is firmly rooted in Hong Kong's nightlife scene. **Fringe Club** (2 Lower Albert Road, Central), one of Hong Kong's most established performing and visual arts venues, showcases local and international talent in a variety of disciplines. Its historical brick building also has spaces for eating and drinking, including a rooftop bar. **Le Rideau Theatre Café** (1/F, Hilltop Plaza, 49 Hollywood Road, SoHo), the self-styled performing arts bistro, is a restaurant, bar, and lounge rolled into one. Quality live music, theatre, and other performances are part of the menu. **Yumla** (Lower Basement, 79 Wyndham Street, Central) presents some of the best local and international DJs, attracting aficionados and unassuming party animals. For dancing to a different rhythm, **Makumba Africa Bar** (G/F, 48–52A Peel Street, Central) is another treasure tucked down a little street in SoHo. Here, the authentic décor includes walls hand-painted with African symbols and live African bands play throughout the week. Those looking to party on past the wee hours can pop down to **Drop** (Basement, On Lok Mansion, 39–43 Hollywood Road, Central), where the DJs reign from a towering booth above the small dance floor, and the cocktails are lethal. Don't even think about arriving before 2 am.

When a quiet drink is in order, there are wine bars such as **DiVino** (73 Wyndham Street, Central), and **Boca** (85 Peel Street, Central) nestled in the cosier SoHo circuit of bars, shops, and restaurants. Nearby, the unmarked **Feather Boa** (38 Staunton Street, SoHo) feels like a cross between a kitsch living room and a speakeasy, but this only adds to its quirky charm. Secret password not required here, but a taste of its delicious strawberry daiquiri most certainly is. The concept has inspired worthy copycats, including the more expansive **Lei Dou** (G/F, 20–22 D'Aguilar Street, Lan Kwai Fong, Central), which offers a welcome alternative to its rowdy neighbours in Lan Kwai Fong.

The words 'hotel bar' might have seedy connotations in many countries, but in Hong Kong, they are elegant meeting places. **The Captain's Bar** (Mandarin Oriental Hong Kong, 5 Connaught Road, Central), the chic and refreshingly quiet **Champagne Bar** (Grand Hyatt Hong Kong, 1 Harbour Road, Wanchai), and the bar at **Felix** (28/F, The Peninsula Hong Kong, Salisbury Road, Tsim Sha Tsui) with its spectacular harbour views, are fine examples of old favourites.

Outdoor space in this urban jungle is rare, but a few havens capitalise on it. Beyond the icy cool interiors of Scandinavian restaurant/bar **FINDS** (2/F, LKF Tower, 33 Wyndham Street) is an open terrace perched above busy Lan Kwai Fong. Spectacular harbour views make the outdoor area at **Isobar** (4/F, ifc mall, 8 Finance Street, Central), ideal for a sunset drink or post-dinner cocktail. For views from the other side of the harbour, the sleek, dark interiors of **Aqua Spirit** (30/F, 1 Peking Road, Tsim Sha Tsui) sparkle with the reflections of stunning harbour and city views.

THIS PAGE: Hip minimalism epitomises the latest clubs in Hong Kong, drawing the movers and shakers of society to their doors in droves.
OPPOSITE (FROM TOP): The plush M1NT exudes decadence, with its centrepiece tank of baby sharks; the exclusive KEE Club pampers its members in lavish fashion.

hong kong: a shopping sensation

Glamorous designer stores within award-winning architectural marvels... Overflowing stalls in bustling street markets... Unique little boutiques concealed inside scruffy old buildings. Hong Kong's distinct districts promise diverse and diverting shopping experiences as the small city continues to grow upwards and outwards. With an incredibly efficient public transport network, it is possible to hop from island to island, district to district, in a matter of minutes.

Despite some of the most expensive real estate on the planet, prices remain competitive in this free port, which still does not impose sales taxes. So it is no surprise that shopping is a favourite pastime of the locals. Indeed, if shopping were an Olympic sport, Hong Kong would be the gold medal winner. It is not just on weekends, either. Even during the week, shops in some areas stay open until 10 pm or later to accommodate long office hours.

And if a specific item cannot be bought, be it a suit, jewellery or shoes, it can be quickly custom-made at reasonable prices.

malls

Gucci, **Louis Vuitton**, **Burberry**, **Prada**, **Chanel**, **Christan Dior**, **Ralph Lauren**, **Cartier**, **Christian Louboutin**, **Bulgari**, **Dolce & Gabbana**, **Marni**, **Versace**, **Lanvin**, **Valentino**—name a luxury brand, and Hong Kong is sure to have at least one store, if not a multiple of them, in its elegant malls. These chic and refined structures, often housing hundreds of shops, are a testament to the wealth in this city. They seem to have taken root everywhere, from the bustling central business district to the former farmlands of Shatin and beyond.

It could take days to navigate the immense **Harbour City** (3–27 Canton Road, Tsim Sha Tsui), which boasts about 700 stores, 50 restaurants, and two cinemas. The newer **Elements** (1 Austin Road West, Kowloon) has staked its claim on shoppers with more than 1 million sq ft (92,903 sq m) of retail space, themed after the five Chinese elements and home to leading international brands.

Malls located out in residential areas, such as the massive **Festival Walk** (80 Tat Chee Avenue, Kowloon Tong), are conveniently linked to the efficient MTR subway system. Catering to the suburban population, Festival Walk houses Hong Kong's largest ice-skating rink, in addition to over 220 shops and restaurants, and a multiplex cinema.

On the Hong Kong side, Central's major shopping malls are connected physically by pedestrian overpasses—to eliminate the need to descend into the streets, especially on hot and humid summer days—and electronically by a comprehensive website, www.CentralHK.com. Each filled with luxury boutiques, the shopping malls include **Prince's Building**, **Alexandra House**, **The Landmark**, **Chater House**, and the light-filled **ifc mall** designed by Cesar Pelli.

Heading eastward, one comes upon another series of linked buildings, this time in Admiralty. **Pacific Place** (88 Queensway, Admiralty) is the undisputed star of the area, where stores graduate from high street labels on the ground floor to the most prestigious brands at the top.

For locals, the true shopping Mecca on the island is frenetic Causeway Bay. While colourful and festive **Times Square** (1 Matheson Street, Causeway Bay) may attract bigger crowds, sophisticated **Lee Gardens** (33 Hysan Avenue, Causeway Bay) has the luxury brands covered.

The iconic **Lane Crawford** has its flagship store (Podium 3, ifc mall, 8 Finance Street, Central) housed in a series of gallery-like spaces. Its vast selection of international designers in fashion, jewellery, home wares, and cosmetics is enlivened by continually evolving visual merchandising displays. Established in 1850, the now ultra-modern retailer has supplied Hong Kong with goods since colonial times. More recently, renowned British store **Harvey Nichols** (G/F–4/F, The Landmark, 15 Queen's Road, Central) entered the market with its own take on international fashion.

The most cutting-edge and avant-garde brand selections can also be found at locally based multi-brand stores, such as **Dmop** (G/F, 11–15 On Lan Street, Central) and the **I.T** chain (2 Kingston Street, Causeway Bay).

boutiques

In the last decade, exciting little shopping streets not unlike those in New York's Nolita have sprouted up, including the dining and entertainment area, SoHo.

On Lan Street in Central has positively exploded with new brands and creative store designs, such as

THIS PAGE (FROM TOP): Homegrown lifestyle brands OVO and G.O.D. (right) make a statement with their daring and imaginative designs.
OPPOSITE: It's luxury labels galore at Pacific Place, one of Hong Kong's top shopping malls.

hong kong: a shopping sensation

those of **Christian Louboutin** (G/F, 7 On Lan Street, Central), **Billionaire Boys Club** (G/F, 14 On Lan Street, Central), **Maison Martin Margiela** (G/F, 18 On Lan Street, Central), and **Comme des Garçons** (G/F, 20 On Lan Street, Central).

But if anyone should be thanked for bringing international designers to Hong Kong, it is Joyce Ma of **Joyce Boutique** (G/F New World Tower, 16 Queens Road, Central), one of the first influential fashion stores in Hong Kong. Now a chain, Joyce Boutique stores are defined by high design not only in their products, but also the fabulous interiors.

Hong Kong's creative talent also shines brightly through ultra-chic stores that originated on home soil, such as **Shanghai Tang** (G/F and Basement, Pedder Building, 12 Pedder Street, Central), which has found success with its daringly redefined Chinese chic. The luxury lifestyle brand features fashion, accessories, home wares, and gift items inspired by Chinese culture, and has also famously collaborated with Philip Treacy, Puma, and others. **Blanc de Chine** (Shop 218–221, The Landmark, 15 Queen's Road, Central) is another Hong Kong native that interprets Chinese fashion and design through its own subtle and sophisticated aesthetic . The irreverent **G.O.D.** (G/F and 1/F, Leighton Centre, 77 Leighton Road, Causeway Bay) is notorious for playing with Chinese words, ideas and design in its home wares and lifestyle items. Even its name is a play on the Cantonese term for the phrase 'to live better'. For casual wear, there is the wildly successful **Giordano** (G/F, Manson House, 74–78 Nathan Road, Tsim Sha Tsui).

Because the thrill of the chase is integral to the true shopper's delight, going off the beaten path to discover charming boutiques and designer ateliers can be very rewarding. **Sin Sin Atelier** (G/F, 52 Sai Street, Sheung Wan) carries conceptual, minimalist clothing, jewellery and accessories that bear the quirky individuality of their creator, Sin Sin. The boutique, located across from her art space and in an old print shop near the Cat Street market, is alone worth the visit. One of Hong Kong's most recognised haute couture and prêt-à-porter designers, **Barney Cheng** (12/F, Worldwide Commercial Building, 34 Wyndham Street, Central), is tucked away inside a commercial building above Central. **Ranee K** (16 Gough Street, Central), a favourite with Chinese celebrities, mixes East and West to create one-of-a-kind fashion, such as her signature cheongsams.

Designer lifestyle store **OVO** (G/F, 16 Queen's Road East, Wanchai) mixes influences to produce elegant, minimalist items for the home. In contrast, but no less distinctive, **Kou** (22/F, Fung House, 19–20 Connaught Road, Central) by socialite and interior designer Louise Kou, presents over-the-top decadence and luxury.

specialist stores

Quaint, conventional local department stores, such as **Chinese Arts & Crafts** (Star House, 3 Salisbury Road, Tsim Sha Tsui), are stocked with traditional Chinese items untainted by designer trends. **Yue Hwa**

Department Store (Main Store, 301–309 Nathan Road, Kowloon) also carries classic Chinese clothing, silks, ceramics, embroidered home items, antique and reproduction furniture, jewellery, and arts and crafts. For a spot of Chinese tea, sample before you buy at specialist **Fook Ming Tong** (Shop 3006, ifc mall, 8 Financial Street, Central).

markets

Colourful street markets are dotted across the city. A treasure chest for those who enjoy soaking up the local atmosphere, they are stocked with interesting merchandise and cheap finds, not to mention countless photo opportunities.

Over on Kowloon, and best seen at night, **Temple Street Night Market** in Jordan proffers goods—often of the kitsch variety—from brightly-lit street stalls, the talents of fortune-tellers, and the occasional Cantonese Opera performance. At the **Jade Market** in Yau Ma Tei, one can find pretty jade, semi-precious, and sometimes plastic trinkets, which are sure to look more impressive away from the dusty stalls.

On Hong Kong Island, **'The Lanes'** is a popular street market set in a series of stalls lining Li Yuen Street East and Li Yuen Street West between the bustling Queen's and Des Voeux roads. **Stanley Market**, on the south side, is a tourist favourite and with good reason—in addition to cheap clothing and souvenirs, the draw includes a wide selection of children's clothing, linens, and discounted luggage in which to pack all of one's new purchases.

THIS PAGE (FROM TOP): Luxurious decorative pieces and furnishings for a lavish lifestyle can be found at the designer lifestyle store, Kou; one of the territory's many colourful night markets.
OPPOSITE: The Hong Kong flagship store of the now-global fashion label Shanghai Tang.

hongkong:ashopping sensation

spas in hong kong

Spa culture is thriving in Hong Kong and Hong Kong, in turn, thrives on it. From some of the world's most luxurious treatments in sumptuous surroundings to amazingly affordable massages in basic but entirely acceptable venues, countless spas offer the antidote to urban stress. And these days, it is not just for women—many offer treatments for men and even treatment rooms designed for couples.

a five-star experience

East-meets-West defines the most popular luxury spas, which merge the best treatments, service, and interior design from both worlds. Treatments at **The Oriental Spa** (The Landmark Mandarin Oriental, Hong Kong, 15 Queen's Road, Central) are designed as a journey to take you from the outer world to the inner world. Its signature Time Ritual is a holistic mix of therapies determined each time by your specific needs on the day. Beginning with a welcome herbal tea, the experience also includes access to a number of facilities, including a relaxation room, vitality pool and amethyst crystal steam room.

At the Grand Hyatt, an entire floor is dedicated to its residential spa, **Plateau** (Grand Hyatt Hong Kong, 1 Harbour Road, Wanchai). Ingeniously designed with overnight rooms, guests can enjoy in-room treatments then continue to relax after the therapist quietly leaves, or even fall asleep for the night.

There is a pattern here: some of the finest spas in Hong Kong are tucked away inside five-star hotels, which also means they stay open later in the evening. **The Spa at the Four Seasons** (Four Seasons Hotel Hong Kong, 8 Finance Street, Central) is an urban sanctuary designed with natural light and clean lines. It offers a number of 'aquatic experiences' in its vitality pool lounge, among other signature treatments.

The Peninsula Spa at the legendary hotel (The Peninsula Hong Kong, Salisbury Road, Kowloon) is a calming retreat with Oriental, Ayurvedic, and traditionally-inspired therapies by spa specialist ESPA.

Another recognisable spa brand, Elemis, lends its name to one of the most established spas in town, **Elemis Day Spa** (9/F, Century Square, 1 D'Aguilar Street, Central). It forms part of the **Paua** group of spas (www.paua.com.hk) with locations around Hong Kong, even one in the Hong Kong Disneyland Hotel in Lantau, the **Victorian Spa** (Level 1 Hong Kong Disneyland Hotel, Hong Kong Disneyland Resort, Lantau Island). The group's newest addition, **Paua Spa** (Centrestage, 108 Hollywood Road, Central), boasts fabulous 'thrones'—raised massage chairs for manicures and pedicures—with views of a green outdoor area or TV screens hanging from above.

small + personal

Even in this brand-obsessed city, several smaller operations offer world-class services. Just off a typical Hong Kong-style stepped street and inside an old Chinese building, **Paul Gerrard Hair & Beauty** (1–2/F, Wah Hing House, 35 Pottinger Street, Central) is a sophisticated little spa and hair salon where every detail is considered. **The Feel Good Factor** (1 Lyndhurst Terrace, Central) has been the go-to nail bar for years, now with an expanded services menu, and ideally located near the Hollywood Road antique shop strip. **Indulgence** (33 Lyndhurst Terrace, Central) takes the lifestyle approach with a shop on the first level, treatment rooms on the second level, and a terrace café serving spa cuisine.

For a Chinese treatment unadulterated by Western notions, there is the immensely popular **Happy Foot Reflexology Centre** (6/F, Jade Centre, 98–02 Wellington Street, Central). These foot massages are Hong Kong's cheap and cheerful spa alternative, set in basic but comfortable rooms, and available until late into the night.

THIS PAGE (FROM TOP): World-class facilities and treatments by spa experts are a signature of The Spa at the Four Seasons; The Grand Hyatt's residential spa, Plateau, offers guests an extensive menu of treatments in spacious yet intimate surroundings; state-of-the-art design and stylish interior décor characterise the latest luxury spas.
OPPOSITE: The beautiful settings and ultra-luxe comforts of hotel spas entice clients to spend the night after a relaxing treatment.

hong kong galleries + museums

Hong Kong might be known for the art of making money, but beyond this one-dimensional reputation, a different kind of art appreciation is making a statement in the territory. An increasingly impressive cultural scene has come to the fore—fine art, music, dance, theatre, and film now fill a comprehensive calendar of exhibitions, performances, and festivals throughout the year. Record-breaking sales at leading international auction houses, such as **Sotheby's** and **Christie's**, continue to validate Hong Kong as the global centre for the trade of Chinese art, spanning antiquities to contemporary art.

The **Asia Art Archive** (11/F, Hollywood Centre, 233 Hollywood Road, Sheung Wan), a pioneering non-profit research centre, leads the way in documenting the phenomenon of Asian contemporary art, which has been rapidly gaining popularity worldwide. One of its key objectives is to promote an understanding of this art form—a noble endeavour it undertakes with the backing of both distinguished curators and art critics among its Board of Directors and Academic Advisory Board. Since its founding in 2000, the organisation has grown to include spacious offices, a library, and research resources, including an informative website.

Experts in the field lead many of Hong Kong's finest galleries. One of the Asia Art Archive's co-founders, Johnson Chang Tsong-zung, is curatorial director of **Hanart TZ Gallery** (202 Henley Building, 5 Queen's Road, Central), where cutting-edge and experimental art from mainland China, Taiwan, and Hong Kong are represented. **Alisan Fine Arts** (Shop 315, Prince's Building, 10 Chater Road, Central), established by gallery director Alice King in 1981, was one of the first Hong Kong galleries to promote contemporary Chinese artists. At **Grotto Fine Art** (2/F, 31C–D Wyndham Street, Central), writer, curator, and lecturer Henry Au-Yeung focuses on local Chinese artists. **Schoeni Art Gallery** (21–31 Old Bailey Street, Central) has represented and supported artists from mainland China ever since it was founded by Manfred Schoeni in 1992; the gallery is now managed by Schoeni's daughter, Nicole. Just across the road, Katie de Tilly's **10 Chancery Lane Gallery** (G/F, 10 Chancery Lane, Central) showcases established and emerging artists from around the world, from paintings by Julian Schnabel to works by local photographers.

Addressing one of the challenges that artists face in this high-rent city—finding a place to show and work—**Para/Site Art Space** (G/F, 4 Po Yan Street, Sheung Wan) is one of Hong Kong's best independent art spaces. At **Cattle Depot Artists Village** (63 Ma Tau Kok Road, To Kwa Wan), a number of independent art organisations have taken up residence, such as **1a space**, **Artist's Commune**, and **On and On Theatre Workshop**. To support emerging artists, the **Jockey Club Creative Arts Centre** offers 9,290 sq m (100,000 sq ft) of space in MTR-accessible Shek Kip Mei. Created with the generous support of The Hong Kong Jockey Club Charities Trust (JCCT), the centre aims to be a self-supporting cultural hub where artists can rent a space and enjoy the support of all the necessary facilities to practice and display their art.

Annual festivals and events further promote the arts, such as the innovative **Hong Kong Art Walk** (www.hongkongartwalk.com). This is the art lover's version of a pub-crawl, during which ticket-holders enjoy open access to over 40 galleries. Participating restaurants provide sustenance for the intrepid 'explorers' as they traipse through a condensed version of Hong Kong's art scene.

In addition to art spaces, there are today an unprecedented number of exhibition venues scattered across Hong Kong, from the commercial centres to remote rural areas. Hong Kong also boasts over 20 museums, about 16 of which are managed by the Leisure and Cultural Services Department. They include **Hong Kong Museum of Art** (10 Salisbury Road, Tsim Sha Tsui), **Hong Kong Space Museum** (10 Salisbury Road, Tsim Sha Tsui), **University Museum and Art Gallery** (The University of Hong Kong, 94 Bonham Road, Pok Fu Lam), **Flagstaff House Museum of Tea Ware** (10 Cotton Tree Drive, Central), **Hong Kong Museum of Coastal Defence** (175 Tung Hei Road, Shau Kei Wan), **Hong Kong Museum of History** (100 Chatham Road South, Tsim Sha Tsui), **Hong Kong Museum of Medical Science** (2 Caine Lane, Mid-Levels), **Hong Kong Science Museum** (2 Science Museum Road, Tsim Sha Tsui East), **The Police Museum** (27 Coombe Road, The Peak), and the **Hong Kong Film Archive** (50 Lei King Road, Sai Wan Ho).

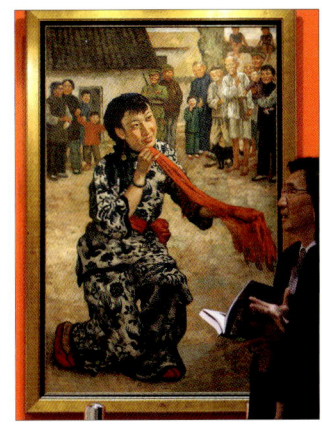

THIS PAGE (CLOCKWISE FROM TOP LEFT): A potential buyer contemplates 'Put Down Your Whip', the famous oil painting by Xu Beihong, one of China's most important artists; a photography exhibition at the University Museum and Art Gallery; Andy Warhol's pop art depictions of Chairman Mao look out over pedestrians from a gallery window; this art piece expresses the West's long fascination with the Orient.

OPPOSITE: Chinese art is a hot commodity in collections around the world today.

four seasons hotel hong kong

THIS PAGE: *Enjoy the best in French cuisine at Caprice.*

OPPOSITE (FROM LEFT): *Lounge by the stunning pool and watch the world go by; the spa is dedicated to luxurious pampering.*

Vibrant Hong Kong, or 'Fragrant Harbour' in Cantonese, is an enchanting city with a plethora of impressive hotels. Against the city's signature skyline, the centrally located Four Seasons Hotel Hong Kong stands out both in terms of architectural presence, and as a sophisticated home away from home.

Plaudits from international publications such as *Institutional Investor* reflect the first-rate facilities the Four Seasons provides. With its exquisite restaurants, rooftop pool, world-class spa, and phenomenal harbour views, it's no wonder that this luxurious establishment was voted by the magazine as the 'Best Hotel in Asia' in 2007.

Guestrooms come fitted with plasma TVs, king-size beds, and high-speed Internet access to ensure as comfortable a stay as possible. Luxury is taken to another level with the Four Seasons Executive and Harbour View Suites, where guests can choose between richly decorated rooms influenced by Chinese traditions, or those with contemporary furniture and a clean Western-inspired look. With stunning views and separate living and work areas, travellers will find their needs met, be they business- or leisure-oriented.

The rejuvenating spa is a sanctuary for self-indulgent travellers. Combining time-honoured oriental traditions and innovative European therapies, the spa offers an extensive variety of facials, massages, baths, wraps, and salon services. There are also crystal steam rooms, ice fountains, and separate vitality lounges for men and women to ensure one attains 'nirvana'.

Even in a city of such cosmopolitan tastes, the hotel's dining options are among the finest. Chef Vincent Thierry's French restaurant Caprice fuses East and West, and classic with contemporary, for an exciting menu featuring only the freshest seasonal ingredients. Dining at Lung King Heen promises to be a Cantonese extravaganza, and The Lounge is ideal for international favourites and sinful desserts. Last but not least, the Blue Bar's fashionable cocktails will end one's evening on a high.

Whether one is in Hong Kong for business or pleasure, rest assured that only the best will be provided at Four Seasons Hotel Hong Kong.

...exquisite restaurants, rooftop pool, world-class spa, and phenomenal harbour views...

rooms
345 rooms • 54 suites

food
Caprice: French • The Lounge: international • Lung King Heen: Cantonese • Pool Terrace: light meals

drink
Blue Bar • Pool Terrace

features
executive club lounge • fitness centre • high-speed Internet access • outdoor pool • satellite TV • spa • vitality lounges

business
24-hour business centre • limousine service • meeting rooms • secretarial services

nearby
Hong Kong Airport • IFC Shopping Mall • Star Ferry Terminal • Victoria Harbour

contact
8 Finance Street, Central, Hong Kong •
telephone: +852.3196 8888 •
facsimile: +852.3196 8899 •
website: www.fourseasons.com/hongkong

grand hyatt hong kong

There are only a handful of truly great metropolitan cities on the planet: the kind that have a certain gravitas, and are so profoundly influential that between them they hold the world's economy in balance. Their names are synonymous with sophistication, glamour, and civilisation. Hong Kong—with its idiosyncratic amalgamation of British-Chinese influences—is undoubtedly one of them.

With Victoria Peak crowning its signature skyline and the phenomenal Victoria Harbour nestled below, Hong Kong's cityscape is one of the brightest stars in the vast Asian sky. A city of this calibre requires a hotel of equal stature, which is why Hyatt International chose to build its flagship property here in 1989. Since then, it has earned a reputation for being one of the finest hotels in the world.

Through this remarkable project, the Grand Hyatt Hong Kong has ingeniously managed to meet the rigorous demands of high-powered business travellers, offering unrivalled personal service and state-of-the-art facilities, at the same time providing the homely details and luxuries sought after by recreational visitors.

Commanding panoramic views over Victoria Harbour, Grand Hyatt Hong Kong makes a monumental contribution to the harbourfront of Hong Kong. With its smooth, polished stone and silvery glass façade, the hotel's exterior reflects the seamless service that has won the hotel a plethora of international awards. In tasteful contrast, the sweeping baroque marble staircases of the lobby hark back to the atmospheric interiors of art deco cruise liners from the 1930s.

THIS PAGE (FROM LEFT):
Get comfortable at Grand Hyatt Hong Kong's signature spa, Plateau; watch the city light up from one's room.
OPPOSITE: *The Plateau's exclusive Water Garden room.*

...a favourite among seasoned travellers.

Within the hotel's rooms, guests can relax in unparalleled comfort and style. With contemporary details such as interactive TVs with high-speed Internet access, it is easy to appreciate why Grand Hyatt Hong Kong is a favourite among seasoned travellers.

In a highly successful bid to attend to guests on business, Grand Hyatt Hong Kong has created a 'hotel within a hotel' concept, where eight floors are reserved exclusively for the Grand Club. Here, guests can enjoy the use of private boardrooms and lounges, full secretarial services and attention from a host of multilingual staff. Understanding that guests are on a tight schedule, rooms are outfitted with step-machines, while CD and DVD players, along with a selection of music and movies, allow the ultra-stressed to unwind.

Indeed, unwinding and relaxing is something the owners of Grand Hyatt Hong Kong know something about. Aside from the staggering array of sporting facilities available, such as tennis and squash courts, a 50-m (164-ft) outdoor heated pool, gym, and driving range, this unrivalled establishment also houses what *Travel & Leisure* magazine rates as one of the top 15 spas in the world.

Plateau is a 7,432-sq-m (80,000-sq-ft) residential spa that is a destination in its own right. Furnished with 23 rooms and suites, and a restaurant, guests are invited to leave the surrounding city behind and immerse themselves in a haven of tranquillity and indulgence. The rooms are a soothing mixture

THIS PAGE: The Pool House is an exceptional venue for private and corporate events.

OPPOSITE (FROM LEFT): JJ's Thai & Grill offers sophisticated cuisine and great music vibes to liven up the evening; the deluxe room encompasses luxury with minimalist accents throughout.

of minimalism and understated luxury, with a king-size futon bedecked in clear, light wood. With a myriad of signature massages, and body and beauty treatments to choose from, pleasant dreams are sure to follow with one's body, mind, and soul at peace.

Clearly, nothing is average at Grand Hyatt Hong Kong, and the dining possibilities are no exception. Gracing the hotel's premises are eight restaurants and bars, guaranteeing something for even the most discerning palate. One Harbour Road is the hotel's legendary Cantonese restaurant. Decorated in the style of a taipan's house in the 1930s, complete with a multi-level interior that assures a breathtaking view of the city for every diner, this is not a meal to be missed.

For a more upbeat evening, Club JJ's offers the ideal combination of mouthwatering dishes and sexy music. Grilled premium steaks and home-style Thai cuisine are served at JJ's Thai & Grill at the lower level, while a vibrant atmosphere is created by a live band performing in JJ's Music Room above. Smooth,

...a monumental contribution to the harbourfront of Hong Kong.

tangy curries are recommended here, with fresh ingredients imported directly from Thailand and masterfully handled by Chef Siriluck, a famed expert in this field.

For those in the mood for a little Japanese, Kaetsu offers the finest sushi and sashimi on the island. Accompanied by a sake menu that features 40 different options, a memorable dining experience awaits.

Western-style dining centres around the exquisite Italian restaurant Grissini, with its flavourful menu of traditional Italian cuisine and extensive wine selection, and at The Grill, where chargrilled specialities are dished up poolside and al fresco. Tired shopaholics looking to while the day away after a morning's worth of intensive shopping will adore Tiffin. Light lunches and afternoon teas are served in true English tradition against the stunning backdrop of Victoria Harbour, a throwback to Hong Kong's colonial past.

Adjacent to the Hong Kong Convention & Exhibition Centre, the Grand Hyatt Hong Kong is minutes from downtown commercial and shopping areas such as Wanchai and Causeway Bay, and guests can stroll down to catch the Star Ferry to neighbouring Kowloon. Hotel employees are also on hand to assist in arranging tours to local points of interest such as Victoria Peak, outlying islands, and beaches, in addition to destinations further afield in China.

Those enthusiastic to explore, but reluctant to leave the luxuries of the Grand Hyatt Hong Kong need not worry: there are Grand Hyatt hotels in Beijing, Shanghai and numerous other Hyatt hotels throughout mainland China.

rooms
497 rooms • 52 suites

food
JJ's Thai & Grill: Thai • Grand Café: international • The Grill: Western grill and al fresco dining • Grissini: Italian • Kaetsu: Japanese • One Harbour Road: Cantonese • Tiffin: afternoon tea, lunch and dessert buffets

drink
Champagne Bar • JJ's Music Room: bar and lounge

features
Plateau residential spa • 24 hour room service • driving range • fitness centre • high-speed Internet access • in-house movies • outdoor heated pool • running track • satellite TV • tennis and squash courts

business
business centre • meeting rooms

nearby
HK Convention & Exhibition Centre • Victoria Harbour • Victoria Peak

contact
1 Harbour Road, Hong Kong •
telephone: + 852.2588 1234 •
facsimile: + 852.2802 0677 •
email: info.ghhk@hyatt.com •
website: www.hongkong.grand.hyatt.com

jia hong kong

THIS PAGE: *Soft lights in the bedroom create a warm, inviting glow.*
OPPOSITE (FROM LEFT): *OPIA is the epitome of stylish dining; JIA Hong Kong's swanky designer lobby.*

For the discerning traveller who wants to live it up in style, home might just be where the Starck is. JIA Hong Kong, which was created out of a refurbished 15-year-old residential building in 2004, bears the distinction of being Hong Kong's—and Asia's—first Philippe Starck-designed boutique hotel. The flamboyant French designer infused the establishment with glamour, luxury, and all things avant-garde. The result is a haven for the hip and upwardly mobile, an abode that's as much about comfort and respite as it is about passion and excitement.

Walk into the 25-storey tower, which stands amid bustling Causeway Bay, and be greeted by the sleek décor bearing Starck's signature style. Nature is the lobby's central theme: the simple elegance of teak wood floors and sheer white curtains act as a backdrop for African artefacts. Dangling chandeliers and satin sofas complete the designer feel of the hotel. Here, guests are invited to mingle as they are served a complimentary continental breakfast, while cakes and wine are on the house during cocktail hour.

Rooms come in three categories: studios, one-bedroom suites, and two-bedroom duplex penthouses, making up a total of 54 rooms. Each room is designed with clearly defined living, dining, and work spaces, delineated by gauzy curtains. The effect of the soft, flowing aesthetic contributes to the rooms' soothing ambience. Designed with both short- and long-term stays in mind, rooms also come with a wide range of modern amenities. From designer kitchens and state-of-the-art home-theatre systems to perks such as complimentary high-speed Internet access and local phone calls, this luxurious abode strives to make guests feel at home as much as possible.

If these homely comforts aren't enough, JIA Hong Kong offers a unique take on in-room dining with its tongue-in-cheek 'Home Delivery' service. Based on a home-style food concept, the menu has extensive selections for both lunch and dinner. Guests receive their orders in special delivery packages just like they would if they were at home, while the rooms' beautiful, fully-equipped arabescato marble-finished kitchens make dining-in a pleasure.

Perfecting the chic, cosmopolitan lifestyle...

However, for a dining experience nonpareil, a meal at OPIA is a must. JIA Hong Kong's signature restaurant and bar has received an impressive number of awards since its launch in 2005, including 'Best Restaurant' at the *South China Morning Post/Harper's Bazaar* Style Awards in 2006. Fusing modern Australian cuisine with Asian influences, OPIA's menu is both innovative and sophisticated. Expect delicious creations such as Crispy Skin Barramundi, Soy Lacquered Wagyu Beef Cheek with Mint and Pomelo Salad, and vegetarian selections like Truffled Potato Cake with Bhutan Wild Honey.

After-hours, OPIA offers a seductive lounge experience with an extensive drinks list prepared by famed 'mixologist' Mark Ward. The Peruvian Punch is a particularly intriguing choice: Captain Morgan's spiced rum shaken with fresh lemon, pineapple and orange juices, and enhanced with antioxidant-rich goji berry syrup and a handful of mint. While others might be neogotiating the traffic home, 'rush hour' at OPIA bar is a pleasant way to kick-start the evening with its trademark cocktails and drinks on promotion.

Perfecting the chic, cosmopolitan lifestyle, the boutique establishment has given its host city an added polish of sophistication: it was the only Hong Kong hotel on *Condé Nast Traveler's* prestigious 'Hot List 2006'. All in all, JIA Hong Kong successfully emulates contemporary Hong Kong: stylish and dynamic, but also familiar and cosy.

rooms
28 studio rooms • 24 suites • 2 duplex penthouses

food
OPIA: modern Australian with Asian influences

drink
OPIA: bar

features
complimentary access to nearby California Fitness gym • flat-screen TV • high-speed Internet access • open-air podium • pantry area • special access to KEE private members' club

business
conference room • audio-visual facilities

nearby
Hong Kong Convention Centre • Hysan Avenue • Lee Gardens • Times Square • Victoria Harbour • Victoria Park

contact
No. 1-5 Irving Street,
Causeway Bay, Hong Kong •
telephone: +852.3196 9000 •
facsimile: +852.3196 9001 •
email: info@jiahongkong.com •
website: www.jiahongkong.com

jw marriott hotel hong kong

Upon first glance, it becomes clear that the award-winning JW Marriott Hotel Hong Kong is no ordinary establishment. Rising 27 floors above street level with a striking angular façade, the edifice is as awe-inspiring as the impeccable service that distinguishes JW Marriott hotels worldwide. Ideally situated at the heart of the city's commercial and business district at Pacific Place, guests have direct access to the world-famous mall with its array of stylish boutiques and restaurants. Being the nexus of such bustling activity, the JW Marriott Hotel Hong Kong is undoubtedly one of the most exclusive hotels the city has to offer.

If the hotel's exterior is impressive, the interior is equally extraordinary. Guests are received in the lobby with a jaw-dropping panoramic view over Hong Kong's spectacular harbour, picturesquely framed by the hotel's immense floor-to-ceiling windows. The resplendent marble floor and natural wood panelling reflect golden light into this majestic space, creating an intimate warmth and a luxurious veneer that aptly characterises the entire building.

In the sumptuous rooms, it becomes clear that the building's distinctive layout allows all guests an unforgettable vista, be it over the

THIS PAGE (FROM LEFT): The spread of international fare is extensive at Marriott Café; the executive floor lounge awaits privileged guests.

OPPOSITE (FROM LEFT): Appreciate Hong Kong's cityscape from the comfort of one's room; the luxurious JW Suite makes guests feel right at home.

...a verdant oasis of tranquillity in the midst of frenetic Hong Kong.

city, the mountains or the harbour itself. Bright and spacious, they have a comfortable, homely feel where deep, soft bedding and pillows ensure complete relaxation. Personal details such as a welcoming cup of tea and a fresh fruit bowl only add to the feeling of being utterly pampered.

Business travellers will want for nothing: all rooms come with high-speed Internet access and data ports. Should time differences require services after-hours, staff at the business centre will be glad to assist on a 24-hour basis. This, in addition to the state-of-the-art audio-visual equipment in the meeting rooms, complete with full secretarial services, make business trips a breeze.

Opportunities to unwind abound at the JW Marriott Hotel Hong Kong. A fully equipped gym allows 24-hour access while a spa complete with steam rooms and a host of treatments are at hand to shake off the stresses of the day. Runners will be tempted by the jogging track in the lush gardens, while water babies will enjoy a dip in the heated outdoor pool or hot tub—a verdant oasis of tranquillity in the midst of frenetic Hong Kong.

True to JW Marriott tradition, the hotel houses six award-winning restaurants, a tantalising variety of eateries, and bars catering to all tastebuds. With the sea just a stone's throw away, seafood gourmands will need little encouragement to head for the Fish Bar. The al fresco feel and simple, yet irresistible menu is sure to delight.

Reputed for its extensive winelist, the signature JW´s California is a fusion of Californian-Asian cuisine in a contemporary setting. Situated within the restaurant is JW's Sushi Bar, offering authentic Japanese cuisine. Marriott Café serves an international menu for all-day dining, while afternoon tea at The Lounge will revive and refresh those feeling tired from an arduous day of sightseeing. For traditional Cantonese fare and seasonal specialities, Man Ho Chinese Restaurant is the place to dine. With favourites such as Steamed Crab Claws and Crispy Fried Chicken, guests will find themselves returning regularly.

Round off the evening by visiting the Q88 Wine Bar, where a vast selection of carefully chosen labels can be savoured along with the accompaniment of live music. The ideal venue to reflect on the day's events and one's good fortune at staying, once again, at the JW Marriott Hotel Hong Kong.

rooms
577 rooms • 25 suites

food
Fish Bar: seafood • JW's California: Californian-Asian • JW's Sushi: Japanese • The Lounge: afternoon tea • Man Ho Chinese Restaurant: Cantonese • Marriott Café: international

drink
Q88 Wine Bar

features
24-hour gym • high-speed Internet access • in-house movies • jogging track • outdoor heated pool • satellite TV • spa

business
24-hour business centre • ballroom • conference facilities • event management team

nearby
botanical gardens • Hong Kong Park • Ocean Park • Pacific Place • The Peak • Tea Ware Museum • Victoria Harbour

contact
Pacific Place, 88 Queensway, Hong Kong • telephone: +852.2810 8366 • facsimile: +852.2845 0737 • email: hotel@marriott.com.hk • website: www.marriott.com

lan kwai fong hotel

THIS PAGE (FROM LEFT): *Buddhist sculptures and contemporary art create an eclectic atmosphere; Lan Kwai Fong Hotel's rooms offer stunning views of Victoria Harbour.*

OPPOSITE (FROM LEFT): *Chill out at Breeze before heading out; Celebrity Cuisine boasts a dramatic interior along with exquisite Cantonese cuisine.*

Once within central Hong Kong's Lan Kwai Fong Hotel, it is hard to decide which is more impressive: the oriental ambience and wonderful hospitality, or its award-winning chic appeal. As Travel Weekly's 'Best Boutique Hotel in Asia', the Lan Kwai Fong Hotel's reputation precedes it, so it is certainly heartening to have one's expectations surpassed upon arrival.

This acclaimed property is situated in Kau U Fong, a small lane in Hong Kong's central business district area, perfectly placed for access to a plethora of entertainment and dining destinations. Previously known for its squatter workshops in the 1960s, Kau U Fong's cobbled lanes have since had a makeover, and its carefully refurbished shophouses are now filled with culture and art. Winding heritage trails and antique streets lead to contemporary art galleries and classy boutiques such as ifc mall, The Landmark, and Prince's Building, bringing cultural vibrancy to the vicinity. With the SoHo and Lan Kwai Fong districts, the Mid-Levels Escalator, and Macau Ferry Terminal all within walking distance, Lan Kwai Fong Hotel is hands-down a winner when it comes to location, location and, well, location.

To relax within the cosy confines of the hotel itself, visit Breeze. This is the place to tuck into a deliciously diverse buffet breakfast or lighter meals throughout the day. Chill out at the restaurant's outdoor terrace and take advantage of Breeze's wireless Internet access, or pore through a variety of magazines with a drink in hand to while away the afternoon. For those craving a satisfying Chinese feast,

Vibrant, individualistic and as stylish as the area it calls home...

Celebrity Cuisine is renowned for its homemade recipes and luxury Chinese ingredients such as abalone, shark's fin, and bird's nest. It hardly comes as a surprise that the restaurant also has a reputation for being a must-visit for celebrities in town.

The hotel's unique décor has unmistakable Chinese accents throughout. The lobby features serenely gleaming Buddhist sculptures with vivid pink lotus flowers adorning its walls. Rooms are home to rich fabrics and intricate wall-mounted mirrors, with hand-carved beds protecting the authentic Chinese artefacts encased in their time-mellowed wood.

Lan Kwai Fong Hotel boasts 157 exquisitely furnished rooms, with city, mountain, and harbour views to choose from. They house top-of-the-range amenities from wireless Internet access to heavenly rainshowers. The best views out over Hong Kong's glittering skyline are from the Lan Kwai Fong Hotel's five highly personalised Harbour View Suites, occupying the hip haven's top two floors. These luxurious rooms have individual balconies that offer panoramic views across Hong Kong's hypnotic Victoria Harbour.

Not content with being supremely easy on the eye, the Lan Kwai Fong Hotel also aims to bring ease to the body with a 24-hour gym. Chinese massage and foot reflexology are also popular diversions. For stressed executives, the hotel's professional therapists are on call until the wee hours of the morning. Vibrant, individualistic and as stylish as the area it calls home, staying at Lan Kwai Fong Hotel is sure to be a unique experience.

rooms
157 rooms • 5 suites

food
Celebrity Cuisine: Cantonese • Breeze: buffet breakfast and light meals

drink
Breeze: bar

features
24-hour gym • in-room reflexology and massage services • satellite TV • wireless Internet access

business
boardroom • computer and mobile phone rental • event planning team • secretarial and translation services

nearby
Exchange Square • Hollywood Road (Antique Street) • ifc mall • Lan Kwai Fong • Macau Ferry Terminal • Mid-Levels Escalator • SoHo • The Centre

contact
3, Kau U Fong, Central Hong Kong •
telephone: +852.3650 0299 •
facsimile: +852.3650 0288 •
email: enquiry@lankwaifonghotel.com.hk •
website: www.lankwaifonghotel.com

hotel le méridien cyberport

THIS PAGE: *Le Méridien Cyberport's rooms successfully blend artistic design with technological function.*
OPPOSITE (FROM TOP): *Gatherings of all sizes are welcome in Prompt's relaxed atmosphere; Nam Fong leads the pack in edgy Cantonese cuisine.*

With its futuristic name, it is implicit that Hotel Le Méridien Cyberport will provide a technological display of the highest specifications. As Travel Weekly's 'Intelligent Building of the Year 2004' and 'Best Hi-Tech Hotel in Asia 2007', this unique waterfront property is located in Cyberport itself, a 'digital city' south of Hong Kong.

In this Andy Tait-designed masterpiece, to check-in is to chill out as the countless dignitaries and public personalities in its A-list guestbook will agree. This sexy hotel boasts 170 Art+Tech-designed guestrooms, each brimming with upscale amenities. The plush, ultra-comfortable beds are encased in pure Egyptian linen and huggable with headboards showcasing a 'Walking through Hong Kong' map—for those who prefer to get their bearings through osmosis, perhaps?

The 142-inch plasma TVs offer satellite TV channels and movies on demand, with high-speed wireless high-speed Internet access and cordless digital telephones allowing connectivity throughout the hotel. The Deluxe Suite and Bayside Premier Suite are enhanced with 'Urban' photos of C.W. Leung, Emma Camden's decorative cast glass, and Hoglund's 'Eclipse' crystal art glasses artfully displayed.

The modish bathrooms are decorated in glass and gleaming chrome, with custom-made lotions and gels by UK-based creators Marietta suspended in sleek translucent holders. Choose between the spacious walk-in rainshower or the roll-top baths, each affording superb views out across the sea. Set the mood with some chilled refreshment from the minibar, served in funky Eva Solo glassware.

Behind the contemporary façade of Le Méridien Cyberport are intriguing tidbits of Hong Kong's pop culture history, seen from the numerous glass etchings of famed 1980s singer Sam Hui's lyrics throughout its foyers. Such nostalgic touches ground Le Méridien Cyberport in Hong Kong, for this multi-faceted establishment is shaped by the inspirational people living in and around it.

In this Andy Tait-designed masterpiece, to check-in is to chill out...

rooms
167 rooms • 3 suites

food
Prompt: high-end dining, al fresco •
Umami: Japanese bar and restaurant •
Nam Fong: contemporary Cantonese

drink
PSI: chill-out bar and lounge • Podium: wine bar

features
cardio-vascular suite • cordless digital telephones • wireless high-speed Internet access • jogging track • landscaped podium • outdoor lap-pool • plasma TV • satellite TV and movies on-demand

business
ballrooms • convention and exhibition centre • function rooms

nearby
Cyberport • central business district • Macau Ferry Terminal • Ocean Park • Repulse Bay

contact
100 Cyberport Road, Hong Kong •
telephone: +852.2980 7788 •
facsimile: +852.2980 7888 •
email: welcome.lmc@lemeridien.com •
website: www.lemeridien.com/hongkong

If planning a conference, Le Méridien Cyberport has all the corporate boxes ticked. Function rooms swathed in abundant natural light are chameleon spaces suitable for intimate soirées, glamorous product launches or theatre-style conferences for up to 350 guests. Sleekly designed working spaces make business trips much more appealing, while boat-trips out to the neighbouring Lamma Island provide a popular diversion.

Le Méridien Cyberport attracts both fitness aficionados and techno-heads. With iPods made available and Randy Cooper steel mesh sculptures adorning the cutting-edge cardio-vascular suite, the outdoor lap pool and natural jogging track need little beckoning.

The gym may well be required, for Le Méridien Cyberport's culinary provision is second to none. PSI chill-out bar looks out to panoramic sunsets over the South China Sea, while Prompt's open gallery kitchen and al fresco terraces are first choice for cosy evening dining. Unwind in the garden of the modern Umami Japanese restaurant, or savour cult wines at the Podium. For Cantonese cuisine with a post-millennial twist, head for the soft, glowing lights of Nam Fong.

Whether as an adventure in hedonistic escapology or as a journey to the forefront of 21st-century technology, Le Méridien Cyberport is, without question, Hong Kong's vision of the future.

kee club

KEE Club was conceived by a group of friends who brought together their own varied experiences and inspiration: an inherent knowledge of fine cuisine from being part of one of Hong Kong's most historic gourmet Chinese restaurants; from parties influenced by stories of great masquerades in Austria; an appreciation of music that can make a club a success; in-depth family knowledge of cinema, and from generations of exposure to classic and contemporary art in Europe and Asia.

This private members' club, situated above the famous Yung Kee restaurant, is a place where friends can gather to appreciate outstanding cuisine, fine wines, great music and art—in other words, the good life. Today, KEE Club is recognised as one of Hong Kong's most sophisticated meeting places, and has become renowned for throwing swanky parties for celebrities such as Sting, The Rolling Stones, and Michael Jordan. Its membership card is a must-have for the city's elite. KEE club extends its hospitality to visitors from out of town, through a special arrangement with a selection of exclusive hotels whose guests are allowed access if booked in advance by the hotel's concierge.

The club's interior is inspired by an eclectic mix of European luxury, New York chic, and African and Asian bohemia. Filled with natural light by day and cast with

THIS PAGE (FROM LEFT): *Appreciate beautiful works of art amid stylish settings; the plush salons are perfect for private parties and intimate meetings.*

OPPOSITE (FROM LEFT): *The dark, sultry bar serves creative cocktails and premium wines; the gilt staircase leading up to the Venetian Dining Room.*

...recognised as one of Hong Kong's most sophisticated meeting places...

long shadows from candlelight by night, it exudes a refined, seductive atmosphere, with a dark wood bar, a Jacobsen's Swan & Egg chair, and a dramatic gilt staircase leading to the Venetian Dining Room. Decked with paintings, sculptures and antiques collected by the owners during their travels, guests can admire works by prominent designers and artists such as Picasso, Topor, and Starck.

On the lower floor there is a bar and lounge that doubles up as a private screening room, and three intimate salons, each with its own distinct décor and ambience. From the peaceful Purple Salon that functions as a library, to the opulent Red and Centurion Salons, each can be transformed to cater to confidential business deals, backgammon championships or private parties. In the lavishness of the Venetian Dining Room, which emulates the glamour of a Venetian Palazzo, KEE Club serves up some of Hong Kong's finest dim sum over an intimate lunch. At dinner, Head Chef Bonelli, whose training has seen him working in the kitchens of some of the world's best restaurants such as Spain's El Bulli and England's The Fat Duck, creates outstanding menus of sublime and contemporary cuisine. House specialities include Boston Lobster and Goose Liver.

Combined with a diverse list of cocktails and one of the city's most prestigious wine cellars, KEE Club is one of Hong Kong's hottest venues for everything from big-ticket events to hip parties featuring international names.

food
contemporary Italian • Cantonese

drink
extensive wine list • cocktails

features
exclusive private member's club (concierges at select five-star hotels can arrange access) • restaurant • lounge bar • private salons • library • screening room • DJs • events • extensive art collection

nearby
Lan Kwai Fong • Star Ferry Terminal • Victoria Peak • Victoria Harbour • Central shopping and business area

contact
6/F, 32 Wellington Street,
Central, Hong Kong •
telephone: +852.2810 9000 •
facsimile: +852.2868 0036 •
email: info@keeclub.com •
website: www.keeclub.com

shanghai tang

Using bold designs, luscious materials and brilliant colours, Shanghai Tang has created a distinctive style that is recognised and admired the world over. Starting out in 1994 as a small tailoring boutique in Hong Kong, it has since become China's world-class luxury brand. With an international following, Shanghai Tang has outlets in the fashion capitals of London, Paris, New York and Tokyo as well as Shanghai—the origin of its inspiration.

1930s Shanghai was known for its extravagant lifestyle and stylish trends. The elegant qi pao, a bodice-hugging dress, was a Shanghainese fashion statement. With the Cultural Revolution in the 1960s, however, the focus moved to Mao suits, dampening the demand for inventive designs. The ancient art of qi pao-making—with its painstaking attention to detail and craftsmanship—dwindled, and tailors turned their concentration to men's suits. Today, Shanghai Tang offers a made-to-measure clothing service that clearly follows in the footsteps of these famed tailors. With the few remaining specialists under its employment, the Chinese haute couture boutique keeps the qi pao in fashion, radically redesigning the classic dress form and taking it to new heights of elegance.

THIS PAGE (FROM LEFT): *Inventive designs are a trademark of Shanghai Tang; modern Chinese details and traditional Chinese décor give the Hong Kong flagship store a stylish touch.*

OPPOSITE (CLOCKWISE FROM LEFT): *Oriental accents influence Shanghai Tang's homeware goods (left), jewellery (right) and handbags (bottom).*

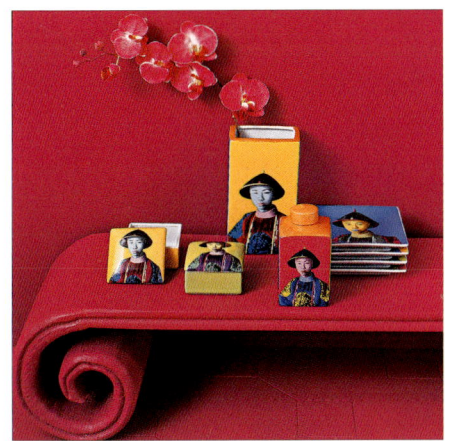

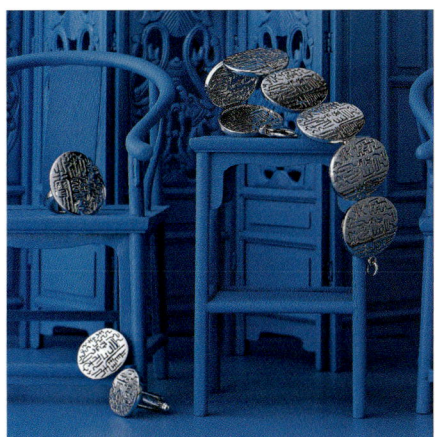

...the epitome of modern Chinese chic.

products
clothing • homeware • accessories

features
custom-design clothing • tailoring services

nearby
The Central • ifc mall • Star Ferry Terminal

contact
Pedder Building, 12 Pedder Street, Central, Hong Kong •
telephone: +852.2537 2888 •
facsimile: +852.2156 9898 •
email: contactus@shanghaitang.com •
website: www.shanghaitang.com

With collections changing every season, Shanghai Tang finds inspiration for all its clothes, homeware and accessory designs in Chinese culture. The luxury label designs with a dynamic and fearless approach to fashion, using exquisite silks, velvets, cashmeres and linens in its trademark vibrant colours. Each design is uniquely cut, with a distinctive quality that makes Shanghai Tang creations the epitome of modern Chinese chic.

Famous for its dignified mandarin-collared jackets and beautiful clothing line, Shanghai Tang also designs children's wear, toys and accessories. In addition, a homeware series is available for those who wish to stamp their homes with the boutique's quirky, tongue-in-cheek style.

Shanghai Tang's Hong Kong flagship store is deemed by many as one of the most prestigious boutiques in the world. The interior of the two-storey shop fills visitors with a sense of splendour and opulence. Its décor includes a dark wooden floor, Chinese art, bespoke wallpaper and vivid clothing collections, all making for a stunning gallery.

For a made-to-measure qi pao, head to the boutique's tailoring department. Soft lights, ceiling fans and lush chaise lounges reflect the Old World charm of traditional Shanghainese couture salons. The adjoining Tearoom allows customers to savour Chinese tea and pastries while expert tailoring consultants assist in the choosing of fabrics and ensure nothing less than the perfect fit.

With smaller stores situated within the airport, Pacific Place, Elements, The Peninsula Hotel, and The InterContinental Hotel in Hong Kong, as well as fine hotels and major shopping districts in Beijing and Shanghai, very few visitors to Hong Kong and China will escape the lure of Shanghai Tang—it would be a real shame if they did.

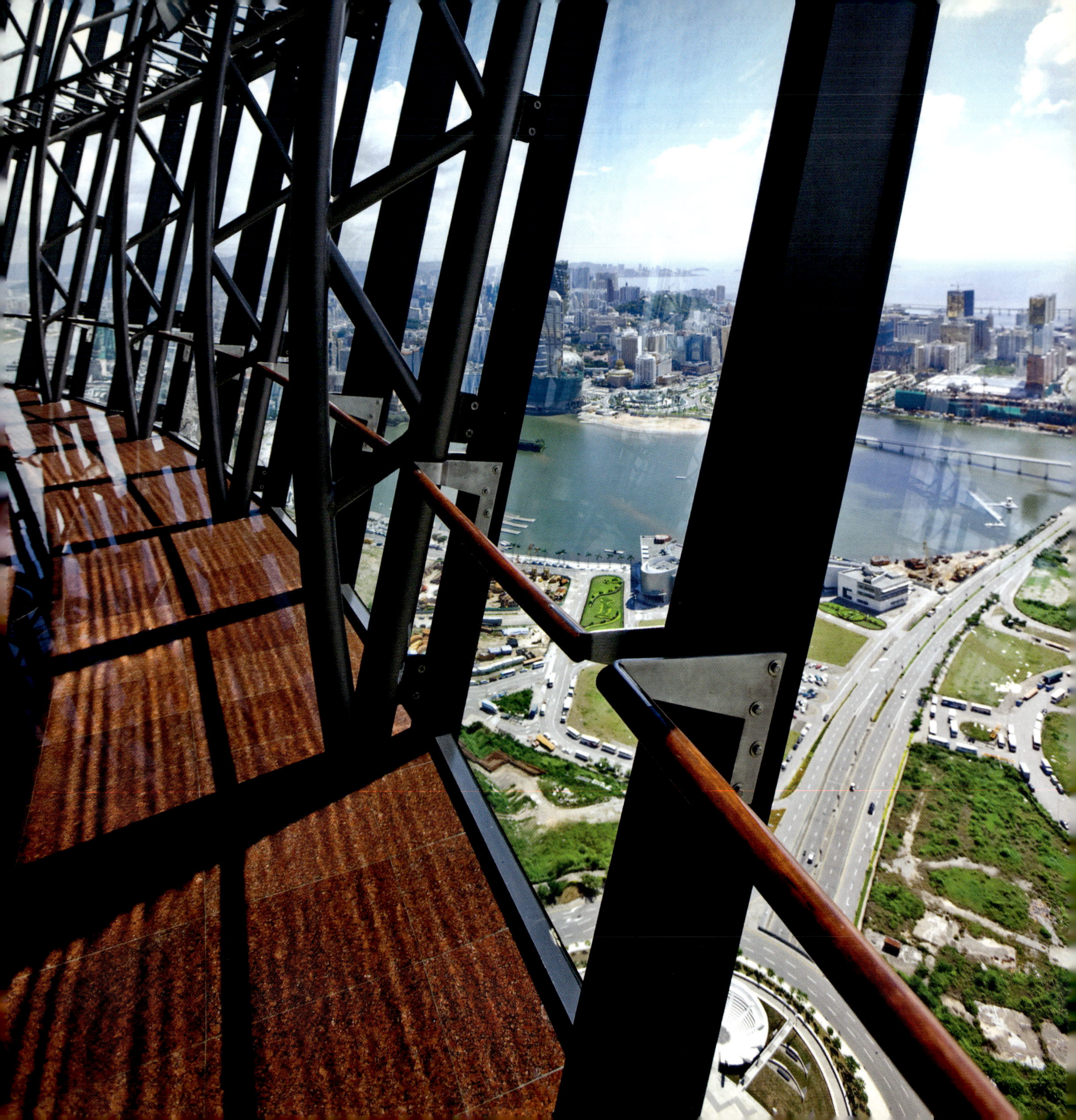

macau

Macau Peninsula

- Rua da Ribeiro do Patane
- Avenida de Horta e Costa
- Flora Gardens
- Rua do Visconde Pato de Arcos
- Ruinas de São Paulo (Ruins of St. Paul's)
- Sofitel Macau at Ponte 16
- Avenida de Almeida Ribeiro
- Rua de Malaca
- Macau Grand Prix Museum
- Macau Wine Museum
- Fisherman's Wharf
- Senado Square
- Dom Pedro V Theatre
- Wynn Macau
- Avenida da Amizade
- Avenida da Praia Grande
- Av. do Infante D. Henrique
- Rua Cidade de Sintra
- Av. do Dr. Mario Soares
- Avenida Dr. Sun Yat-sen
- Rua da Almirante Sergio
- Macau Culture Centre
- Avenida de Sagres
- Avenida Zheng Guan Ying
- Avenida 24 de Junho
- Av. Marginal da Baia Nova
- Avenida da Republica
- Rua da Praia do Bom Parto
- Nam Van Lake
- Ponte Governador Nobre de Carvalho
- Avenida Dr. Sun Yat-sen
- Lan Kwai Fong
- Kun Iam Statue
- Sai Van Lake
- Temple da A-ma (A-ma Temple)
- Ponte de Sai Van
- Macau Tower
- To Taipa

Inset: Taipa / Cotai / Coloane

- Crown Macau
- Taipa
- Macau Jockey Club
- Cotai
- Coloane
- Coloane Village
- Hac Sa Beach

Legend

- Expressway
- Main Road
- Other Road
- Water
- Airport

0 km — 0.3 — 0.6 — 0.9 km

0 km — 0.5 — 1.0 — 1.5 km

macau metamorphosis

Few could have imagined the incredible metamorphosis Macau has experienced in less than a decade. Once upon a time, the territory was largely known as a seedy colonial outpost of gambling dens, crime, and other indiscretions. Since then, a surge in tourism and foreign investment has transformed the former Portuguese enclave into a flourishing gaming, entertainment, and dining destination that rivals Las Vegas. It has also managed to retain some of its more charming colonial characteristics.

Macau is just 28.6 sq km (11 sq miles) in size, comprising the Macau Peninsula and the Taipa and Coloane islands. On the Macau Peninsula, also known as Downtown Macau, European-style architecture makes a striking contrast against Asian elements such as temples with burning joss sticks. The quieter and calmer Taipa is now merged with Coloane by Cotai, reclaimed land that bridges the 3-km (2-mile) Taipa-Coloane Causeway. Cotai exemplifies the new Macau, home to famous US brand casinos such as The Venetian, with countless others under construction.

The population of just over half a million is predominantly ethnic Chinese, with smaller numbers of Portuguese descendants, Eurasians, and expatriates. Macau's Eurasian community can trace its history back at least a century to the union between Portuguese and Chinese ancestors. Chinese and Portuguese are official languages, but English is widely used in business.

entertainment + gaming

Electronics, textiles, and toys are important industries in Macau but tourism has had, by far, the greatest impact. Visitor numbers have nearly quadrupled in the last decade, with approximately 55 per cent from mainland China, who flood into Macau in ever greater numbers, enjoying more relaxed travel restrictions and indulging their legendary appetite for gambling. Contemporary annual events help to draw visitors to this tiny but dynamic destination, such as music festivals and the famous Macau Grand Prix, but it is the casinos that pull in the record crowds.

Macau's gaming industry began in the 1960s and grew much like a weed—with little control and giving life to the seedy businesses that tend to sprout up around it. By the 1990s, the territory was infamous for its various scandals. Then came the Handover back to China in 1999. The monopoly held by casino mogul Stanley Ho's Sociedade de Jogos de Macau came to an end as gaming licenses were made available to other companies for the first time in almost 40 years.

PAGE 204: *The view from the observation deck of the Macau Tower, one of the territory's modern landmarks.*

THIS PAGE (FROM TOP): *The dramatic Sai Van Bridge links Taipa to the Macau Peninsula; the Macau Grand Prix attracts the world's top racing names to its prestigious Formula Three World Cup every year.*

macau 207

The arrival of foreign casinos has catapulted the gaming industry into the stratosphere. Revenues now surpass those of the Las Vegas Strip and are predicted to exceed US$15 billion by the end of 2010. The onslaught of these gaming powerhouses has, however, put pressure on Macau's older casinos. Stanley Ho still controls about 18 of the 27 casinos in the gambling Mecca, but few operate on the scale of the newer developments. The planned redevelopment of the landmark Lisboa Hotel is a sign of the times, its revenues having long been eclipsed by Sands and others.

Those who aren't mesmerised by the flashing lights of the Cotai Strip can find an alternative form of enjoyment in the numerous highlights and enduring reminders of Macau's past. UNESCO listed the 'Historic Centre of Macau', which consists of over 20 historic monuments and buildings, as a World Heritage Site in 2005. It includes some of China's oldest examples of Western architecture. Two of Macau's most widely recognised buildings, the iconic Ruínas de São Paulo (Ruins of St. Paul's) and the well-loved Templo de A-Ma (A-Ma Temple) are among the preserved monuments of the Historic Centre.

building on the past

With plans to enhance Macau as a luxury destination well on the way, the territory appears to be heading towards a golden age, but it would not be the first time. Around the period that the first settlers were known to have arrived from Fujian and Guangdong, Macau was known as 'Ou Mun' or 'trading gate' as it was an access point on the Silk Road, favourably positioned downstream from Guangdong on the west bank of the Pearl River Delta. The Portuguese made the entrepôt port the first European colony in East Asia in 1557 and named it Macau, a name adapted from 'A Ma Gao', the patron goddess of seafarers. Macau thrived, acting as the key trading port where Chinese silks and tea, African ivory, Indian spices, Brazilian gold, and Japanese crafts all passed through on their way to Portugal, Spain, Italy, and beyond.

This golden era ended in the 1800s as the Dutch and the British founded their own colonial outposts and began to dominate trading in the region. British-ruled Hong Kong, with its deep harbour just 60 km (37 miles) away, soon overshadowed Macau. Macau never returned to its more prosperous days in the intervening years, and by the time Portugal returned Macau to China in 1999, it had become known as a gambling destination coloured by crime. However, before seceding power to China, the Portuguese carried out several infrastructure projects, including land reclamation, new bridges, and an international airport, which would put the territory in good stead for the future development of the tourism and gaming industries.

THIS PAGE (FROM TOP): Modern-day statues adorn the square at the foot of Ruínas de São Paulo, one of Macau's most famous sights; greyhound races are held at the Canidrome in Macau.

OPPOSITE: Work continues around the clock on Macau's glitzy new casinos, each gunning for a larger slice of the territory's phenomenal gaming revenues.

...a flourishing gaming, entertainment, and dining destination...

macau: dining out

For such a small territory, Macau offers a remarkably vast range of dining options spanning many cultures and price ranges. Like much of the city, restaurants may be divided into the old and the new, but all of them showcase the influences of the city's colourful history.

pure macanese

Macanese cuisine has developed over the centuries, a delicious combination of traditions from Portuguese, Chinese, and sometimes Malay cooking. Its use of spices and chilli can be traced back to Portugal's colonial history in Africa and India. The distinct flavours blend beautifully in hearty meals that consist of such classics as chorizo (sausage), bacalhau (salt cod), African chicken, feijoada, and curried prawns, all enjoyed with fresh bread and Portuguese wines.

Arguably the most famous Macau restaurant is **Restaurante Fernando** (Praia de Hac Sa 9, Coloane), an open, casual space located near Hac Sa beach. **A Lorcha** (298 Rua do Almirante Sergio, Inner Harbour, Macau) is another immensely popular destination for a classic Portuguese and Macanese meal. **Restaurante Litoral** (261A Rua do Almirante Sergio, Macau) is considered one of the best and offers a convivial ambience with dark wood floors and whitewashed walls. The private **Clube Militar de Macau** (975 Avenida da Praia Grande, Downtown, Macau) allows non-members into its dining room for a taste of old Macau in its nostalgic colonial building. At Fisherman's Wharf, **Camoes** (Shop 101, Lisbon-Evora, Macau Fisherman's Wharf, Macau) makes authentic Portuguese food and takes advantage of the fresh supply of seafood from nearby waters. **Nga Tim Café** (Rua Caetano, 8, Coloane Village, Coloane) leans towards a more Chinese take on Macanese food, which is served in a bustling open-air pavilion. Located in the main square of Coloane Village, it is also an excellent spot to people-watch and meet locals.

Of course, no meal—indeed, no visit to Macau—would be complete without a taste of the legendary Portuguese egg tart or pastel de nata. It has a light, flaky casing filled with an egg custard—just like its Hong Kong cousin—but with the added delight of a caramelised top reminiscent of a crème brûlée. An ongoing competition for the best egg tart title continues to rage between the former partners behind **Lord Stow's Bakery** (1 Rua da Tassara, Coloane Town Square, Macau) and **Margaret's Café e Nata** (Edificio Kam Loi, Nam Van, Macau). But these treats are so delicious, it is the perfect excuse to indulge in more than just one by sampling from both bakeries!

chinese cuisine

The Cantonese food of southern China thrives in Macau. **Fat Siu Lau** (Rua da Felicidade, Downtown, Macau) has been a popular destination for reasonably priced Cantonese and Macanese food for over 100 years. **Long Kei** (7B Largo do Senado, Downtown, Macau) is another old faithful specialising in Cantonese classics such as roast pork.

At the other end of the spectrum, **Portas do Sol** (2/F, Hotel Lisboa, 2–4 Avenida de Lisboa, Downtown, Macau) is an elegant choice for dim sum and Chinese food. For yum cha (a gathering of friends and/or family where dim sum is served), there is also the subtly lit, contemporary **Lua Azul** (3/F, Macau Tower, Largo da Torre de Macau, Downtown, Macau).

asian cuisine

No gourmand city would be worth its salt without fabulous Japanese restaurants—and Macau is no exception. Connoisseurs applauded the arrival of famous Tokyo restaurant, **Tenmasa** (11/F, Crown Macau, Avenida de Kwong Tung at Avenida Dr. Sun Yat Sen, Taipa), where fresh ingredients are flown in almost daily from Japan. Catering to the intense demand for Japanese dining, a second Japanese restaurant in the Crown Macau, **Kira** (10/F, Crown Macau, Avenida de Kwong Tung at Avenida Dr. Sun Yat Sen, Taipa), serves meticulously prepared creations by Chef Hiroshi Kagata within a setting by designers Hashimoto Yukio and David Sung. **Okada** (Wynn Macau, Rua Cidade de Sintra, NAPE, Macau) takes a traditional perspective on Japanese cuisine, but presents it in a sleek, contemporary interior.

international

A plethora of fine dining venues has followed the flood of high rollers and visitors to Macau. Acclaimed chef Joel Robuchon opened the exclusive **Robuchon a Galera** (3/F, Hotel Lisboa, 2–4 Avenida de Lisboa, Downtown, Macau) in 2001, and returns frequently to oversee the seasonal menu and extensive wine list. **Aurora** (10/F, Crown Macau, Avenida de Kwong Tung at Avenida Dr. Sun Yat Sen, Taipa) draws food-lovers for its modern French cuisine, sophisticated ambience, a terrace with lovely views, and a fantastic champagne brunch on Sundays. Chef Claude Durant serves true French classics at **Le Bistrot** (G/F, Block 27, Nova Taipa Garden, Taipa).

The Italians have also made their mark. Chef Alfonso Laccarino brings generations of secret Italian recipes to **Don Alfonso 1890—Macau** (Grand Lisboa Hotel, Avenida de Lisboa, Macau). Southern Italian cooking also informs the elegant meals at **Il Teatro** (Wynn Macau, Rua Cidade de Sintra, NAPE, Macau). A dramatic setting replete with private balconies and VIP rooms serves as the stage for the classic menu. Near Macau's nightlife hub, **Antica Trattoria da Ise** (40–46 Avenida Sir Anders Ljungstedt, Edificio Vista Magnifica Court, Macau) is where one can kick back and enjoy wonderful Italian food.

The Churrascaria concept of dynamic cooking and presentation is alive and well at **Fogo Samba** (Shop 2410, Grand Canal Shoppes, The Venetian Macao, Estrada da Baia de N. Senhora da Esperanca, Taipa), where the Brazilian barbecue is fired up in the open kitchen.

And for those days when only a juicy grain-fed, prime-aged American steak will do, there is always **Morton's of Chicago** (Shop 1016, Grand Canal Shoppes, The Venetian Macao, Estrada da Baia de N. Senhora da Esperanca, Taipa)!

THIS PAGE (FROM TOP): *A bold contemporary setting complements the Chinese cuisine at Fat Siu Lau; Macau offers the best of the world's cuisines, both sweet and savoury.*
OPPOSITE: *A warm sophisticated ambience characterises Aurora.*

macau:diningout 211

macau's nightlife

Macau entertains all night long with a myriad of bars, nightclubs, restaurants, casinos, concerts, and more. While the saunas and burlesque shows of old are still there for those who seek them out, hip new Macau also comes with cosmopolitan spots for fun after dark.

Many of the territory's latest watering holes are found in the new five- and six-star casino resorts. At the MGM Grand Macau, one can enjoy pre-dinner cocktails or kick back and relax at the **M Bar** (G/F, MGM Grand Macau, Avenida Dr. Sun Yat Sen, NAPE, Macau), where plush surroundings and live music are accompanied by a wide selection of beverages. For a sip of bubbly, champagne-lovers have a choice of the intimate **Champagne Bar** (MGM Grand Macau, Avenida Dr. Sun Yat Sen, NAPE, Macau), which also houses a glass cellar filled with fine vintages, and the glamourous **Veuve Clicquot Lounge** (MGM Grand Macau, Avenida Dr. Sun Yat Sen, NAPE, Macau).

For a quiet drink away from the hustle and bustle, **Lumina Bar** (5/F, Crown Macau, Avenida de Kwoong Tung at Avenida Dr. Sun Yat Sen, Taipa) at the Crown Macau serves a selection of refreshing cocktails, while the **Crystal Club** (38/F, Crown Macau, Avenida de Kwoong Tung at Avenida Dr. Sun Yat Sen, Taipa) offers panoramic views with an extensive drinks menu from its perch on the top level of the hotel.

The Venetian Macao has two bars on its casino floor to better serve its busy gaming clientele: the more casual **Bar Florian** (Shop 1043, The Venetian Macao, Estrada da Baia de N. Senhora da Esperanca, Taipa), which serves light snacks and cocktails; and the **Bellini Lounge** (Shop 1041, The Venetian Macao, Estrada da Baia de N. Senhora da Esperanca, Taipa) for those taking a break to catch some live music and refreshment. Also located on the casino level, the funky **blue frog bar & grill** (Shop 1037, The Venetian Macao, Estrada da Baia de N. Senhora da Esperanca, Taipa), sister to the popular Shanghai establishment, offers an extensive drinks menu and live performances within a stylishly cosy setting. For business drinks, the Wynn Macau lobby lounge **Cinnebar** (Wynn Macau, Rua Cidade de Sintra, NAPE, Macau) is ideal.

Outside the realm of hotels, **'Lan Kwai Fong'** is a main bar area near the Cultural Centre along Avenida

Dr. Sun Yat Sen, named, of course, after Hong Kong's famous nightlife hub. Live music spills out of the windows of pubs and into the streets, creating an infectious party atmosphere along the strip. **Moonwalker** (Avenida Dr. Sun Yat Sen, Outer Harbour, Macau) is famous among the bars and pubs. Also in the area, the charismatic **Casablanca** (1373–1369, Avenida Dr. Sun Yat Sen, Outer Harbour, Macau) is distinctive with its dim lighting, movie posters and velvet curtains, and always an old film flickering from the projector.

For clubbing, **Sky21** (21/F, AIA Tower, 251A–301 Avenida Comercial de Macau, Macau) is the place to be. Spread over 1,858 sq m (20,000 sq ft) on three levels, it also has outdoor bar terraces taking advantage of the spectacular views from atop AIA Tower. Revellers who make it past 3 am inevitably meet at **D2** (2/F, AIA Tower, 251A–301 Avenida Comercial de Macau, Macau), where the party is in full swing by then.

The **Jazz Club** (9 Rua das Alabardas, Macau) is something of a local institution. Drinks are reasonably-priced but the live jazz is the real draw here. A visit on the weekend is recommended.

In addition to nightspots, Macau offers entertainment in the form of concerts and performances. The 15,000-seat **Venetian Arena** (The Venetian Macao, Estrada da Baia de N. Senhora da Esperanca, Taipa) is Macau's premier venue for world-class acts, which have included Celine Dion, The Police, Jose Carreras, and Beyonce. For a romantic evening at the ballet or the theatre, the **Macao Cultural Centre** (Avenido Xian Xing Hai, NAPE, Macau) offers a year-long calendar of art house movies, opera, and music and dance performances. The 19th-century **Dom Pedro V Theatre** (Largo de Santo Agostinho, Macau), refurbished and restored to its original grandeur, now also serves as a concert hall for classical and symphonic performances. An evening at this historic building is a treat in itself.

Those looking for even more gaming excitement outside the confines of the casinos can pay a visit to the **Macau Jockey Club** (Estrada Governador Albano da Oliveira, Taipa), where horse races are held in the evening during the racing season.

THIS PAGE (FROM TOP): *It's not just the glamorous casinos but Macau's hip and happening bars that draw the crowds too; luxury champagne is the poison of choice for Macau's high-rollers.*
OPPOSITE: *Revellers party the night away at a nightclub; there are also elegant venues for a quiet drink or meal away from the crowds.*

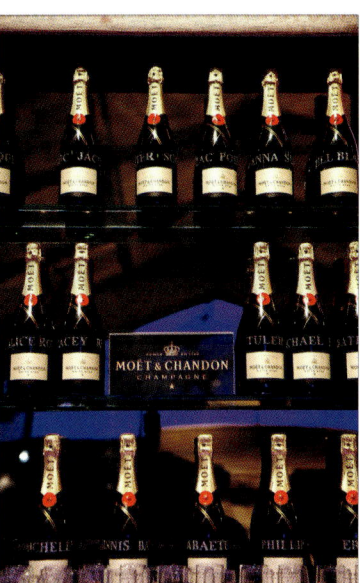

macau'snightlife 213

macau: a shopping sensation

From Chinese handicrafts to Italian handbags, from Portuguese wines to Parisian haute couture, there are wonderfully diverting forms of retail therapy in this tax-free port. Indeed, in the span of just a few years, Macau has begun to emerge from the shadow of Hong Kong, historically the region's retail giant, as far as shopping goes. Yet, here again, the contrast between old and new is like night and day. The pre-existing quaint little boutiques, free from the sway of the big city, have been joined by ultra-chic stores and the biggest players in the luxury game, often housed within the new mega casino resorts.

malls

Luxury brands have leapt at the opportunity to enter the shopping scene in tandem with the exponential growth in tourism. The colossal new casinos were strategically developed to enhance the luxury shopping experience. The **Wynn Esplanade** (Rua Cidade de Sintra, NAPE, Macau), for example, boasts the biggest names in designer jewellery and fashion, among them, **Tiffany**, **Piaget**, **Van Cleef and Arpels**, **Chanel**, **Prada**, **Rolex**, **Dior**, **Dunhill**, **Giorgio Armani**, **Hermes**, **Hugo Boss**, **Bulgari**, and **Fendi**. It is by no means the most extensive display of luxury, however. The **Grand Canal Shoppes at The Venetian Macao** (The Venetian Macao, Estrada da Baia de N. Senhora da Esperanca, Taipa) has that honour. A giant among giants, this Baroque-themed mall houses 350 stores, 20 restaurants, and a 'Streetmosphere' programme of musicians, performers and, yes, singing gondoliers.

specialist stores

Intense interest in Chinese antiques has almost emptied the casual collector's market, but Macau continues to surprise with a nice selection of antique (or simply old), restored and reproduced pieces. Furniture, ceramics and other works of art are still good buys, and are sold at prices often lower than those in neighbouring Hong Kong. The shops, concentrated around the area of **Fortaleza do Monte**, **Rua de São Paulo**, **Rua das Estalagens**, and **Rua St. António** sometimes arrange shipment for customers who live abroad. **Wing Tai** (1A Avenida de Almeida Ribeiro, Macau) is a reputable, established dealer, where the staff takes the time to share their knowledge with customers. **Asian Artefacts** (9 Rua dos Negociantes, Coloane) carries restored pieces from around the region, and makes it a point to clearly detail each item's history.

Macau may have returned to China in 1999, but it retains certain charming characteristics of its centuries-old relationship with Europe, including a fabulous assortment of Portuguese wines. Rather a well-kept secret, they are only now gaining worldwide recognition. The **Macau Wine Museum** (Tourism Activities Centre, 431 Rua Luis Gonzaga Gomes, Macau) provides an excellent pre-shopping introduction. Supermarkets, and even the small grocery stores, will have a few bottles for sale, but the **Pavilions** wine cellar (417 Avenida da Praia Grande, Downtown, Macau) is well worth a visit.

Those with a sweet tooth will enjoy browsing among the many bakeries selling traditional cookies along streets like **Rua de São Paulo** and **Avenida Infante D. Henrique**. Just follow your nose!

markets

Street markets and fairs add to the colour of Macau. Flea markets near St. Paul's or near the old Chinese Bazaar by the Hong Kung Temple sell a hodgepodge of merchandise. On weekend evenings, the shopping action is in a square on **Estrada do Reouso**, near the Cinema Allegria, where the neighbourhood association stages a night market. Every Sunday, the **Islands' Weekly Fair** is held between Bombeiros and Camoes Squares on Taipa, offering an eclectic mix of toys, food, traditional crafts, clothes, and miscellanea. If reasonably-priced clothing is on the agenda, a search among the old Portuguese shophouses of **Senado Square** is a must for casual wear and an impressive array of children's clothes. Off the square, **Avenida de Almeida Ribeiro** is a popular shopping street where one can find both boutiques selling well-known international brands and traditional Chinese stores selling all manner of dried goods. **Avenida Horta e Costa** is good for a stroll and some window-shopping. It starts at the **Red Market**, where food and fresh produce are sold, and ends at **Flora Gardens**. Along the way and in neighbouring streets, treasure-seekers can browse through a wide array of shops selling jewellery, electronics, clothes, and other interesting finds.

THIS PAGE (FROM TOP). *It is a feast for the senses at the Grand Canal Shoppes at The Venetian Macao; a local shows off his sense of style outside one of Macau's traditional biscuit shops; bustling Senado Square at dusk.*

OPPOSITE: *Louis Vuitton, just one of the galaxy of luxury brands housed in the Wynn Esplanade.*

spas in macau

An authentic luxury spa experience in Macau rivals the very best in the world. However, one would have to forgive a raised eyebrow or an amused grin at the very mention of the word, 'spa'. It has rather salacious connotations here, which harks back to a time before the recent surge of five-star hotels and resorts. Nowadays, the popular perception of spas is changing and with countless treatments to indulge in, one is literally spoilt for choice.

a five-star experience

For years, **The Spa at the Mandarin Oriental Macau** (956–1110 Avenida da Amizade, Macau) was the only oasis in the desert, a light-filled, Mediterranean-inspired haven with beautiful, green outdoor spaces, a heated pool and waterfall. The spa has devised a full menu of treatments with UK brand Aromatherapy Associates, which combines the techniques and philosophies of Chinese, European, Japanese and Thai cultures. The signature Ritual treatments offer a holistic, highly personalised experience that is not to be missed.

New on the scene, the **Six Senses Spa** (3/F, MGM Grand Macau, Avenida Dr. Sun Yat Sen, NAPE, Macau) describes its philosophy as a pyramid of the senses, starting with a foundation of sight, sound, and touch, and graduating to smell and taste, and finishing with a sense of elation. Only natural ingredients are used during treatments, and heating facilities include the standard sauna and steam room, plus a hammam and a laconium.

The decadent **Spa at Wynn Macau** (Rua Cidade de Sintra, NAPE, Macau) was singled out in the *Condé Nast Traveler* Hot List of spas for 2007. In addition to its welcoming, luxurious design, the spa provides truly unique treatments, many rooted in local culture. Reminiscent of its Portuguese colonial past, the Macanese Massage, for example, is done on a heated bed using warm olive oil. The hotel's beauty and fitness facilities include a fully equipped fitness centre and a salon for hair and nail services overlooking a grand 'tropical' swimming pool.

While ancient health and beauty traditions inspire the treatments at **The Spa at Crown** (Crown Macau, Avenida de Kwong Tung at Avenida Dr. Sun Yat Sen, Taipa), thoroughly contemporary design sets the calming mood of its interiors. Spread over 6,000 sq m (64,583 sq ft) on two floors, the sanctuary encompasses a rasul, vitality pools, saunas, crystal steam, and a hair salon. The full list of treatments offers pampering from head to toe, including the signature Gold body treatment, which ends with a light dusting of the precious metal.

small + personal

Beyond the hotel sphere, **Spa Philosophy** (327–331 Avenida Xian Xing Hai, Nam On Garden, Macau) stands out as one of Macau's first and finest day spas. Not only does it offer a host of pampering services for the face and body, it provides a serene, oxygenated environment to battle the effects of daily exposure to pollution.

THIS PAGE (FROM TOP): *Macau's spas offer exotic and luxurious treatments, even using ingredients such as champagne (left) and chocolate (right); spa-goers can enjoy a soothing tropical view while having a manicure at the hair and nail salon of Spa at Wynn Macau.*
OPPOSITE: *The ultra-modern premises of Spa Philosophy, one of Macau's premier day spas.*

spasinmacau 217

macau's casino scene

Glitzy, larger-than-life casinos, their names up in flashing lights, a 24-hour programme of world-class entertainment, meals at restaurants by famed international chefs and, yes, all forms of gaming. Las Vegas? No. This is Macau, where gaming revenues have already surpassed those of the Las Vegas Strip. This is not the den of debauchery that you may have come to expect from Macau. The territory has changed politically, economically and culturally at a breathtaking pace. What's left is a new, polished version—with one constant: gaming. And the recent influx of the biggest names in casino development is helping to ensure that the high-rollers keep rolling in. In addition to the gaming rooms, these companies have brought with them luxurious resort facilities, award-winning restaurants, high-end shopping, and phenomenal artists from around the globe.

The first foreign-owned casino was opened by Las Vegas tycoon Sheldon Addelson in 2004, the **Sands Macao** (203 Largo de Monte Carlo, Macau). The gleaming golden edifice sprawls across 90,120 sq m (970,069 sq ft) with several gaming floors, 289 rooms, and entertainment venues.

Stephen Wynn launched the **Wynn Macau** in 2006 (Rua Cidade de Sintra, NAPE, Macau) with the distinctive architecture and sloping roof of its antecedent in Las Vegas. Inside, there are over 9,290 sq m (100,000 sq ft) of gaming pleasure, 600 rooms, luxury brand shopping, a spa, fine dining, and all the frills of a high-end US-style casino. It is located on Macau's reclaimed Cotai Strip.

The year 2007 saw several significant new additions. Australian James Packer brought the Crown concept to Macau in a joint venture with Stanley Ho's son, Lawrence Ho. The six-star **Crown Macau** (Avenida de Kwong Tung at Avenida Dr. Sun Yat Sen, Taipa) has honed the luxury experience with exceptional dining and spa facilities. Interestingly, it is one of the casinos not located near the Cotai Strip.

Las Vegas Sands introduced **The Venetian Macao** (Estrada da Baia de N. Senhora da Esperanca, Taipa), a US$2.4 billion palatial resort hotel. The world's largest casino, it is home to 1,150 gaming tables, 7,000 slot machines, 3,000 hotel suites, and convention and performance venues. With it came yet another benefit of Las Vegas-style casinos: world-class entertainment. In the short time since it opened, The Venetian bill has featured the likes of the Pussycat Dolls, Jose Carreras, The Police, Cirque du Soleil, and Macau's first-ever heavyweight boxing title bout.

The MGM Mirage group and Pansy Ho, one of Stanley Ho's most prominent offspring, upped the ante at the end of 2007 with the **MGM Grand Macau** (Avenida Dr. Sun Yat Sen, NAPE, Macau). The 35-storey complex was inspired by Macau's Portuguese history and is styled after Lisbon's central train station with an enormous glass-ceiling atrium.

Not to be outdone, Stanley Ho's Sociedade de Jogos de Macau also opened the flamboyant lotus flower-shaped **Grand Lisboa** (2–4 Avenida de Lisboa, Macau), sister to the landmark Casino Lisboa.

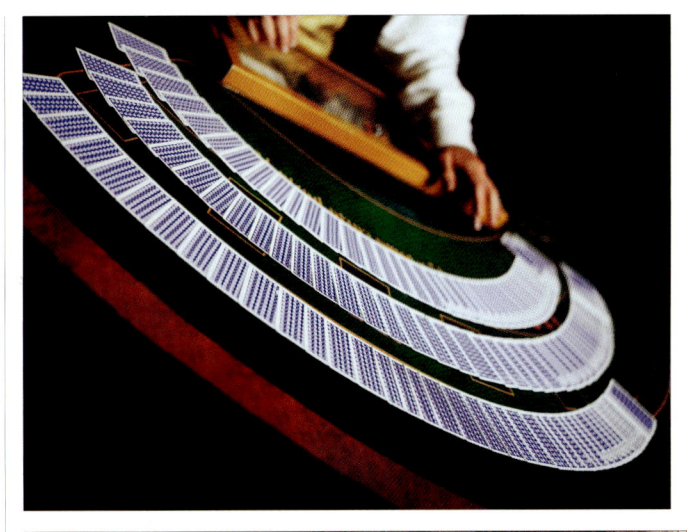

THIS PAGE (FROM TOP): *A 24-hour programme of gaming is on the cards in casino capital Macau; it's bright lights and big money in the Crown Macau casino.*
OPPOSITE: *Keeping up with the times—Grand Lisboa is the new flagship of casino mogul Stanley Ho's Sociedade de Jogos de Macau.*

macau's casino scene

crown macau

THIS PAGE: *Crown Macau's minimalist gardens exude style and sophistication.*

OPPOSITE: *Aurora's extensive wine collection on display.*

Since the arrival of the Portuguese in the 16th century, Macau has been a true cultural melting pot: a unique and charming mélange of ancient Portuguese influences with an exotic Asian slant. Drawing obvious comparisons with Hong Kong, not least because they are only one hour apart by ferry, Macau stakes its individuality not only on its rich history, but also on its world-famous casinos. The peninsula attracts soaring numbers of visitors with its high-end gaming facilities that outstrip even Las Vegas in revenues. One of the newest and most impressive casino complexes to grace its enchanting shores is Crown Macau.

This stunning modern edifice is located on the northern coast of Taipa Island, housing an impressive array of first-class restaurants and bars, a wide variety of gaming options,

...offers guests an oasis of tranquillity...

as well as the lavishly appointed Crown Towers hotel. While the multi-level casino alone is noteworthy—featuring private gaming salons as well as gaming tables and machines—it is the combination of impressive casino facilities and luxury amenities found within the Crown Towers hotel that makes Crown Macau stand out from the crowd.

Situated in the tallest building on Taipa Island, Crown Towers offers guests an oasis of tranquillity, a soothing respite from the excitement of the casinos or from a hectic day spent sightseeing. With interiors created by award-winning designer Peter Remedios, this hotel blends absolute comfort with understated sophistication.

The hotel's lobby is located on the 38th floor of the Crown Macau complex, with breathtaking views of the peninsula seen through floor-to-ceiling windows—a stunning backdrop to its sleek, contemporary interiors. Abundant light filters through the spacious lobby and lounge areas, which feature plush brown and gold furnishings accentuated by the polished, dark stone floors. Wooden Oriental screens with grid-like patterns are seen gracing the lobby's surroundings, while exquisite orchids and bamboo plants further highlight the Asian theme.

Crown Towers features 208 rooms and suites in addition to eight exclusive, private villas, each of them spectacularly decorated. The warm earth tones of the wooden floors and rich fabrics of the upholstery make the interiors irresistibly cosy, yet extremely elegant. Furthermore, all rooms are equipped with just about every high-tech gadget imaginable.

Space is not an issue at Crown Towers, and all rooms have a beautifully appointed lounge area complete with high-speed Internet access, plasma-screen TVs, and cable channels, making them ideal for quiet evenings spent indoors. However, the entertainment options do not stop there: iHome units are also a standard feature, allowing guests to personalise their living environment with their choice of music.

THIS PAGE: *The Premier Suite commands a spectacular view of the peninsula.*

OPPOSITE (FROM TOP): *Relax and enjoy The Spa at Crown's range of soothing treatments; the rooms here provide every modern convenience for a comfortable stay.*

Bathrooms could not be more sumptuous with Japanese-style showers and circular, hand-crafted stone tubs complemented by extravagant designer toiletries. As unbelievable as it may seem, these bathrooms also have individual television screens that can be viewed from the comfort of a warm bath.

The management team at Crown Towers has taken every last detail into consideration when it comes to customer service, so it is no surprise that the hotel features a fully-equipped business centre, complete with full secretarial services at hand.

Exercise fanatics, or those who simply want to stretch their legs, will be bowled over by the hotel's fitness centre on the 16th floor. Reserved for Crown Towers guests and members, state-of-the-art cardiovascular and weights machines are provided, with personal trainers on hand to assist. Also included is a

...one of the best reasons to visit the Asian continent...

pilates and yoga studio to work out one's stiff muscles. Little encouragement will be needed to take a dip in a 25-m (82-ft) indoor infinity-edge pool that looks over the island below.

The Spa at Crown's awe-inspiring facilities is yet another example of how the owners of this exceptional hotel have managed to take luxury to a whole new dimension. Designed in collaboration with German spa engineers Deckelmann Wellness, The Spa at Crown is a two-storey sanctuary of renewal and revival to beat all others. Here, ancient health and beauty rituals are recreated in a stylish, modern setting that includes 12 exquisitely appointed treatment rooms and a separate VIP area for those seeking a little more privacy.

Wet spa facilities go beyond the realm of imagination. Vitality pools, crystal streams, saunas, ice fountains and rasul are but a few of the options available, while the innovative 'experience' showers introduce aromatherapy and colour light therapy to the pleasures of bathing.

The tempting array of treatments available use the ultra-exclusive Elemis line of skincare products and spa therapies, all tailored to suit individual needs. Guests are invited to pamper the senses with a coconut and milk bath wrap, a hot stone massage or any number of other enticing choices to ensure complete relaxation.

Without a doubt, one of the best reasons to visit the Asian continent is to savour the delicacies of the diverse range of cuisines

THIS PAGE: *It's a toss-up between signature Japanese restaurants Tenmasa (left) and Kira (right).*

OPPOSITE (FROM LEFT): *Ying, the benchmark of Chinese fine-dining in Macau; the chic Crystal Club offers cocktails and is a great vantage point over the peninsula.*

available and, in this respect, Crown Macau promises nothing short of a culinary nirvana. The hotel's four signature restaurants offer tantalising menus developed by talented chefs, who combine the freshest local produce with imported ingredients that ensure the authenticity of every dish.

Exquisite Cantonese food is found at Ying, where traditional dishes feature alongside innovative contemporary interpretations. Using home-style Chinese cuisine as an inspiration, award-winning Chef Tam Kwok Fung dazzles guests not only with the unsurpassed quality of his creations, but also with their stunning artistic presentations. The restaurant's striking, modern interiors are bedecked in crimson and gold fabrics, while silk panels and beaded curtains provide the perfect setting for an intimate gourmet meal in graceful surroundings.

Japanese food lovers will be thrilled at the prospect of two specialised, highly-acclaimed restaurants at Crown Towers. Kira offers well-loved dishes such as sushi, teppanyaki and sukiyaki, in addition to offering kaiseki—Japanese haute cuisine. Fresh seafood dishes and the finest cuts of Wagyu beef can be experienced in an atmosphere of sophisticated elegance as the minimalist décor is further emphasised by the still water feature surrounding the restaurant's exterior. With al fresco dining available on pristine wooden decks overlooking Japanese gardens and pavilions, this is the choice for diners in search of a romantic dinner under the stars.

The sensational Tenmasa tempura restaurant originated in Tokyo in 1937 and has been opened exclusively at Crown Macau by the grandson of the original owner. Drawing on three generations of expertise in Japanese

...Crown Macau promises nothing short of a culinary nirvana.

cuisine, the highly skilled chefs work their art before diners, presenting each dish straight from the fryer, piping hot, to be relished immediately. Amid a traditional Japanese environment complete with delicate screens and natural, light wood finishes, guests may be fooled into thinking that they are indeed dining in the land of the rising sun.

Finally, for those hankering for some European food, Aurora offers fantastic brasserie cuisine. Open for dinner and an extravagant Sunday brunch, the restaurant's sumptuous dishes and seasonal menus will please the eye as much as the palate. This chic brasserie offers an array of contemporary choices to pick from, while guests can choose between a casual bistro, or fine dining setting. Not to be outdone, Aurora's wine lounge is home to one of the largest collections in Macau, featuring rare vintages and premium labels to impress even the most discerning connoisseur.

Open 24 hours, Crown Macau's Crystal Club is the place to have a drink while appreciating unrivalled views of the Macau Peninsula. Nestled on the 38th storey, the club offers indoor and outdoor seating for guests to chill out, while an impressive cocktail menu and live DJ performances beckon. Be it to celebrate a special occasion or to have a private moment alone, sipping a martini in the cool evening air is undoubtedly the most fitting way to end another beautiful day at Crown Macau.

rooms and suites
184 rooms • 24 suites • 8 private villas

food
Ying: Cantonese • Tenmasa: tempura • Kira: Japanese • Aurora: brasserie

drink
Aurora: wine lounge and bar • Crystal Club: bar

features
The Spa at Crown • casino • fitness centre • iHome units • infinity-edge indoor pool • satellite TV

business
business centre • secretarial services

nearby
Coloane Island • Cotai district • downtown Macau

contact
Avenida de Kwong Tung, Taipa, Macau •
telephone: +853.2886 8888 •
facsimile: +853.2886 8666 •
email: enquiries@crown-macau.com •
website: www.crown-macau.com

sofitel macau at ponte 16

The glitz of Macau is embodied in the Sofitel Macau at Ponte 16, one of the newest hotels to grace the island's shores. Within the hotel's grand structure, guests can expect nothing less than exquisite indulgence and luxury, two qualities that the world has come to identify with the Sofitel brand.

The five-star hotel sits on the waterfront of Macau's Inner Harbour, within the sprawling grounds of the Ponte 16 casino resort. The celebrated Ruins of St Paul's, the historic A-Ma Temple, and the famous Macau Tower are within walking distance. The ferry terminal and international airport are also minutes away, giving the establishment a peerless advantage in terms of its excellent location.

Contemporary furnishings in relaxing shades of chocolate and cream decorate the rooms of the Sofitel Macau at Ponte 16, creating a soothing ambience for guests to unwind in. The rooms also come with views of the glittering cityscape or picturesque scenes of the Zhuhai River below. While Macau never sleeps, guests who choose to do so will be luxuriously provided for. Combining sumptuous comforts with hi-tech bedding materials, Sofitel's signature 'MyBed' concept focuses on giving guests a truly restful 'sleep' experience. MyBeds are padded with luscious feather-down duvets and quilted top-mattresses, inviting one to sink in and drift off into a deep, peaceful slumber.

THIS PAGE (FROM TOP):
The Sofitel Macau at Ponte 16's grand lobby; from afar, the hotel lights up the Macau night scene.

OPPOSITE (FROM LEFT): *Relax by one of the hotel's swimming pools; rooms come complete with luxurious amenities.*

...expect nothing less than exquisite indulgence and luxury...

rooms
364 rooms • 25 suites • 19 presidential apartments

food
Mistral: French and Mediterranean

drink
Pool Bar • Rendezvous: lounge • Vin Bar

features
Club Sofitel • fitness centre • high-speed Internet access • satellite TV • spa • pools

business
ballroom • business centre • conference rooms

nearby
A-Ma Temple • Macau Tower • Ponte 16 casino • Ponte 16 shopping arcade • Ruins of St Paul's • Wanzai (Zhuhai)

contact
Rua do Visconde Paco de Arcos, Macau • telephone: +853.8861 0016 • facsimile: +853.8861 0018 • email: sales@sofitelmacau.com • website: www.sofitel.com.cn

To see guests through their waking hours, there are all the modern conveniences of a sophisticated hotel. High-speed Internet access allows easy connectivity with the world, while satellite TV makes a perfect companion for quiet nights in. For an added touch of luxury, spacious bathrooms come with bath products from French brand L'Occitane, yet another instance of how the Sofitel Macau at Ponte 16 indulges its guests.

Those with work on their minds can take advantage of the fully-equipped business centre. The Sofitel Macau at Ponte 16 also provides versatile conference facilities, which can be configured to host small functions as well as large conventions. Leisure-oriented guests can head to the fitness centre, swimming pools, or spa to while the day away as they refresh and recharge. Alternatively, a visit to the adjacent high-end shopping arcade and world-class casino is bound to give guests a healthy dose of excitement.

Dining at Sofitel Macau at Ponte 16 is a multi-sensory experience. Mistral serves refined French and Mediterranean cuisine on an impressive colonnaded terrace overlooking the Zhuhai River. Vin Bar serves some of the world's finest cheeses and wines along with live entertainment in the evenings. Rendezvous has an extensive drinks menu, while the Pool Bar is the place to enjoy cocktails al fresco. Dusk is the magical hour, where guests can watch the sun set with a trademark Sofitini in hand.

There may already be numerous luxury accommodations in Macau. However, it is the exclusivity and attention to detail that makes Sofitel Macau at Ponte 16 a cut above the rest.

wynn macau

THIS PAGE: *Enjoy authentic Cantonese cuisine in Wing Lei's majestic interior.*
OPPOSITE: *Chefs at work in the bustling kitchen of Il Teatro.*

Self-styled Las Vegas of the East, Macau was the oldest European territory in East Asia's entire history, being administered by the Portuguese from the 16th century until 1999. Like its neighbour Hong Kong, Macau is now one of China's two Special Administrative Regions. As top resorts like Wynn Macau prove, Macau is taking full advantage of this status to transform itself into the hottest commercial and tourist capital in China.

For the history enthusiast, Macau holds endless appeal. Churches, fortresses, and the almost anachronistic Mediterranean-style that are vestiges of Portugal's long colonial rule remain highly visible in the country. Business travellers are lured by its extensive conference calendar, excellent infrastructure and the profitable magnets of its electronics and textiles industries. For the adrenalin-seeker, Macau crams an entire life's worth of hedonism in a few square kilometres that teem with the bright lights of restaurants, mega casinos, sports and music stadia.

At the heart of this burgeoning destination is Wynn Macau, China's—indeed, Asia's—first fully integrated resort. It is draped in Las Vegas-style glamour, with plush accommodations, an exciting gaming space

...draped in Las Vegas-style glamour.

and stylishly clad guests. This luxurious one-stop destination exceeds every expectation in terms of boutique shopping, fine dining, indulgent spa treatments and cutting-edge meeting facilities with no less than five exquisite restaurants and cosy cafés.

Wynn Macau is the brainchild of Steve Wynn, the celebrated casino developer credited with the phenomenal success of the Las Vegas Strip during the 1990s. The Strip's iconic architecture includes the seminal Mirage resort, the Bellagio, and the Wynn. With the Wynn Macau, Steve brings his inimitable style to the very heart of Asia.

The 600 rooms and suites at Wynn Macau are rooms with a view par excellence, boasting stunning floor to ceiling vistas of the glittering South China Sea, Nam Van Lake or Macau's mesmerising skyline. Complete with pillow-top Wynn signature beds, each room is luxuriously appointed with fine Egyptian cotton, futuristic drapery controls, and the latest in-room entertainment.

The suites and grand deluxe rooms offer VIP check-in and private access to the hotel's Wynn Club for exclusive entertainment and dining. These rooms are impeccably furnished, and provide spacious bathrooms with specially commissioned Desert Bambu toiletries. If the sky is the limit, opt for the vast 278-sq-m (2,992-sq-ft) Sky Suite, a two-bedroom apartment with 24-hour butler service, separate media room and an in-room spa therapy suite.

Back on ground level, the Wynn Macau boasts a hypnotic performance lake that produces choreographed son et lumière displays. Concealing 1,000 lights and holding over 3 million l (659,908 gal) of water, it is a spectacular sight at any time of the day or night. Yet in true Las Vegas style, the glittering casino is Wynn Macau's pièce de résistance. It features themed slot machines and traditional and contemporary table games from Blackjack and Caribbean Stud to Roulette, with many popular types of Baccarat available too. Using Wynn's Red Card in the casino benefits guests as they get to earn complimentary hotel accommodation, meals, and invitations to exclusive events.

Escape the drama and suspense of the casino for some relaxation at the landscaped luxury of Wynn Macau's heated pools, whirlpools, or jacuzzi. For more personalised pampering, select from the extensive menu of treatments at The Spa, whose skilled professionals include a certified Chinese physician for traditional spa therapies. Following total rejuvenation, guests can opt for a brand new look with a glamorous makeover at the hotel's exclusive salon.

When it comes to fine dining, Wynn Macau's range is second to none. The master chef impresses his guests with signature teppanyaki and robatayaki dishes at the Okada restaurant, while Ristorante Il Teatro is first port of call for a uniquely Italian dining experience. The stylishly decorated Wing Lei creates exquisite Cantonese fare, and guests can head to Red 8 for some Asian noodles and congee. From casual cocktail bars to the sophisticated Cinnebar, Wynn Macau has a distinctive day or evening venue in which to titillate any palate.

Last but not least, Wynn Macau is home to a 2,415-sq-m (26,000-sq-ft) shopping esplanade, showcasing high-end boutiques from Bulgari to Prada, Asia's only anchor Rolex store, and Macau's very first Wynn Signature Shop. As a creator of big winners as well as a Mecca for big spenders, Steve Wynn's attentively designed and luxuriously appointed Macau resort will be the highlight of any trip to this unique corner of China.

THIS PAGE: *The Wynn Macau's breathtaking façade at night.*
OPPOSITE (FROM LEFT): *With fine furnishings and stylish décor, the suites provide the best of modern comforts; take a leisurely swim or relax by the pool cabana.*

...the highlight of any trip to this unique corner of China.

rooms
460 rooms • 140 suites

food
Café Esplanada: international •
Il Teatro: Italian • Okada: Japanese •
Red 8: Asian • Wing Lei: Cantonese

drink
Cinnebar • Wing Lei Lounge

features
casino • tropical garden • pool • spa • gym • jacuzzi • high-speed Internet access •

business
ballroom • business centre • laptop rental • limousine service

nearby
Nam Van Lake • Kun Iam Ecumenical Centre

contact
Rua Cidade de Sintra, NAPE, Macau •
telephone: +853.8986 9966 •
facsimile: +853.2832 9966 •
email: roomreservations@wynnmacau.com •
website: www.wynnmacau.com

macau/hotels

index

Numbers in *italics* denote pages where pictures appear. Numbers in **bold** denote profile pages.

88 Xintiandi, **98–99**

A
Andy Tait, **198**
Annabel Lee Shanghai, *89*, **120–121**
Annly Chan, **122–123**
Annly's China, **122–123**
antiques, 68–69, 70–71, 122–123, 128–129
architecture, 16
art,
    Chinese, 14–15, *15*
    Creative Centre, Bund18, **125**
    Peking Opera, 36–37
Asian cuisine, 49, 60, 101

B
Bank of New York, 38
bars,
    Aqua Spirit, 177
    Armani Bar, 177
    Attica, 87
    Bar Florian, 212
    Bar Rouge, 86, 87
    Bellini Lounge, 212
    blue frog bar & grill, 212
    Boca, 177
    British Bulldog, 86
    Canidrome, 213
    Captain's Bar, The, 177
    Casablanca, 213
    Castle Oktober, 86
    Centro, 28
    Champagne Bar (Hong Kong), 177
    Champagne Bar (Macau), 212
    Cinnebar, 212, **230**
    Crystal Club, 212
    D2, 213
    DiVino, 177
    Dom Pedro V Theatre, 213
    Drop, 177
    Face (Beijing), 28, 29
    Face Bar (Shanghai), 86
    Feather Boa, 177
    Felix, 177
    FINDS, 177
    Garden Brasserie, 137
    Isobar, 177
    Jazz Club, 213
    Lan Kwai Fong, 212
    Le Rideau Theatre Café, 177
    Lei Dou, 177
    Lumina Bar, 212
    M Bar (Beijing), 28
    M Bar (Macau), 212
    Macau Cultural Centre, 213
    Macau Jockey Club, 213
    Makumba Africa Bar, 177
    Manifesto Lounge, 87
    Mint, 87
    Moonwalker, 213
    O'Malley's, 86
    Paulaner Brauhaus, 86
    Red Moon, *28, 29,* **46**
    Shintori, 86
    Sky21, 213
    TMSK, 87, *87*
    Venetian Arena, 213
    Veuve Clicquot Lounge, 212
    World of Suzie Wong, The, 29
    Xintiandi, 87
    Yumla, 177

Bayhood No. 9, **40–43**
Beihai Park, 38
Beijing, 18–75
    galleries + museums, 34–35
    history, 21–22
    hotels, **40–61**
    nightlife, 28–29
    restaurants, 24–27, **62–67**
    shopping, *15,* 30–31
    shops, **68–73**
    spas, 32–33, **74–75**
    theatres, 37
Beijing Capital International Airport, *12*
Bird's Nest, *17*, 22
British in Hong Kong, 169
Bund18, 83, 84, *86*, 87, **124–127**, *124–127*
Bund, The, 79, 80, *81*, 96, 97, *97*, **102–105**
Butterfly Valley, 161

C
Cantonese cuisine, 46, 54, 58, 101, 109, 126, 145, 148, 163, 165, 190, 195, 197, 199, 201, 224, 230
casinos, 207, 208, 218–219
CCTV Tower, 39
Central Business District, Beijing, 39
Charlie Soong, 153
Chen Kaige, 15
China-Singapore Suzhou Industrial Park (SIP), **145**, 148
Chinese cuisine, 24–26, **46**, 64–65, 66–67, 82–83, 105, 172–173, 210
Chinese garden, *130*, 133, 140–141, 148
cinema, 15–16
clubs,
    dragon i, 177
    Fringe Club 177
    Halo, 176
    KEE Club, 176, *176*
    LAN Club, 29
    M1NT, 176, *176*
    Racks, 176
    Volar, 176
Commune by The Great Wall Kempinski, **44–45**
Communist Party of China (CPC), 14, 21
Confucianism, 170
Cotai, 207
Cottage Boutique, **68–69**
Cottage Warehouse, **70–71**
Crown Macau, *210, 211, 211, 212, 217, 219, 219*, **220–225**
Cuandixia, 39
Cultural Revolution, 14, 21–22, *202*
Customs House, Shanghai, 96

D
Dadonghai Bay 160
Darryl W. Goveas, **59**
Deng Xiaoping, 14, 22
design, 16
Ditan Park, 39
Dr Sun Yat-sen, 134, 153
    Mausoleum, 141, *141*
Downtown Macau, 207
Dushu Lake, 147
dynasties, 13, 133, 134

E
eco-hotel, **112–113**
Edmund N. Bacon, 21
End of the Earth, 160
Expo 2010, 79–80

F
Five Finger Mountain, 161
Forbidden City, 21, 38, *39*

Four Seasons Hotel Hong Kong, 175, 183, **186–187**
Four Seasons Hotel Shanghai, 84, **100–101**
French Concession, 97, 112, *186*
French cuisine, 27, 49, 51, 62–63, 127, 211, 227

G
galleries,
    10 Chancery Lane Gallery, 184
    50 Moganshan Road, 94
    Art Scene, 94
    Asia Art Archive, 184
    Alisan Fine Arts, 184
    CAAW (Chinese Art and Archives Warehouse), 34
    Cattle Depot Artists Village, 184
    Christie's, 184
    Dashanzi Art District, 34
    Eastlink Gallery, 95
    Grotto Fine Art, 184
    Hanart TZ Gallery, 184
    Hong Kong Art Walk, 185
    Jockey Club Creative Arts Centre, 184
    One Moon Gallery, 34
    Para/Site Art Space, 184
    Pekin Fine Arts, 34
    Red Gate Gallery, 34
    Schoeni Art Gallery, 184
    ShangART, 94
    Sotheby's, 184
gaming industry, 207–208
Gary Chang, **44**
golf, **40–43**, 158–159
Grand Canal, 133
Grand Hyatt Beijing, 26, 29, **46–47**
Grand Hyatt Hong Kong, 177, 182, *183*, **188–191**
Grand Lisboa, 208, 210, 211, *218*, **219**
Great Hall of the People, *14*
Great Wall, The, 13, 39, **44–45**
Guilling Stone House, 141

H
Hainan, 150–165
    history, 153
    hotels, **162–165**
    restaurants, 156–157
Hong Kong, 166–203
    galleries + museums, 184–185
    geography, 169
    history, 169
    hotels, **186–199**
    nightlife, 176–177
    restaurants, 172–175, **200–201**
    shopping, 178–181
    shops, **202–203**
    spas, 182–183
Hong Kong and Shanghai Bank Building, 96
Hotel Le Méridien Cyberport, **198–199**
hot springs, 159
history, 13–14, 21–22
Hu + Hu, **128–129**
Humble Administrator's Garden, 140
Hyatt On The Bund, 83, **102–105**

I
international cuisine, 46, 55, 58, 60, 83–85, 101, 105, 109, 114–115, 145, 157, 165, 186, 195
International Wedding Festival, 154
Italian cuisine, 46, 51, 107, 126, 191, 201, 211, 230

J
Jaan at Raffles Beijing Hotel, **62–63**
Japanese cuisine, 27, 55, 60, 84, 101, 145, 174, 191, 195, 199, 211, **224–225**, 230
JIA Hong Kong, 175, **192–193**
JIA Shanghai, *83*, **106–107**

Jia Zhangke, 16
Jinji Lake, **147**
JW Marriott Hotel Beijing, **48–49**
JW Marriott Hotel Hong Kong, **194–195**
JW Marriott Shanghai, 84, 92, **108–109**

K
Kangle Garden HNA Resort, 159
Kathleen's 5 Rooftop Restaurant + Bar, *84, 85,* **114–115**
Kathleen Lau, 114
Kayumanis Nanjing, **142–143**
KEE Club, 176, *176,* **200–201**
Kempinski Hotel Suzhou, **144–147**
Kengo Kuma, **60**
Kowloon, 169
Kuomintang (KMT), 21

L
Lan Kwai Fong Hotel, **196–197**
Legation Quarter, 38
Lingering Garden, 141
Linggu Temple, 141
Longevity Hill, 39
Luhuitou Park, 161

M
Macanese cuisine, 210
Macau, 204–231
    gaming industry, 207–208
    casinos, 207, 208, 218–219
    history, 209
    hotels, **221–231**
    nightlife, 212–213
    restaurants, 210–211
    shopping, 214–215
    spas, 216–217
Macau Grand Prix, *207,* 207
malls,
    Alexandra House, 179
    Chater House, 179
    Citic Square, 88
    Cloud Nine, 88
    Elements, 179
    Festival Walk, 179
    Grand Canal Shoppes at The Venetian Macao, 214, *215*
    Grand Gateway Mall, 88
    Harbour City, 179
    ifc mall, 179
    Landmark, The, 179
    Lee Gardens, 179
    Malls at Oriental Plaza, The, 30
    Pacific Place, *178,* 179
    Place, The, 30
    Plaza 66, 88
    Prince's Building, 179
    Raffles City, 88
    Shinkong Place, 30
    Superbrand Mall, 88
    Times Square, 179
    Wynn Esplanade, *214,* 215
Mandarin Oriental, Sanya, **162–163**
Mao Zedong, 14, 21
Marco Polo, 133
markets, 31, 89–91, 139, 181
massacre of Nanjing, 134
    Memorial to the Victims of the Nanjing Massacre, 141, *141*
Master of Nets Garden, 140
Mediterranean cuisine, **60**
Mei Lanfang, 37
Mingxiao Ling Tomb, 141
MGM Grand, 212, 216, 219,
museums,

232 chinachic

index

Beijing Mumingtang Ancient Porcelain Museum, 35
Beijing Planning Exhibition Hall, 35
Capital Museum, 35, 37
Hong Kong Film Archive, 185
Hong Kong Museum of Art, 185
Hong Kong Museum of Coastal Defence, 185
Hong Kong Museum of History, 185
Hong Kong Museum of Medical Science, 185
Hong Kong Science Museum, 185
Flagstaff House Museum of Tea Ware, 185
Macau Wine Museum, 215
Mei Lanfang Museum, 37
Military Museum of Chinese People's Revolution, 21
Museum of Contemporary Art (MoCA), 94
National Art Museum of China, 35
Police Museum, 185
Poly Art Museum, 35
Shanghai Art Museum, 94, 97, 114
Shanghai Museum, 94, 95, 97
Shanghai Museum of Arts and Crafts, 95
Shanghai Science and Technology Museum Pudong, 94–95
Suzhou Museum, 140
Suzhou Silk Museum, 139
University Museum and Art Gallery, 185, 185
Xu Beihong Memorial Museum, 35
My Humble House at China Central Place, 64–65
My Humble House at The Oriental Plaza, 66–67

N
Nanjing, 134, 135, 142–143
Nanjing Road, 80, 88
Nanshan Cultural Centre, 160
Nanwan Monkey Peninsula, 161
National Grand Theatre, 16
New Territories, 169

O
Old Summer Palace, 39
Olympics, 13, 14, 22
Opposite House, The, 60–61
Oriental Pearl Tower, 13, 76

P
Parkyard Hotel Shanghai, 110–111
Party People, The, 117–118
Pearl River Nantian Hot Spring Resort, 159
People's Park, 97
Peter Remedios, 221
Philippe Starck, 106, 192, 201
Pudong, 96–97, 96, 110–111
Purple Mountain, 141

Q
Qianmen Street, Beijing, 23

R
Raffles Beijing Hotel, 26, 50–51
Rear Lakes, 38
Rebecca Hsu, 68–69, 70–71
restaurants,
  .IZE, 156, 156
  1912, 137
  A FuturePerfect, 85
  A Lorcha, 210
  Antica Trattoria de Ise, 211
  Aqua Luna, 173
  Aqua, 172
  Aurora, 210, 211
  Bellagio (Beijing), 26
  Bellagio (Nanjing), 137
  California Grill, 84

Camoes, 210
Caprice, 175
Celestial Court, 136, 137
Chez Patrick, 175
China Club, 175
Chinese Restaurant, 157
Chocolux, 175
Chunyuan Seafood Square, 156
Cinecittà, 175
Classified, 175
Clipper Lounge, The, 175
Club Militar de Macau, 210
Cococabana, 175
Da Domenico, 175
Dadong Kaoya, 25
Deyue Lou, 136
Dim Sum, 173
Din Tai Fung, 25
Don Alfonso 1890 – Macau, 211
Dongjiao Palm Tree Seafood Restaurant, 156
East 33, 26, 51
Fat Siu Lau, 210, 211
Feipo Seafood Restaurant, 156
Fogo Samba, 211
Fook Lam Moon, 173
Gaia, 175
Garden Brasserie, 137
Gugong Yushan, 25
Guibin Lou, 137
Guo Yao Xiaoju, 26
Hatsune, 25, 27
Huang Ting, 24
Hutong, 173, 173
Il Teatro, 211
Indochine, 157, 157, 165
Ingredients, 175
Jade on 36, 84
Jinying Dajiulou, 137
Jitang Mian Guan, 136
Kathleen's 5 Rooftop Restaurant & Bar, 84, 85, 114–115
Kira, 211
Kong Yiji Shangyan, 25
L'Atelier de Joel Robuchon, 174, 174
Lan, 25, 26
Laris, 84
Le 5 Sens, 137
Le Bistrot, 211
Le Pré Lenôtre, 27, 27
Liguo Restaurant, 157
Lobby, The, 175
Lord Stow's Bakery, 210
Lost Heaven Yunnan, 82
Lua Azul, 210
Luk Yu Tea House, 173
Lung King Heen, 173
M at the Fringe, 175
M on the Bund, 84
Made in China, 26, 46
Mandarin Grill + Bar, The, 175, 175
Mare, 211
Margaret's Café e Nata, 210
Maxim's Palace, 173
Mesa Restaurant & Manifesto Lounge, 83, 85
MoCA Caffé, 85
Morton's of Chicago, 211
My Humble House, 25, 26, 64–67
New Heights, 84–85
Nga Tim Café, 210
Nobu, 174
Okada, 211
OPIA, 175, 193
Osmanthus Restaurant, 157
People 8, 26

Pierre, 174, 174
Portas do Sol, 210
Press Room, 175
Red Capital Club, 24
Restaurante Fernando, 210
Restaurante Litoral, 210
Robuchon a Galera 211
Roma Pizzeria, 157
Sampan Seafood Restaurant, 156
Sens & Bund, 82, 84
Shintaro, 84, 85
Shui Hu Ju, 173
Sichuan Huigan, 25
Skyways Bakery and Deli, 137
SOAHC Restaurant & Tea Garden, 83
Songhe Lou, 136
Source, The, 26
South Beauty (Nanjing), 137
South Beauty 881 (Shanghai), 82
Spice Garden, 157
Spoon, 174
Spring Moon, 173
Tan Wai Lou, 83, 83
Tenmasa, 211
Tiandi Yijia, 24
Top Deck, 175
Tribute, 175
Versailles Restaurant, 157
Xi Yan Sweets, 175
Xi Yan, 173
Xindalu, 83, 84
Xintiandi, 83
XTC Gelato, 175
Yotsuba, 27
Yuan Qi Lou, 157
Yung Kee, 173
Zuma, 174
Ritan Park, 39
river cruise, 54
Ruinas de São Paulo, 208, 208

S
St. Michael's Catholic Church, 38
Sands Macau, 218
Sanya, 154, 155
Sanya Bay, 158, 159, 160
Sanya Marriott Resort + Spa, 157, 157, 164–165
Sanya Padi Diving, 159
Sanya Surf Club, 159
sea sports, 159
Shanghai, 76–129
  architecture, 80
  galleries + museums, 94–95
  hotels, 98–113
  nightlife, 86–87
  restaurants, 82–85, 114–119
  shopping, 88–91
  shops, 120–129
  spas, 92–93
Shanghai Tang, 180, 202–203
Shanghai Urban Planning Exhibition Hall, 79
Shangri-La Hotel, The, Beijing, 52–55
Shangri-La's Kerry Centre Hotel, Beijing, 56–59
Sheraton Suzhou Hotel + Towers, 136, 137, 148–149
Shi Mao Building, 97
shikumen houses, 99
silk production, 138–139
Simply The Group, 116–119
S.Miura, 67
Sofitel Macau at Ponte 16, 226–227
Soong sisters, 153
spas,
  Anantara Spa, 45
  Banyan Tree Spa, 93

CHI, The Spa, 32, 33, 53–54, 92
Club Oasis, 32, 32
Diva Life, 93, 93
Dragonfly, 93
Elemis Day Spa, 183
Feel Good Factor, The, 183
Happy Foot Reflexology Center, 183
Indulgence, 183
I Spa, 32
Mandara Spa, 92, 92, 109
Oriental Spa, The, 182
Oriental Taipan, 33
Paua Spa, 183
Paul Gerrard Hair & Beauty, 183
Peninsula Spa by ESPA, 32, 183
Plateau, 182, 183, 189–190
Quan Spa, 49, 164–165
Ritz-Carlton Spa, 33
St. Regis Spa and Club, 33
Six Senses Spa, 216
Spa at Crown, The, 217, 223
Spa at the Four Seasons, The, 183, 183
Spa at the Mandarin Oriental Macau, The, 216
Spa at Wynn Macau, 217
Spa Philosophy, 216, 217
Village Retreat, 119
Yuan Spa, 104
Zenspa, 33, 33, 74–75
Stanley Ho, 207, 208
statue of Guanyin, 160
Steve Wynn, 229
Summer Palace, 39
Sun Valley Sanya Golf Resort, 158
Suzhou, 133, 144–149
Suzhou and Nanjing, 130–149
  hotels, 143–149
  restaurants, 136–137
  shopping, 138–139

T
Taipa, 207, 215, 220, 221
Temple of Heaven, 11, 22, 38, 39
Templo de A-Ma, 208
Thai cuisine, 116–117, 190
Tomorrow Square, 97, 108

U
UNESCO Asia-Pacific Heritage Award, 125, 127
UNESCO World Heritage Site, 133, 208
URBN Hotels Shanghai, 112–113

V
Venetian Macao, 207, 211, 212, 213, 214, 215, 219
Village at Sanlitun, The, 72–73

W
Wang Xiaoshuai, 16
Water Cube, 18, 22
Western cuisine, 49, 101, 105,
Wynn Macau, 211, 212, 217, 218, 228–231

X
Xinglong Tropical Botanical Garden, 161

Y
Yalong Bay, 160, 164
Yalong Bay Golf Club, 158
Yokohama Species Bank, 38

Z
Zenspa, 74–75
Zhang Huimin, 154
Zhang Yimou, 15
Zhang Yuan, 16

index 233

picture credits + acknowledgements

88 Xintiandi front cover (screen), 98–99
Alex Hofford/epa/Corbis 207 (top)
Alvin Mak/urbanimpressions.hk 169 (top)
Andrea Pistolesi/Getty Images 171
Annabel Lee Shanghai back cover (store interior), 120–121
Annly's China 122–123
Aqua 173 (bottom)
Bayhood No. 9 40–43
blue jean images/Getty Images 137 (bottom left)
Bund18 front cover (Bar Rouge), 82, 83 (top), 86, 87 (top left), 124–127
Cancan Chu/Getty Images 31 (top), 39 (bottom)
China Photos/Getty Images back cover (lattice window, National Stadium), 1, 5 (right), 8, 9, 13 (bottom), 16 (top and bottom), 17 18, 21 (bottom), 22 (top), 35 (bottom), 37 (top and bottom), 38, 91 (bottom left), 94, 134 (top), 138, 139 (top), 141 (top), 153 (top)
China Tourism Press/Getty Images 154, 158 (left)
Commune by the Great Wall Kempinski 44–45
Cottage Boutique 68–69
Cottage Warehouse 70–71
Crown Macau back cover (spa beds), 210, 211 (bottom), 219 (bottom), 220–225
Dana Shek/urbanimpressions.hk 181 (bottom)
David Hartung/OnAsia Images 36 (top)
Diva Life 92 (bottom left), 93 (top)
Donovan Reese/Getty Images 166
EIGHTFISH/Getty Images 87 (bottom)
Eng Koon/AFP/Getty Images 21 (top)
Face Bar 29 (bottom)
Feng Li/Getty Images 12, 23
Fernando Bueno/ Getty Images 80 (top)

Flip Chalfant/Getty Images 139 (bottom left)
Four Seasons Hotel Hong Kong 183 (top), 186–187
Four Seasons Hotel, Shanghai 85 (top right), 100–101
Frank Lukasseck/Corbis 161 (middle)
Frans Lemmens/Getty Images 88
Frederic J. Brown/AFP/Getty Images 15 (top)
G.O.D. 179 (bottom)
Gareth Brown/Corbis 204
Getty Images 13 (top)
Getty Images/Getty Images for Moet & Chandon 213 (bottom)
Gideon Mendel/Corbis 29 (top)
Gilles Sabrie 37 (middle), 79 (top and bottom)
Glowimages/Getty Images 133 (bottom), 134 (bottom), 138 (right), 219 (top)
Goh Chai Hin/AFP/Getty Images 135
Grand Hyatt Beijing 24, 27 (bottom), 28, 32, 46–47
Grand Hyatt Hong Kong 183 (bottom right), 188–191
Grant Faint/Getty Images front cover (Great Wall), 2
Greg Elms/Getty Images 87 (top right)
Guang Niu/Getty Images 14 (top), 22 (bottom), 36 (bottom), 39 (top), 173 (top)
Hatsune 25 (top)
Hilton Sanya Resort and Spa 156
Hotel Le Méridien Cyberport 198–199
Hu & Hu 128–129
Hyatt on the Bund 84 (right), 86 (top), 102–105
IMAGEMORE Co.,Ltd./Getty Images 155, 159 (bottom), 160
InterContinental Hong Kong 173 (top and middle)
Jaan at Raffles Beijing Hotel 62–63

Jeff Rotman/Getty images 158 (right)
JIA Hong Kong 175 (top right and bottom), 192–193
JIA Shanghai 83 (bottom left), 106–107
Jochen Schlenker/Getty Images 133 (top)
Jodi Cobb/Getty Images 170 (bottom)
Joe McNally/Getty Images 213 (top)
Jon Hicks/Corbis 208 (top)
Jörg Sundermann 177 (bottom)
Julian Smith/Corbis 212 (top)
Justin Guariglia/Getty Images 91 (bottom right)
JW Marriott Hotel Beijing 33 (top right), 48–49
JW Marriott Hotel Hong Kong 194–195
JW Marriott Shanghai 92 (top and bottom right), 93 (bottom), 108–109
Kathleen's 5 Rooftop Restaurant and Bar 84 (left), 85 (bottom), 114–115
Kayumanis Nanjing 142–143
KEE Club 176 (bottom), 200–201
Kempinski Hotel Suzhou 144–147
Keren Su/ Getty Images front cover (boat), 81, 96 (bottom), 97 (middle and bottom), 140, 141 (bottom)
Kou 181 (top)
L'Atelier de Joel Robuchon 174 (top left), 175 (top)
Lan Kwai Fong Hotel 196–197
Liu Jin/AFP/Getty Images front cover (exhibit, mask), 80 (bottom), 95 (middle left, top right, and bottom)
Liu Liqun/Corbis 161 (top)
Luke Duggleby/OnAsia Images 150, 153 (bottom), 161 (bottom), 178 (top)
M1NT 176 (top)
Macduff Everton/Getty Images 215
Mandarin Oriental Hong Kong 172, 175 (bottom)
Mandarin Oriental, Sanya 162–163

Mark Ralston/AFP/Getty Images back cover (Oriental Pearl Tower), 76, 89 (top)
Mesa Restaurant & Manifesto Lounge 83 (bottom right)
Michael Freeman/Corbis 130
Michel Setboun/Corbis 215 (middle)
Mike Clarke/AFP/Getty Images back cover (lady), 15 (bottom), 184, 208 (bottom), 209, 214
MN Chan/Getty Images 218
My Humble House at China Central Place 64–65
My Humble House at The Oriental Plaza 25 (bottom), 66–67
Natalie Behring/OnAsia images 34 (bottom)
Nicholas Pitt/Getty Images 30 (top)
Pacific Place 178 (bottom)
Parkyard Hotel Shanghai 110–111
Pascal Rondeau/Allsport/Getty Images 207 (bottom)
Paua Spa 183 (bottom left)
Paul Chesley/Getty Images 39 (middle)
Pete Turner/Getty Images 170 (top)
Peter Parks/AFP/Getty Images 14 (top), 31 (bottom)
Picture This Gallery 185 (bottom left)
Piecework Productions/Getty Images 169 (bottom)
Raffles Beijing Hotel 26, 50–51
Restaurant Fat Siu Lau 211 (top)
Richard Nowitz/Getty Images 31 (middle), 137 (top left)
Sanya Marriott Resort & Spa 157 (top left, top right and bottom), 164–165
Scott R. Barbour/Getty Images 95 (top left)
Sens & Bund 85 (top left)
Shanghai Tang 180, 202–203
Shangri-La's Kerry Centre Hotel, Beijing 56–59

Sheraton Suzhou Hotel & Towers 136, 148–149
Siegfried Layda/Getty Images 90 (bottom)
Simply The Group 116–119
Sofitel Macau at Ponte 16 226–227
Sofitel Wanda Beijing 27 (top)
Spa Philosophy 216, 217 (top left and top right)
Starstreet 179 (top)
Steven Morris/Getty Images 139 (middle left)
STR/AFP/Getty Images 30 (bottom), 34 (top)
Stuart Franklin/Getty Images 159 (top)
Ted Aljibe/AFP/Getty Images 185 (bottom right), 214
Teh Eng Koon/AFP/Getty Images 4
The Opposite House front cover (bath tub), 60–61
The Peninsula Hong Kong 182
The Shangri-La Hotel, Beijing 33 (top left), 52–55
The Village at Sanlitun 72–73
Tim Flach/Getty Images front cover (bull), 35 (top)
ULTRA.F/Getty Images 90 (top), 91 (top)
University Museum and Art Gallery 185 (top right)
URBN hotels Shanghai 112–113
Wilfried Krecichwost/Getty Images 97 (top)
Woody Wu/AFP/Getty Images 185 (top left)
Wynn Macau 212 (bottom), 228–231
Yang Xi/ChinaFotoPress/Getty Images 139 (bottom)
Zenspa 33 (bottom), 74–75

The publishers would like to thank Annette Tan, Kathrynn Koh, Mark Wong and Zoe Jacques for their help and support during the production of this book.

directory

BEIJING

HOTELS

Bayhood No. 9 (page 40)
9 Anwai Beihu
Chaoyang District, Beijing 100012
telephone : +86.10.6491 8888
facsimile : +86.10.6498 0078
info@bayhood9.com
www.bayhood9.com

Commune by the Great Wall (page 44)
The Great Wall Exit at Shuiguan
Badaling Highway, Beijing 100022
telephone : +86.10.8118 1888
facsimile : +86.10.8118 1866
reservation@commune.com.cn
www.commune.com.cn

Grand Hyatt Beijing (page 46)
1 East Chang'an Avenue
Dongcheng District, Beijing 100738
telephone : +86.10.8518 1234
facsimile : +86.10.8518 0000
grandhyattbeijing@hyatt.com
beijing.grand.hyatt.com

JW Marriott Hotel Beijing (page 48)
83 Jianguo Road, China Central Place
Chaoyang District, Beijing 100025
telephone : +86.10.5908 6688
facsimile : +86.10.5908 6699
mhrs.bjsjw.sr.reservation1@marriott.com
www.jwmarriottbeijing.com

Raffles Beijing Hotel (page 50)
33 East Chang'an Avenue
Dongcheng District, Beijing 100004
telephone : +86.10.6526 3388
facsimile : +86.10.6527 3838
beijing@raffles.com
www.beijing.raffles.com

The Shangri-La Hotel, Beijing (page 52)
29 Zizhuyuan Road
Haidian District, Beijing 100089
telephone : +86.10.6841 2211
facsimile : +86.10.6841 8002/3
slb@shangri-la.com
www.shangri-la.com

Shangri-La's Kerry Centre Hotel, Beijing (page 56)
1 Guanghua Road
Chaoyang District, Beijing 100020
telephone : +86.10.6561 8833
facsimile : +86.10.6561 2626
hbkc@shangri-la.com
www.shangri-la.com

The Opposite House (page 60)
Building 1, 11 Sanlitun Road,
Beijing 100027
telephone : +86.10.6417 6688
facsimile : +86.10.6417 7799
answers@theoppositehouse.com
www.theoppositehouse.com

RESTAURANTS

Jaan at Raffles Beijing Hotel (page 62)
33 East Chang'an Avenue
Dongcheng District, Beijing 100004
telephone : +86.10.6526 3388
facsimile : +86.10.6527 3838
beijing@raffles.com
www.beijing.raffles.com

My Humble House at China Central Place (page 64)
2/F, Club House, Block 19, China Central Place,
89 Jianguo Road, Chaoyang District,
Beijing 100025
telephone : +86.10.6530 7770
facsimile : +86.10.6530 7771
mhh@tunglok.com
www.tunglok.com

directory

My Humble House at The Oriental Plaza (page 66)
Beijing Oriental Plaza, Podium Level, W3,
#01-07, 1 East Chang'an Avenue,
Dongcheng District, Beijing 100738
telephone : +86.10.8518 8811
facsimile : +86.10.8518 6249
mhh@tunglok.com
www.tunglok.com

SHOPS

Cottage Boutique (page 68)
4 North Ritan Road
Chaoyang District, Beijing 100020
telephone : +86.10.8561 1517
facsimile : +86.10 8561 1517
rebecca0929@yahoo.com
www.cottage-china.com

Cottage Warehouse (page 70)
4 North Ritan Road
Chaoyang District, Beijing 100020
telephone : +86.10.8561 1517
facsimile : +86.10.8561 1517
rebecca0929@yahoo.com
www.cottage-china.com

The Village at Sanlitun (page 72)
11 and 19 Sanlitun Road,
Chaoyang District, Beijing 100027
telephone : +86.10.6536 0588
www.thevillage.com.cn

SPAS

Zenspa (page 74)
House 1, 8A Xiaowuji Road
Chaoyang District, Beijing 100023
telephone : +86.10.8731 2530
facsimile : +86.10.8731 2539
info@zenspa.com.cn
www.zenspa.com.cn

BEIJING: DINING OUT

Aria
2/F, China World Hotel
1 Jianguomenwai Avenue
Chaoyang District, Beijing 100004
telephone : +86.10.6505 2266 ext 36
facsimile : +86.10.6505 3163
cwh@shangri-la.com
www.shangri-la.com

Bellagio
6 Gongti East Road
Chaoyang District, Beijing 100027
telephone : +86.10.6551 3533
facsimile : +86.10.6551 1769
www.bellagiocafe.com.cn

Dadong Kaoya
1–2 Nanxincang Guoji Dasha
22A Dongsi Shitiao
Dongcheng District, Beijing 100007
telephone : +86.10.5169 0329
facsimile : +86.10.5169 0326
dadongduck@sina.com

Da Giorgio
Grand Hyatt Beijing, 1 East Chang'an Avenue
Dongcheng District, Beijing 100738
telephone : +86.10.8518 1234
facsimile : +86.10.8518 0000
grandhyattbeijing@hyatt.com
beijing.grand.hyatt.com

Din Tai Fung
22 Hujiayuan, Yibei Building
Dongcheng District, Beijing 100027
telephone : +86.10.6462 4512
facsimile : +86.10.6462 4503
www.dintaifung.com.cn

East 33
Block E, Raffles Beijing Hotel
33 East Chang'an Avenue
Dongcheng District, Beijing 100004
telephone : +86.10.6526 3388 ext 5171
facsimile : +86.10.8500 4380
beijing@raffles.com
beijing.raffles.com

Gugong Yushan
Room 620, Wangfu Century Building
55 Dong'anmen Avenue
Dongcheng District, Beijing 100006
telephone : +86.10.6559 2490 ext 806
facsimile : +86.10.6559 2481
fiona@fccd.cn

Guo Yao Xiaoju
58 Bei Santiao, Jiaodao Kou,
Andingmennei Avenue
Dongcheng District, Beijing 100007
telephone : +86.10.6403 1940
bjguoyaoxiaoju@tom.com

Hatsune
2/F, Heqiao Building C, 8A Guanghua Road
Chaoyang District, Beijing 100026
telephone : +86.10.6581 3939
facsimile : +86.10.6583 2133

Huang Ting
The Peninsula Beijing
8 Jinyu Hutong, Wangfujing
Dongcheng District, Beijing 100006
telephone : +86.10.8516 2888 ext 6707
facsimile : +86.10.6510 6311
pbj@peninsula.com
beijing.peninsula.com

Kong Yiji Shangyan
8 Chaoyang Park Road
Chaoyang District, Beijing 100026
telephone : +86.10.6508 2228
facsimile : +86.10.6508 5829

Lan
4/F, Twin Towers
B-12 Jianguomenwai Avenue
Chaoyang District, Beijing 100022
telephone : +86.10.5109 6012
facsimile : +86.10.6566 2086
www.lanbeijing.com

Le Pré Lenôtre
Sofitel Wanda Beijing, Tower C,
Wanda Plaza. 93 Jianguo Road
Chaoyang District, Beijing 100022
telephone : +86.10.8599 6528
facsimile : +86.10.8599 6501
leprelenotre@sofitelwandabj.com
www.sofitel.com.cn

Mare
14 Xindong Road
Chaoyang District, Beijing 100027
telephone : +86.10.6417 1459
facsimile : +86.10.6417 1459
marebeijing@hotmail.com
marebeijing@soho.com

Made in China
1/F, Grand Hyatt Beijing
1 East Chang'an Avenue
Dongcheng District, Beijing 100738
telephone : +86.10.8518 1234 ext 3608
facsimile : +86.10.8518 0000
grandhyattbeijing@hyattintl.com
beijing.grand.hyatt.com

People 8
18 Jianguomenwai Avenue
Chaoyang District, Beijing 100022
telephone : +86.10.6515 8585
facsimile : +86.10.6538 4895
www.shintori.com.tw

Red Capital Club
66 Dongsi Jiutiao
Dongcheng District, Beijing 100010
telephone : +86.10.6402 7150
facsimile : +86.10.6402 7153
info@redcapitalclub.com.cn
www.redcapitalclub.com.cn

Sichuan Huiguan
2/F, Guohua Touzi Daxia
3 Dongzhimen South Avenue
Dongcheng District, Beijing 100007
telephone : +86.10.5819 9892
facsimile : +86.10.5819 9890
www.sichuanfood.com

Tiandi Yijia
140 Nanchizi Avenue
Dongcheng District, Beijing 100006
telephone : +86.10.8511 5556
facsimile : +86.10.6559 9374
info@tiandigroup.com

The Source
14 Banchang Hutong, Kuanjie
Dongcheng District, Beijing 100009
telephone : +86.10.6400 3736
source_beijing@hotmail.com
www.yanclub.com

Yotsuba
2 Xinzhong Jie Xili
Chaoyang District, Beijing 100006
telephone : +86.10.6467 1837

BEIJING'S NIGHTLIFE

Centro
1/F, Shangri-La's Kerry Centre Hotel Beijing
1 Guanghua Road
Chaoyang District, Beijing 100020
telephone : +86.10.6561 8833 ext 42
facsimile : +86.10.6561 2626
hbkc@shangri-la.com

Face
26 Dongcao Yuan, Gongti South Road
Chaoyang District, Beijing 100020
telephone : +86.10.6551 6788
facsimile : +86.10.6551 6739
beijing@facebars.com
www.facebars.com

Lan Club
4/F, Twin Towers, B-12 Jianguomenwai Avenue
Chaoyang District, Beijing 100022
telephone : +86.10.5109 6012
facsimile : +86.10.6566 2086
www.lanbeijing.com

M Bar
6/F, Sofitel Wanda Beijing Tower C,
Wanda Plaza, 93 Jianguo Road
Chaoyang District, Beijing 100022
telephone : +86.10.8599 6666 ext 6525
facsimile : +86.10.8599 6686
sofitel@sofitelwandabj.com
www.sofitel.com.cn

Red Moon
1/F, Grand Hyatt Beijing
1 East Chang'an Avenue
Dongcheng District, Beijing 100738
telephone : +86.10.8518 1234 ext 6366
facsimile : +86.10.8518 0000
grandhyattbeijing@hyattintl.com
beijing.grand.hyatt.com

The World of Suzie Wong
1A South Nongzhanguan Road
West Gate, Chaoyang Park
Chaoyang District, Beijing 100026
telephone : +86.10.6590 3377
facsimile : +86.10.6593 6049
clubsuziewong@263.net
www.suziewong.com.cn

BEIJING: A SHOPPING SENSATION

Beijing Curio City
21 Dongsanhuan South Road
Chaoyang District, Beijing 100053
telephone : +86.10.6774 7711,

C.L. Ma Furniture
Room 109–110, Building 4
6 Chaoyang Park South Road
Chaoyang District, Beijing 100027
telephone : +86.10.6466 7040,
facsimile : +86.10.6530 6473
clmabj@clmafurniture.com

Hongqiao Market
46 Tiantan East Road
Chongwen District, Beijing 100061
telephone : +86.10.6713 3354
facsimile : +86.10.6713 3354
hongqiao565@sohu.com
www.hongqiao-pearl-market.com

Panjiayuan Market
18 Huawei Li, Panjiayuan Road
Chaoyang District, Beijing 100021
telephone : +86.10.6775 2405
www.panjiayuan.com

Qianxiangyi
5 Zhubaoshi, Qianmen Avenue
Xuanwu District, Beijing 100051
telephone : +86.10.6301 6658
facsimile : +86.10.6304 8963
qxysilk@qianxiangyi.com
www.qianxiangyi.com

Ruifuxiang
5 Dashilan Street, Qianmen Wai
Xuanwu District, Beijing 100051
telephone : +86.10.6303 5313
facsimile : +86.10.6304 1702

Shinkong Place
87 Jianguo Road
Chaoyang District, Beijing 100025
telephone : +86.10.6530 5888
www.shinkong-place.com

The Malls at Oriental Plaza
1 East Chang'an Avenue
Dongcheng District, Beijing 100738
telephone : +86.10.8518 6363
www.orientalplaza.com

The Place
9A Guanghua Road
Chaoyang District, Beijing 100021
telephone : +86.10.6587 1188

Torana Gallery
Lobby, Kempinski Hotel Beijing
50 Liangmaqiao Road
Chaoyang District, Beijing 100016
telephone : +86.10.6465 3388 ext 5542
gallery@toranahouse.com
www.toranahouse.com

SPAS IN BEIJING

CHI, The Spa
Shangri-La Hotel, Beijing,
29 Zizhuyuan Road, Beijing 100089
telephone : +86.10.6841 2211
facsimile : +86.10.6841 8002/3
slb@shangri-la.com
www.shangri-la.com

Club Oasis
Grand Hyatt Beijing,
1 East Chang'an Avenue
Dongcheng District, Beijing 100738
telephone : +86.10.8518 1234
facsimile : +86.10.8518 0000
reservation.belgh@hyattintl.com
www.beijing.grand.hyatt.com

I-Spa
InterContinental Beijing Financial Street
11 Financial Street
Xicheng District, Beijing 100034
telephone : +86.10.5852 5888
facsimile : +86.10.5852 5999
icbeijing@interconti.com
www.intercontinental.com

Oriental Taipan
Sunjoy Mansion, 6 Ritan Road
Chaoyang District, Beijing 100032
telephone : +86.10.6502 5722
www.taipan.com.cn

St Regis Spa and Club
St Regis Beijing, 21 Jianguomenwai Avenue
Chaoyang District, Beijing 100020
telephone : +86.10.6460 6688
facsimile : +86.10.6460 3299
stregis.beijing@stregis.com
www.stregis.com

Peninsula Spa by ESPA
The Peninsula Beijing
8 Jinyu Hutong, Wangfujing
Dongcheng District, Beijing 100006
telephone : +86.10.8516 2888
facsimile : +86.10.6510 6311
pbj@peninsula.com
beijing.peninsula.com

The Ritz-Carlton Spa
The Ritz-Carlton Beijing, Financial Street
1 Jinchengfang East Street
Xicheng District, Beijing 100032
telephone : +86.10.6629 6660
facsimile : +86.10.6629 6687
www.ritzcarlton.com

Zenspa
House 1, 8A Xiaowuji Road
Chaoyang District, Beijing 100023
telephone : +86.10.8731 2530
facsimile : +86.10.8731 2539
info@zenspa.com.cn
www.zenspa.com.cn

BEIJING GALLERIES + MUSEUMS

Beijing Mumingtang Ancient Porcelain Museum
1 Huashi Beili Dongcu
Chongwen District, Beijing 100062
telephone : +86.10.6718 7266

Beijing Planning Exhibition Hall
20 Qianmen East Avenue
Chongwen District, Beijing 100051
telephone : +86.10.6701 7074
facsimile : +86.10.6705 7756
www.bjghzl.com.cn

CAAW
East End Art District
Nangao Road, Caochangdi Village
Chaoyang District, Beijing 100102
telephone : +86.10.8456 5152
facsimile : +86.10.8456 5152
caaw@public.gb.com.cn
www.archivesandwarehouse.com

Capital Museum
16 Fuxingmenwai Road
Xicheng District, Beijing 100045
telephone : +86.10.6337 0492
bjmuseum@126.com
www.capitalmuseum.org.cn

Dashanzi Art District
4 Jiuxianqiao Road, Dashanzi
Chaoyang District, Beijing 100015
telephone : +86.10.6437 6248
facsimile : +86.10.6437 6248
info@798space.com
www.798space.com

directory

National Art Museum of China
1 Wusi Road
Dongcheng District, Beijing 100010
telephone : +86.10.6401 7076
facsimile : +86.10.6403 4953
www.namoc.org

One Moon Gallery
Ditan Park Andingmenwai
Dongcheng District, Beijing 100011
telephone : +86.10.6427 7748
facsimile : +86.10.6427 7817
info@onemoonart.com
www.onemoonart.com

Pékin Fine Arts
241 Cui Ge Zhuang Xiang
Caochangdi Village
Chaoyang District, Beijing 100015
telephone : +86.10.5127 3220
info@pekinfinearts.com
www.pekinfinearts.com

Poly Art Museum
9/F, New Poly Plaza
1 Chaoyangmen North Street
Dongcheng District, Beijing 100010
telephone : +86.10.6408 2001

Red Gate Gallery
Levels 1 and 4, Dongbianmen Watchtower
Chongwen District, Beijing 100600
telephone : +86.10.6525 1005
facsimile : +86.10.6432 2624
redgategallery@aer.net.cn
www.redgategallery.com

Xu Beihong Memorial Museum
53 Xinjiekou North Road
Xicheng District, Beijing 100035
telephone : +86.10.6225 2042
www.xubeihong.org

PEKING OPERA

Chang'an Grand Theatre
7 Jianguomen Nei Road
Dongcheng District, Beijing 100005
telephone : +86.10.6510 1310
facsimile : +86.10.6510 1308

Huguang Guildhall
3 Hufang Road
Xuanwu District, Beijing 100051
telephone : +86.10.6351 8284
facsimile : +86.10.6351 8284
www.beijinghuguang.com

Laoshe Tea House
3 Qianmen West Road
Xuanwu District, Beijing 100050
telephone : +86.10.6303 6830
facsimile : +86.10.6301 7529
www.laosheteahouse.com

Liyuan Theatre
Qianmen Hotel, 175 Yongan Road
Xuanwu District, Beijing 100050
telephone : +86.10.6301 6688 ext 8860
facsimile : +86.10.6303 2301

Mei Lanfang Grand Theatre
32 Ping'anli West Road
Xicheng District, Beijing 100034
telephone : +86.10.5833 1288
www.mlfdjy.cn

Mei Lanfang Memorial Museum
9 Huguosi Street
Xicheng District, Beijing 100035
telephone : +86.10.6618 3598
info@meilanfang.com.cn
www.meilanfang.com.cn

Tianqiao Happy Tea House
A1 Beiwei Road
Xuanwu District, Beijing 100050
telephone : +86.10.6304 0617

SHANGHAI

HOTELS

88 Xintiandi (page 98)
380 Huang Pi Nan Road, Shanghai 200021
telephone : +86.21.5383 8833
facsimile : +86.21.5383 8877
inquiry@88xintiandi.com
www.88xintiandi.com

Four Seasons Shanghai (page 100)
500 Weihai Road, Shanghai 200041
telephone : + 86.21.6256 8888
facsimile : +86.21.6256 5678
reservations.shg@fourseasons.com
www.fourseasons.com/shanghai

Hyatt On The Bund (page 102)
199 Huangpu Road, Shanghai 200080
telephone : +86.21.6393 1234
facsimile : +86.21.6393 1313
info.shang@hyatt.com
www.shanghai.bund.hyatt.com

JIA Shanghai (page 106)
931 West Nanjing Road, Shanghai 200041
telephone : +86.21.6217 9000
facsimile : +86.21.6287 9001
info@jiashanghai.com
www.jiashanghai.com

JW Marriott Shanghai (page 108)
399 Nanjing West Road,
Shanghai 200003
telephone : +86.21.5359 4969
facsimile : +86.21.6375 5988
mhrs.shajw.reservations@marriotthotels.com
www.marriotthotels.com/shajw

Parkyard Hotel Shanghai (page 110)
699 Bi Bo Road, Zhangjiang Hi-Tech Park,
Shanghai 201203
telephone : +86.21.6162 1168
facsimile : +86.21.6162 1169
service@sh.parkyard.net
www.parkyard.net

URBN Hotels Shanghai (page 112)
183 Jiaozhou Road, Shanghai 200040
telephone : +86.21.5153 4600
facsimile : +86.21.5153 4610
info@urbnhotels.com
www.urbnhotels.com

RESTAURANTS

Kathleen's 5 Rooftop Restaurant + Bar (page 114)
5th Floor, Shanghai Art Museum
325 Nanjing West Road,
Shanghai 200003
telephone : +86.21.6327 2221
facsimile : +86.21.6327 0004
info@kathleen5.com
www.kathleen5.com.cn

Simply The Group (page 116)
facsimile : +86.21.6431 6334
goodtimes@simplythegroup.com
www.simplythegroup.com

Simply Thai (French Concession)
5C Dong Ping Road, Shanghai 200031
telephone : +86.21.6445 9551

Simply Thai (Xintiandi)
Corner of Madang Road and Xing Ye Road,
Shanghai 200021
telephone : +86.21.6326 2088

Simply Thai (Hong Mei)
28 Hong Mei Road, Lane 3338,
Shanghai 200021
telephone : +86.21.6465 8955

Simply Thai (Jin Qiao)
Jin Qiao Pudong, Green Sports and
Leisure Centre, Shanghai 200021
telephone : +86.21.5030 1690

Pin Chuan
French Concession, 47 Tao Jiang Road,
Shanghai 200031
telephone : +86.21.6437 9361

Simply Life flagship store
159 Madang Road, Shanghai 200021
telephone : +86.21.6326 2088

Simply Life
9 Dong Ping Road, Shanghai, 200021
telephone : +86.21.34060509

The Village
6 Dong Ping Road, Shanghai 200031
telephone : +86.21.6466 5123

The Party People
3 Future Island, level 1, Sui De Road,
Shanghai, 200333
telephone : +86.21.5477 0998

SHOPS

Annabel Lee Shanghai (page 120)
facsimile : +86.21.6323 0093
press@annabel-lee.com
www.annabel-lee.com

Bund flagship store
No. 1, Lane 8, Zhongshan Dong Yi Lu
(The Bund), Shanghai 200002
telephone : +86.21.6445 8218

Xintiandi store
Unit 3, House 3, North Block, Xintiandi,
Lane 181, Taicang Road, Shanghai 200021
telephone : +86.21.6320 0045

Anny's China (page 122)
No. 68, Lane 7611, Zhong Chun Road,
Shanghai 201101
telephone : +86.21.6406 0242
facsimile : +86.21. 6405 7322
annlyschina@gmail.com
www.annlychina.com

Bund 18 (page 124)
18 Zhongshan East Road, Shanghai 200002
telephone : +86.21.6323 8099
facsimile : +86.21.6323 3099
info@bund18.com
www.bund18.com

Hu + Hu (page 128)
Cao Bao Road, Alley 1885, No. 8
Shanghai 201101
telephone : +86.21.3431 1212
facsimile : +86.21.5486 2160
hu-hu@online.sh.cn
www.hu-hu.com

SHANGHAI: DINING OUT

a FuturePerfect
House 16, Lane 351, Huashan Rd
telephone : +86.21.6248 8020
www.afutureperfect.com.cn

California Grill
40/F, JW Marriott Hotel Shanghai
399 Nanjing West Road, Shanghai 200003
telephone : +86.21.5359 4969
facsimile : +86.21.6375 5565
www.marriotthotels.com

Jade on 36
36/F, Tower 2, Pudong Shangri-La Hotel
33 Fucheng Road, Pudong, 200120
telephone : +86.21.6882 8888
facsimile : +86.21.6882 6688
www.jadeon36.com

Kathleen's 5 Rooftop Restaurant & Bar
5/F, 325 Nanjing West Road
Shanghai 200003
telephone : +86.21.6327 2221
facsimile : +86.21.6327 0004
www.kathleen55.com.cn

Laris
6/F, Three on the Bund
3 Zhongshan Dong Yi Road,
Shanghai 200002
telephone : +86.21.6321 9922
facsimile : +86.21.6329 0810
www.threeonthebund.com

Lost Heaven Yunnan
38 Gaoyou Rd (near Fuxing West Rd)
telephone : +86.21.6433 5126
facsimile : +86.21.6433 8574

M on the Bund
7/F, 5 Zhongshan Dong Yi Road
Shanghai 200002
telephone : +86.21.6350 9988
facsimile : +86.21.6322 0099
www.m-onthebund.com

Mesa Restaurant & Manifesto Lounge
748 Julu Rd, Shanghai 200040
telephone : +86.21.6289 9108
facsimile : +86.21.6289 9138
www.mesa-manifesto.com

MoCA Caffé
Gate 7, People's Park, 231 Nanjing West Road, Shanghai 200003
telephone : +86.21.6327 0856
facsimile : +86.21.6327 1257
mocacaffe@mocashanghai.org
www.mocashanghai.org

New Heights
7/F, Three on the Bund
3 Zhongshan Dong Yi Road,
Shanghai 200002
telephone : +86.21.6321 0909
facsimile : +86.21.6329 0916
www.threeonthebund.com

Sens & Bund
6/F, Bund18, 18 Zhongshan Dong Yi Road
Shanghai 200002
telephone : +86.21.6323 9898
facsimile : +86.21.6323 8797
www.volgroup.com.cn

Shintaro
2/F, Four Seasons Hotel, Shanghai
500 Weihai Road, Shanghai 200041
telephone : +86.21.6256 8888
facsimile : +86.21.6256 5678
www.fourseasons.com

SOAHC Restaurant & Tea Garden
House 3, Lane 123, Xingye Road
South Block Xintiandi
telephone : +86.21.6385 7777

South Beauty 881
881 Central Yan'an Rd
telephone : +86.21.6247 5878
facsimile : +86.21.6222 0118
www.qiaojiangnan.com

Tan Wai Lou
5/F, Bund18, 18 Zhongshan Dong Yi Road
Shanghai 200002
telephone : +86.21.6339 1188
facsimile : +86.21.6323 8789
www.volgroup.com.cn

Xindalu–China Kitchen
1/F, Hyatt on the Bund, 199 Huangpu Rd,
Shanghai 200080
telephone : +86.21.6393 1234 ext 6318
facsimile : +86.21.6393 1313
www.shanghai.bund.hyatt.com

SHANGHAI'S NIGHTLIFE

Attica
11/F, 15 The Bund
15 Zhongshan Dong Er Road
Shanghai 200002
telephone : +86.21.6373 3588
enquiry@attica-shanghai.com
www.attica-shanghai.com

Bar Rouge
7/F, Bund18, 18 Zhongshan Dong Yi Road
Shanghai 200002
telephone : +86.21.6339 1199
www.rest018.com

British Bulldog
1 Wulumuqi South Road
telephone : +86.21.6466 7878
www.britishbulldogpub.com

Castle Oktober
39 Taojiang Road, Shanghai 200031
telephone : +86.21.6433 0186
facsimile : +86.21.6431 5918
www.castle-oktober.com

Face Bar
Ruijin Hotel Shanghai, Building 4,
118 Ruijin Er Road, Shanghai 200020
telephone : +86.21.6466 4328
facsimile : +86.21.6415 8913
shanghai@facebars.com
www.facebars.com

Manifesto Lounge
748 Julu Rd, Shanghai 200040
telephone : +86.21.6289 9108
facsimile : +86.21.6289 9138
www.mesa-manifesto.com

Mint
2/F, 333 Tongren Road
telephone : +86.21.6247 9666
mint@mintclub.com.cn
www.mintclub.com.cn

O'Malley's Irish Pub
42 Taojiang Road
Shanghai 200031
telephone : +86.21.6474 4533
fascsimile : +86.21.6466 4598
www.omalleys-shanghai.com

Paulaner Brauhaus
150 Fenyang Road, Xuhui District
Shanghai 200031
telephone : +86.21.6474 5700
facsimile : +86.21.6445 9189
paulaner-fenyangroad@bln.com.cn
www.bln.com.cn

Shintori
803 Julu Road
telephone : +86.21.5404 5252

TMSK
Unit 2, House 11 Beili, Xintiandi Square
Lane 181, Taicang Road
telephone : +86.21.6326 2227
facsimile : +86.21.6326 2237
service@tmsk.com
www.tmsk.com

SHANGHAI: A SHOPPING SENSATION

Plaza 66
1266 Nanjing West Road, Shanghai 200040
telephone : +86.21.5306 8888

CITIC Square
1168 Nanjing West Road, Shanghai 200041
telephone : +86.21.6218 0180

directory

Super Brand Mall
168 Lujiazui West Road, Shanghai 200122
telephone : +86.21.6887 7888
facsimile : +86.21.6887 1199
web@superbrandmall.com
www.superbrandmall.com

Cloud Nine
1018 Changning Road, Shanghai 200042
telephone : +86.21.5237 8275

Raffles City
268 Xizang Central Road, Shanghai 200001
telephone : +86.21.6340 3600
facsimile : +86.21.6340 3008
www.rafflescity-shanghai.com

Grand Gateway Mall
1 Hongqiao Road, Shanghai 200030
telephone : +86.21.6407 0111
facsimile : +86.21.6407 2800
master@grandgateway.com
www.grandgateway.com

Uniqlo
300 Huaihai Central Road
telephone : +86.21.3308 0427
www.uniqlo.com

Hongqiao International Pearl City
3721 Hongmei Road, Shanghai 201103
telephone : +86.21.62623851,
facsimile : +86.21.62623702
sales@hqpearl.com
www.shhqpearl.com

Yu Yuan Bazaar
218 Anren Street, Old Town,
Shanghai 200010
telephone : +86.21.6355 5025

Fuyou Market
457 Fangbang Road

SPAS IN SHANGHAI

Banyan Tree Spa Shanghai
3/F, The Westin Shanghai, Bund Centre
88 Henan Central Road, Shanghai 200002
telephone : +86.21.6335 1888
facsimile : +86.21.6335 1113
spa-shanghai@banyantree.com
www.banyantreespa.com/shanghai

CHI, The Spa
Pudong Shangri-La, 33 Fucheng Road
Shanghai 200120
telephone : +86.21.5877 1503
facsimile : +86.21. 6882 6688
www.shangri-la.com

Diva Life
266 Ruijin Er Road
telephone : +86.21.5465 7291
www.mydivalife.com

Dragonfly
20 Donghu Road, Xuhui District
telephone : +86.21.5405 0008
www.dragonfly.net.cn

Mandara Spa
6/F, JW Marriott Hotel Shanghai
399 Nanjing West Road, Shanghai 200003
telephone : +86.21.5359 4969
facsimile : +86.21.6375 5560
ms_jwms@minornet.com
www.mandaraspa.com

SHANGHAI GALLERIES + MUSEUMS

Art Scene
2/F, Building 4, 50 Moganshan Road
Shanghai 200060
telephone : +86.21.6277 4940
facsimile : +86.21.6433 8403
art@artscenechina.com
www.artscenewarehouse.com

Eastlink Gallery
5/F, Building 6 , 50 Moganshan Road
Shanghai 200060
telephone : +86.21.6276 9932
facsimile : +86.21.6276 6313
www.eastlinkgallery.cn

Museum of Contemporary Art (MoCA)
Gate 7, People's Park, 231 Nanjing West
Road, Shanghai 200003
telephone : +86.21.6327 9900
facsimile : +86.21.6327 1257
info@mocashanghai.org
www.mocashanghai.org

Shanghai Art Museum
325 Nanjing West Road, Shanghai 200003
telephone : +86.21.6327 2829
www.sh-artmuseum.org.cn

Shanghai Museum
201 Renmin Boulevard, Shanghai 200003
telephone : +86.21.6372 3500
www.shanghaimuseum.net

Shanghai Museum of Arts and Crafts
79 Fenyang Road, Luwan District
telephone : +86.21.6431 4074,

Shanghai Science and Technology Museum
2000 Century Avenue, Pudong
telephone : +86.21.6862 2000
www.sstm.org.cn

ShanghART
Buildings 16 & 18, 50 Moganshan Road
Shanghai 200060
telephone : +86.21.6359 3923
facsimile : +86.21.6359 4570
info@shanghartgallery.com
www.shanghartgallery.com

SUZHOU + NANJING

HOTELS

Kayumanis Nanjing (page 142)
Sizhuang Village, Tangshan Town
Nanjing, Jiangsu 211131
telephone : +86.25.8410 7777
facsimile : +86.25.8410 2666
nanjing@kayumanis.com
www.kayumanis.com

Kempinski Hotel Suzhou (page 144)
168 Guobin Road, Suzhou Industrial Park,
Suzhou, Jiangsu 215021
telephone : +86.512.6289 7888
facsimile : +86.512.6289 7866
info.suzhou@kempinski.com
www.kempinski-suzhou.com

Sheraton Suzhou Hotel + Towers
(page 148)
259 Xin Shi Road, Suzhou, Jiangsu 215007
telephone : +86.512.6510 3388
facsimile : +86.512.6510 0888
sheraton.suzhou@sheraton.com
www.sheraton.com/suzhou

SUZHOU + NANJING: DINING OUT

Bellagio
Building A1, 52 Taiping North Road
1912 District, Nanjing, Jiangsu 210008
telephone : +86.25.8452 2281
facsimile : +86.25.8452 2792

Celestial Court
Sheraton Suzhou Hotel + Towers
259 Xin Shi Road, Suzhou, Jiangsu 215007
telephone : +86.512.6510 3388
facsimile : +86.512.6510 0888
www.starwoodhotels.com/sheraton

Deyue Lou
43 Taijian Alley, Guanqian Street
Suzhou, Jiangsu 215005
telephone : +86.512.6522 2230

Garden Brasserie
Sheraton Suzhou Hotel + Towers
259 Xin Shi Road, Suzhou, Jiangsu 215007
telephone : +86.512.6510 3388
facsimile : +86.512.6510 0888
www.starwoodhotels.com/sheraton

Guibin Lou
12 Chao Ku Street, Qinhuai District
Nanjing, Jiangsu 210006
telephone : +86.25.5223 1770,
facsimile : +86.25.5221 7321

Jinying Dajiulou
3–4/F Jianhua Building, 56 Shigu Road
Nanjing, Jiangsu 210005
telephone : +86.25.8473 8868
facsimile : +86.25.8473 8818

Jitang Mian Guan
1 Hanzhong Road, Suzhou, Jiangsu 210088
telephone : +86.25.8472 1517

Le 5 Sens
52–1 Hankou Road, Nanjing, Jiangsu 210000
telephone : +86.25.8359 5859

Skyways Bakery and Deli
10 Taipingmen Street
Nanjing, Jiangsu 210016
telephone : +86.25.8481 2002
facsimile : +86.25.8481 2002

Songhe Lou
41 Guanqian Street, Pingjiang District
Suzhou, Jiangsu 215000
telephone : +86.512.6770 0688

South Beauty
Building 17, 8 Changjiang Hou Street
1912 District, Nanjing, Jiangsu 210018
telephone : +86.25.8451 1777

SUZHOU + NANJING: A SHOPPING SENSATION

Deji Plaza
18 Zhongshan Road,
Nanjing, Jiangsu 210000
telephone : +86.800.828 9598
www.dejiplaza.com

Dong Wu Silk Weaving Mill
782 Binhe Road, Suzhou, Jiangsu 215011
telephone : +86.512.8518 7900
facsimile : +86.512.6808 6712
dongwu@publicl.sz.js.cn
www.dongwu.com

Suzhou Kaidi Silk Co.
1965 Renmin Road, Suzhou, Jiangsu 215001
telephone : +86.512.6753 4587
facsimile : +86.512.6752 1812
www.szkdsilk.com

Suzhou Museum
204 Dong Bei Street,
Suzhou, Jiangsu 215001
telephone : +86.512.6757 5666
facsimile : +86.512.6754 4232
www.szmuseum.com

Suzhou Silk Museum
2001 Renmin Road, Suzhou, Jiangsu 215001
telephone : +86.512.6753 6506
facsimile : +86.512.6754 6221

HAINAN

HOTELS

Mandarin Oriental, Sanya (page 162)
12 Yuhai Road, Sanya, Hainan 572000
telephone : +86 898 8820 9999
facsimile : +86 898 8820 9393
mosan-reservations@mohg.com
www.mandarinoriental.com/sanya

Sanya Marriott Resort + Spa (page 164)
Yalong Bay National Resort District
Sanya, Hainan 572000
telephone : +86.898.8856 8888
facsimile : +86.898.8856 7111
sanyaresort@marriotthotels.com
www.marriott.com/SYXMC

HAINAN: DINING OUT

.IZE
Hilton Sanya Resort & Spa
Yalong Bay National Resort District
Sanya, Hainan 572000
telephone : +86.898.8858 8888
facsimile : +86.898.8858 8588
www.sanya.hilton.com

Chinese Restaurant
Mangrove Tree Resort,
Yalong Bay National Resort District
Sanya, Hainan 572000
telephone : +86.898.8855 8888
facsimile : +86.898.8855 8800

Chunyuan Seafood Square
Hexi Road, near City Park
Sanya, Hainan 572000
telephone : +86.898.8818 1102

Dongjiao Palm Tree Seafood Restaurant
109 Yuya Avenue, Dadonghai Tourist
District, Sanya, Hainan 572000
telephone : +86.898.8821 0999
facsimile : +86.898.8821 5039

Feipo Seafood Restaurant
Shengli Road, Hainan 572000
telephone : +86.898.3189 8828

Indochine
1/F, Building A, Sanya Marriott Resort &
Spa, Sanya, Hainan 572000
telephone : +86.898.8856 8888 ext. 6618
facsimile : +86.898.8856 1176
www.marriott.com

Liguo Restaurant
Hexi Road, Sanya, Hainan 572000
telephone : +86.898.8825 9099

Osmathus Restaurant
Resort Golden Palm
Yalong Bay National Resort District
Sanya, Hainan 572000
telephone : +86.898.8856 9988
facsimile : +86.898.8856 9999

Roma Pizzeria
1 Haiyun Road, Dadonghai Tourist District
Sanya, Hainan 572000
telephone : +86.898.8867 7871
facsimile : +86.898.8867 8822

Sampan Seafood Restaurant
Gloria Resort Sanya
Yalong Bay National Resort District
Sanya, Hainan 572000
telephone : +86.898.8856 8855
facsimile : +86.898.8856 8533
www.gloriaresort.com

Spice Garden Pan Asian Restaurant
Sheraton Sanya
Yalong Bay National Resort District
Sanya, Hainan 572000
telephone : +86.898.8855 8855
facsimile : +86.898.8855 8866

Versailles Restaurant
Hexi Road, Sanya, Hainan 572000
telephone : +86.898.3888 8881
facsimile : +86.898.3888 8882

Yuan Qi Lou
Nanshan Cultural Tourism Zone
Sanya, Hainan 572025
telephone : +86.898.8883 7923

HAINAN'S GREAT OUTDOORS

Kangle Garden HNA Resort
Xinglong Town, Wanning, Hainan 571533
telephone : +86.898.6256 8888
facsimile : +86.898.6256 6666
www.kangleresort.com

Pearl River Nantian Hot Spring Resort
Tenggiao Expressway Entrance
Sanya, Hainan 572013
telephone : +86.898.8881 9888
facsimile : +86.898.8881 9292
www.nantian-hot-spring.com

Sanya PADI Diving
Crowne Plaza Hotel Sanya
Yalong Bay International Resort District
Sanya, Hainan 572000
telephone : +86.898.8855 1836

Sanya Surf Club
2/F, Room 8219, Yindu Hotel
8 Huyuan Road
Dadonghai Tourist District
Sanya, Hainan 572000
telephone : +86.898.8821 3353,
facsimile : +86.898.8821 3353
www.surfinghainan.com

Sun Valley Sanya Golf Resort
Yalong Bay National Resort District
Sanya City, Hainan 572010
telephone : +86.898.8856 4488
facsimile : +86.898.8856 6699
info@sunvalleysanya.com
www.sunvalleygolfresort.com

Yalong Bay Golf Club
Yalong Bay National Resort District
Sanya, Hainan 572010
telephone : +86.898.8856 5888
facsimile : +86.898.8856 5052
welcome@yalongbaygolfclub.com
www.yalongbaygolfclub.com

HONG KONG

HOTELS

Four Seasons Hong Kong (page 186)
8 Finance Street, Central, Hong Kong
telephone : +852.3196 8888
facsimile : +852.3196 8899
www.fourseasons.com/hongkong

Grand Hyatt Hong Kong (page 188)
1 Harbour Road, Hong Kong
telephone : + 852.2588 1234
facsimile : + 852.2802 0677
info.ghhk@hyatt.com
www.hongkong.grand.hyatt.com

JIA Hong Kong (page 192)
No. 1–5 Irving Street,
Causeway Bay, Hong Kong
telephone : +852.3196 9000
facsimile : +852.3196 9001
info@jiahongkong.com
www.jiahongkong.com

directory

JW Marriott Hotel Hong Kong (page 194)
Pacific Place, 88 Queensway, Hong Kong
telephone : +852.2810 8366
facsimile : +852.2845 0737
hotel@marriott.com.hk
www.marriott.com

Lan Kwai Fong Hotel (page 196)
3, Kau U Fong, Central Hong Kong
telephone : +852.3650 0299
facsimile : +852.3650 0288
enquiry@lankwaifonghotel.com.hk
www.lankwaifonghotel.com

Hotel Le Méridien Cyberport (page 198)
100 Cyberport Road, Hong Kong
telephone : +852.2980 7788
facsimile : +852.2980 7888
welcome.lmc@lemeridien.com
www.lemeridien.com/hongkong

RESTAURANTS

KEE Club (page 200)
6th Floor, 32 Wellington Street, Central
telephone : +852 2810 9000
facsimile : +852 2868 0036
info@keeclub.com
www.keeclub.com

SHOPS

Shanghai Tang (page 202)
Pedder Building, 12 Pedder Street, Central
telephone : +852.2537 2888
facsimile : +852.2156 9898
contactus@shanghaitang.com
www.shanghaitang.com

HONG KONG: DINING OUT

Aqua Luna
telephone : +852.2116 8821
aqualuna@aqua.com.hk
www.aqua.com.hk

Caprice
Four Seasons Hotel Hong Kong
8 Finance Street, Central
telephone : +852.3196 8888
facsimile : +852.3196 8899
www.fourseasons.com/hongkong

Chez Patrick
8–9 Sun Street, Wanchai
telephone : +852.2527 1408
sunstreet@chezpatrick.hk
www.chezpatrick.hk

Chocolux
57 Peel Street, Central
telephone : +852.2858 8760
chocolux8@yahoo.com
www.chocoluxcafe.com

Cinecittà
9 Star Street, Wanchai
telephone : +852.2529 0199
cin@elite-concepts.com
www.elite-concepts.com

Cococabana
UG/F, Beach Building,
Island Road, Deep Water Bay
telephone : +852.2812 2226
facsimile : +852.2813 6218
cocobay@biznetvigator.com
www.toptables.com

Da Domenico
G/F Sunning Plaza,
10 Hysan Avenue, Causeway Bay
telephone : +852.2882 8013
facsimile : +852.2890 6003

Dim Sum
63 Sing Woo Road, Happy Valley
telephone : +852.2834 8893

Fook Lam Moon
35–45 Johnston Road, Wanchai
telephone : +852.2866 0663
facsimile : +852.2865 0165
teresawong@fooklammoon-grp.com
www.fooklammoon-grp.com

Gaia
G/F, Grand Millennium Plaza
181 Queen's Road, Central
telephone : +852.2167 8200
facsimile : +852.2167 8220
contactus@gaiagroup.com.hk
www.gaiaristorante.com

Hutong
28/F, One Peking Road, Tsim Sha Tsui
telephone : +852.3428 8342
hutong@aqua.com.hk
www.aqua.com.hk

Ingredients
23–29 Wing Fung Street, Wanchai
telephone : +852.2544 5133
facsimile : +852.2544 9588
ingredients@netvigator.com
www.ingredients.com.hk

L'Atelier de Joel Robuchon
4/F, The Landmark
15 Queen's Road Central, Central
telephone : +852.2166 9000
www.joel-robuchon.com

Luk Yu Tea House
24–26 Stanley Street, Central
telephone : +852.2523 5464
facsimile : +852.2524 8683

Lung King Heen
Four Seasons Hotel Hong Kong
8 Finance Street, Central
telephone : +852.3196 8888
facsimile : +852.3196 8899
www.fourseasons.com/hongkong

M at the Fringe
1/F, South Block,
2 Lower Albert Road, Central
telephone : +852.2877 4000
facsimile : +852.2877 0135
www.m-restaurantgroup.com

Mandarin Grill + Bar
1/F, Mandarin Oriental Hong Kong
5 Connaught Road, Central
telephone : +852.2825 4004
mohkg-grill@mohg.com
www.mandarinoriental.com/hongkong

Maxim's Palace
2/F, Low Block, City Hall
Connaught Road, Central
telephone : +852.2521 1303

Nobu
InterContinental Hong Kong
18 Salisbury Road, Tsim Sha Tsui
telephone : +852.2721 1211
facsimile : +852.2739 4546
hongkong@interconti.com
www.noburestaurants.com

OPIA
JIA Hong Kong,
1–5 Irving Street, Causeway Bay
telephone : +852.3196 9100
facsimile : +852.3196 9010
info@jiahongkong.com
www.jiahongkong.com

Pierre
Mandarin Oriental Hong Kong
5 Connaught Road, Central
telephone : +852.2825 4001
mohkg-pierre@mohg.com
www.pierre-gagnaire.com

Press Room
108 Hollywood Road, Central
telephone : +852.2525 3444
facsimile : +852.2525 3445
info@thepressroom.com.hk
www.thepressroom.com.hk

Shui Hu Ju
G/F, 68 Peel Street, Central
telephone : +852.2869 6927
shuihuju@aqua.com.hk
www.aqua.com.hk

Spoon
InterContinental Hong Kong
18 Salisbury Road, Tsim Sha Tsui
telephone : +852 2313 2256
facsimile : +852 2739 4546,
www.alain-ducasse.com

Spring Moon
The Peninsula Hong Kong,
Salisbury Road, Tsim Sha Tsui
telephone : +852.2315 3160
facsimile : +852.2315 3140
diningphk@peninsula.com
www.peninsula.com

The China Club
13/F, Old Bank of China Building
Bank Street, Central
telephone : +852.2521 8888
facsimile : +852.2522 6611

The Clipper Lounge
Mandarin Oriental Hong Kong
5 Connaught Road, Central
telephone : +852.2825 4007
mohkg-clipperlounge@mohg.com
www.mandarinoriental.com

The Lobby
The Peninsula Hong Kong
Salisbury Road, Tsim Sha Tsui
telephone : +852.2920 2888
facsimile : +852.2722 4170
diningphk@peninsula.com
www.peninsula.com

Top Deck
Top Floor, Jumbo Floating Restaurant
Shum Wan Pier Drive
Wong Chuk Hang, Aberdeen
telephone : +852.2553 9111
facsimile : +852.2553 0527
sales-hk@jumbokingdom.com
www.jumbo.com.hk

Tribute
G/F, 13 Elgin Street, Central
telephone : +852.2135 6645
facsimile : +852.2135 6602
tribute@tribute.com.hk
www.tribute.com.hk

Xi Yan
3/F, 83 Wanchai Road, Wanchai
telephone : +852.2575 6977
facsimile : +852.2575 6955
www.xiyan.com.hk

Xi Yan Sweets
G/F, 8 Wing Fung Street, Wanchai
telephone : +852.2833 6299
facsimile : +852.2833 6696
www.xiyan.com.hk

XTC Gelato
Shop B, 45 Cochrane Street, Central
telephone : +852.2541 0500
facsimile : +852.2540 0205
info@xtc.com.hk
www.xtc.com.hk

Yung Kee
32–40 Wellington Street, Central
telephone : +852.2522 1624
facsimile : +852.2840 0888
info@yungkee.com.hk
www.yungkee.hk

Zuma
5–6/F, The Landmark,
15 Queen's Road, Central
telephone : +852.3657 6388
facsimile : +852.3657 6399
info@zumarestaurant.com.hk
www.zumarestaurant.com

HONG KONG'S NIGHTLIFE

Aqua Spirit
30/F, 1 Peking Road, Tsim Sha Tsui
telephone : +852.3427 2288
aqua@aqua.com.hk
www.aqua.com.hk

Armani Bar
2/F, Chater House, 11 Chater Road, Central
telephone : +852.2805 0028
facsimile : +852.2805 0025

Boca
85 Peel Street, Central
telephone : +852.2548 1717
facsimile : +852.2548 1727
tapasandwine@boca.com.hk
www.boca.com.hk

Champagne Bar
Grand Hyatt Hong Kong
1 Harbour Road, Wanchai
telephone : +852.2588 1234 ext. 7321
facsimile : +852.2802 0677
web: www.hongkong.grand.hyatt.com

DiVino
73 Wyndham Street, Central
telephone : +852.2522 1002
facsimile : +852.2167 7333
divino@divino.com.hk
www.divino.com.hk

dragon i
UG/F, The Centrium,
60 Wyndham Street, Central
telephone : +852.3110 1222
facsimile : +852.3110 1223
info@dragon-i.com.hk
www.dragon-i.com.hk

Drop
Basement, On Lok Mansion
39–43 Hollywood Road, Central
telephone : +852.2543 8856
info@drophk.com
www.drophk.com

Feather Boa
38 Staunton Street, SoHo
telephone : +852.2857 2586

Felix
28/F, The Peninsula Hong Kong
Salisbury Road, Tsim Sha Tsui
telephone : +852.2315 3188
facsimile : +852.2315 3140
phk@peninsula.com
www.peninsula.com

FINDS
2/F, LKF Tower, 33 Wyndham Street
telephone : +852.2522 9318
facsimile : +852.2521 9818
info@finds.com.hk
www.finds.com.hk

Fringe Club
2 Lower Albert Road, Central
telephone : +852.2521 7521
enquiry@hkfringeclub.com
www.hkfringeclub.com

Halo
LG/F, 10–12 Stanley Street, Central
telephone : +852.2110 1274
facsimile : +852.2810 2179
reservations@halo.hk
www.halo.hk

Isobar
4/F, ifc mall, 8 Finance Street, Central
telephone : +852.2383 8765
facsimile : +852.2383 8622
info@isolabarandgrill.com
www.isolabarandgrill.com

KEE Club
6/F, 32 Wellington Street, Central
telephone : +852.2810 9000
facsimile : +852.2868 0036
info@keeclub.com
www.keeclub.com

Le Rideau Theatre Cafe
1/F, Hilltop Plaza, 49 Hollywood Road, SoHo
telephone : +852.2850 8833
info@lerideau.hk
www.lerideau.hk

Lei Dou
G/F, 20–22 D'Aguilar Street
Lan Kwai Fong, Central
telephone : +852.2521 6188

M1NT
108 Hollywood Road, Central
telephone : +852.2261 1111
facsimile : +852.2980 3737
info@M1NT.com.hk
www.m1nt.com.hk

Makumba Africa Bar
G/F, 48–52A Peel Street, Central
telephone : +852.2522 0544
facsimile : +852.2522 0744
makumba@biznetvigator.com
www.makumba-hk.com

Racks
7/F, 2–8 Wellington Street
telephone : +852.2868 3762
info@racksmdb.com
www.racksmdb.com

The Captain's Bar
Mandarin Oriental Hong Kong
5 Connaught Road, Central
telephone : +852.2825 4006
mohkg-captain@mohg.com
www.mandarinoriental.com/hongkong

Volar
Basement, 38–44 D'Aguilar Street, Central
telephone : +852.2810 1272
facsimile : +852.2810 1279
intoxicated@volar.com.hk
www.volar.com.hk

Yumla
Lower Basement, 79 Wyndham Street,
Central
telephone : +852.2147 2382
contact@yumla.com
www.yumla.com

HONG KONG: A SHOPPING SENSATION

Alexandra House
18 Chater Road, Central
atam@hkland.com
www.CentralHK.com

Barney Cheng
12/F, Worldwide Commercial Building
34 Wyndham Street, Central
telephone : +852.2530 2829
facsimile : +852.2530 2835
info@barneycheng.com
www.barneycheng.com

Blanc de Chine
218–221, The Landmark
15 Queen's Road Central, Central
telephone : +852.2104 7934
www.blancdechine.com

Billionaire Boys Club
G/F, 14 On Lan Street, Central
telephone : +852.2526 7166
www.bbicecream.com

Chater House
8 Connaught Road, Central
atam@hkland.com
www.CentralHK.com

Chinese Arts & Crafts
Star House, 3 Salisbury Road, Tsim Sha Tsui
telephone : +852.2839 1100
hotline@crcretail.com
www.chineseartsandcrafts.com.hk

Christian Louboutin
G/F, 7 On Lan Street, Central
telephone : +852.2118 0016
www.christianlouboutin.fr

Comme des Garçons
G/F, 20 On Lan Street, Central
telephone : +852.2869 5906
www.ithk.com

Dmop
G/F, 11–15 On Lan Street, Central
telephone : +852.2840 0822
www.d-mop.com.hk

Elements
1, Austin Road West, Kowloon
telephone : +852.2735 5234
www.elementshk.com

Festival Walk
80 Tat Chee Avenue, Kowloon Tong
telephone : +852.2844 2223
facsimile : +852.2265 8112
fwshopping@swireproperties.com
www.festivalwalk.com.hk

Fook Ming Tong
Shop 3006, ifc mall
8 Financial Street, Central
telephone : +852.2295 0368
www.fookmingtong.com

G.O.D.
G/F and 1/F, Leighton Centre
77 Leighton Road, Causeway Bay
telephone : +852.2890 5555
facsimile : +852.2882 2832
www.god.com.hk

Giordano
G/F, Manson House
74–78 Nathan Road, Tsim Sha Tsui
telephone : +852.2926 1681
www.giordano.com.hk

Harbour City
3–27 Canton Road, Tsim Sha Tsui
telephone : +852.2118 8666
cs@harbourcity.com.hk
www.harbourcity.com.hk

Harvey Nichols
Shop G–4/F, The Landmark
15 Queen's Road Central, Central
telephone : +852.3695 3388
customer_relations@harveynichols.com.hk
www.harveynichols.com

ifc mall
8 Finance Street, Central
atam@hkland.com
www.CentralHK.com

I.T
2 Kingston Street, Causeway Bay
telephone : +852.2881 6102
www.ithk.com

Joyce Boutique
G/F, New World Tower
16 Queens Road, Central
telephone : +852.2869 5816

Kou
22/F, Fung House
19–20 Connaught Road, Central
telephone : +852.2530 2234
facsimile : +852.2849 4771
info@kouconcept.com
www.kouconcept.com

Lane Crawford
Podium 3, ifc mall, 8 Finance Street, Central
telephone : +852.2118 7777
customerrelationship@lanecrawford.com
www.lanecrawford.com

Lee Gardens
33 Hysan Avenue, Causeway Bay
telephone : +852.2830 5169
www.leegardens.com.hk

Maison Martin Margiela
G/F, 18 On Lan Street, Central
telephone : +852.2869 7707
www.ithk.com

OVO
G/F, 16 Queen's Road East, Wanchai
telephone : +852.2526 7226
www.ovo.com.hk

Pacific Place
88 Queensway, Admiralty
telephone : +852.2844 8900
facsimile : +852.2918 0417
ppshopping@swireproperties.com
www.pacificplace.com.hk

Prince's Building
10 Chater Road, Central
atam@hkland.com
www.CentralHK.com

Ranee K
16 Gough Street, Central,
telephone : +852.2108 4068
raneek@netvigator.com
www.raneek.com

Shanghai Tang
G/F and Basement, Pedder Building,
12 Pedder Street, Central
telephone : +852.2525 7333
facsimile : +852.2530 1888
hkorder@shanghaitang.com
www.shanghaitang.com

Sin Sin Atelier
G/F, 52 Sai Street, Sheung Wan
telephone : +852.2521 0308
facsimile : +852.2764 0406
info@sinsin.com.hk
www.sinsin.com.hk

The Landmark
15 Queen's Road Central, Central
atam@hkland.com
www.CentralHK.com

Times Square
1, Matheson Street, Causeway Bay
telephone : +852.2118 8900
www.timessquare.com.hk

Yue Hwa Department Store
301–309 Nathan Road, Kowloon
telephone : +852.3511 2222
info3@yuehwacp.com
www.yuehwa.com

SPAS IN HONG KONG

Elemis Day Spa
9/F, Century Square
1 D'Aguilar Street, Central
telephone : +852.2521 6660
facsimile : +852.2521 0016
elemisdayspa@paua.com.hk
www.elemisdayspa.com.hk

Happy Foot Reflexology Centre
6/F, Jade Centre
98–02 Wellington Street, Central
telephone : +852.2544 1010

Indulgence
33 Lyndhurst Terrace, Central
telephone : +852.2815 6600

Paua Spa
Centrestage,
108 Hollywood Road, Central
telephone : +852.2522 3054
pauaspacs@paua.com.hk
www.paua.com.hk

Paul Gerrard Hair & Beauty
1–2/F, Wah Hing House
35 Pottinger Street, Central
telephone : +852.2869 4408
facsimile : +852.2869 4438
info@paulgerrard.com
www.paulgerrard.com

Plateau
Grand Hyatt Hong Kong
1 Harbour Road, Wanchai
telephone : +852.2584 7688
facsimile : +852.2584 7738
plateau.ghhk@hyattintl.com
www.hongkong.grand.hyatt.com

The Feel Good Factor
1 Lyndhurst Terrace, Central
telephone : +852.2530 0610
info@feelgoodfactor.com
www.feelgoodfactor.com.hk

The Oriental Spa
The Landmark Mandarin Oriental,
Hong Kong, 15 Queen's Road, Central
telephone : +852.2132 0011
lmhkg-spa@mohg.com
www.mandarinoriental.com

The Peninsula Spa
The Peninsula Hong Kong
Salisbury Road, Kowloon
telephone : +852.2315 3322
facsimile : +852.2315 3325
spaphk@peninsula.com
www.peninsula.com

The Spa at the Four Seasons
Four Seasons Hotel Hong Kong
8 Finance Street, Central
telephone : +852.3196 8888
facsimile : +852.3196 8799
www.fourseasons.com

Victorian Spa
1/F, Hong Kong Disneyland Hotel,
Hong Kong Disneyland Resort,
Lantau Island
telephone : +852.3510 6388
facsimile : +852.3510 6670
victorianspa@paua.com.hk
www.victorianspa.com

HONG KONG GALLERIES + MUSEUMS

1a space
Unit 14, Cattle Depot Artist Village
63 Ma Tau Kok Road, To Kwa Wan
telephone : +852.2529 0087
facsimile : +852.2529 0072
admin@oneaspace.org.hk
www.oneaspace.org.hk

10 Chancery Lane Gallery
G/F, 10 Chancery Lane, Central
telephone : +852.2810 0065
info@www.10chancerylanegallery.com
www.10chancerylanegallery.com

Alisan Fine Arts
Shop 315, Prince's Building
10 Chater Road, Central
telephone : +852.2526 1091
info@alisan.com.hk
www.alisan.com.hk

Artist's Commune
Unit 12, Cattle Depot Artist Village
63 Ma Tau Kok Road, To Kwa Wan
telephone : +852.2104 3322
facsimile : +852.2104 9515
m63@artist-commune.com
www.artist-commune.com

Asia Art Archive
11/F, Hollywood Centre
233 Hollywood Road, Sheung Wan
telephone : +852.2815 1112
facsimile : +852.2815 0032
info@aaa.org.hk
www.aaa.org.hk

Cattle Depot Artist Village
63 Ma Tau Kok Road, To Kwa Wan

Christie's
22/F, Alexandra House,
16–20 Chater Road, Central
telephone : +852.2521 5396
facsimile : +852.2845 2646
www.christies.com

Flagstaff House Museum of Tea Ware
10 Cotton Tree Drive, Central
telephone : +852.2869 0690
facsimile : +852.2810 0021
enquiries@lcsd.gov.hk
www.lcsd.gov.hk

Grotto Fine Art
2/F, 31C–D Wyndham Street, Central
telephone : +852.2121 2270
facsimile : +852.2121 2269
info@grottofineart.com
www.grottofineart.com

Hanart TZ Gallery
202 Henley Building,
5 Queen's Road, Central
telephone : +852.2521 9019
facsimile : +852.2521 2001
tzchang@hanart.com
www.hanart.com

Hong Kong Art Walk
telephone : +852.2854 1018
batten@netvigator.com
www.hongkongartwalk.com

Hong Kong Film Archive
50 Lei King Road, Sai Wan Ho
telephone : +852.2739 2139
facsimile : +852.2311 5229
hkfa@lcsd.gov.hk
www.filmarchive.gov.hk

Hong Kong Museum of Art
10 Salisbury Road, Tsim Sha Tsui
telephone : +852.2721 0116
facsimile : +852.2723 7666
enquiries@lcsd.gov.hk
www.lcsd.gov.hk

Hong Kong Museum of Coastal Defence
75 Tung Hei Road, Shau Kei Wan
telephone : +852.2569 1500
facsimile : +852.2569 1637
hkmcd@lcsd.gov.hk
http://hk.coastaldefence.museum

Hong Kong Museum of History
100 Chatham Road South, Tsim Sha Tsui
telephone : +852.2724 9042
facsimile : +852.2724 9090
hkmh@lcsd.gov.hk
http://hk.history.museum

Hong Kong Museum of Medical Sciences
2 Caine Lane, Mid-Levels
telephone : +852.2549 5123
facsimile : +852.2559 9458
info@hkmms.org.hk
www.hkmms.org.hk

Hong Kong Science Museum
2 Science Museum Road,
Tsim Sha Tsui East
telephone : +852.2732 3232
facsimile : +852.2311 2248
enquiries@hk.science.museum
www.lcsd.gov.hk

Hong Kong Space Museum
10 Salisbury Road,
Tsim Sha Tsui
telephone : +852.2721 0226
facsimile : +852.2311 5804
spacem@space.lcsd.gov.hk
http://hk.space.museum

Jockey Club Creative Arts Centre
telephone : +852.2353 1311
facsimile : +852.2353 1269
jccac@hkbu.edu.hk
www.hkbu.edu.hk/jccac

On and On Theatre Workshop
Unit 7, Cattle Depot Artist Village
63 Ma Tau Kok Road, To Kwa Wan
telephone : +852.2503 1630
facsimile : +852.2503 1654
onandon@onandon.org.hk
www.onandon.org.hk

Para/Site Art Space
G/F, 4 Po Yan Street, Sheung Wan
telephone : +852. 2517 4620
facsimile : +852.2517 6850
info@para-site.org.hk
www.para-site.org.hk

Schoeni Art Gallery
21–31 Old Bailey Street, Central
telephone : +852.2869 8802
facsimile : +852.2522 1528
gallery@schoeni.com.hk
www.schoeni.com.hk

Sotheby's
Suites 3101–3106, 31/F, 1 Pacific Place
88 Queensway
telephone : +852.2524 8121
facsimile : +852.2810 6238
www.sothebys.com

The Police Museum
27 Coombe Road, The Peak
telephone : +852.2849 7019
facsimile : +852.2849 4573
www.police.gov.hk/hkp-home/english/museum/

University Museum and Art Gallery
The University of Hong Kong
94 Bonham Road, Pok Fu Lam
telephone : +852.2241 5500
facsimile : +852.2546 9659
museum@hkusua.hku.hk
www.hku.hk/hkumag/

MACAU

HOTELS

Crown Macau (page 220)
Avenida de Kwong Tung at Avenida
Dr. Sun Yat Sen, Taipa
telephone : +853.2886 8888
facsimile : +853.2886 8666
enquiries@crown-macau.com
www.crown-macau.com

Sofitel Macau at Ponte 16 (page 226)
Rua do Visconde Paco de Arcos, Macau
telephone : +853.8861 0016
facsimile : +853.8861 0018
sales@sofitelmacau.com
www.sofitel.com.cn

Wynn Macau (page 228)
Rua Cidade de Sintra, NAPE, Macau
telephone : +853.8986 9966
facsimile : +853.2832 9966
roomreservations@wynnmacau.com
www.wynnmacau.com

MACAU: DINING OUT

A Lorcha
298 Rua do Almirante Sergio
Inner Harbour, Macau
telephone : +853.2831 3195
facsimile : +853.2896 6842

Antica Trattoria da Ise
40–46 Avenida Sir Anders Ljungstedt
Edificio Vista Magnifica Court, Macau
telephone : +853.2875 5102

Aurora
10/F, Crown Macau,
Avenida de Kwong Tung at Avenida
Dr. Sun Yat Sen, Taipa
telephone : +853.2886 8868
facsimile : +853.2886 8666
enquiries@crown-macau.com
www.crown-macau.com

Camoes
Shop 101, Lisbon-Evora
Macau Fisherman's Wharf, Macau
telephone : +853.2872 8818

Clube Militar de Macau
975 Avenida da Praia Grande
Downtown, Macau
telephone : +853.2871 4000
cmm@macau.ctm.net
home.macau.ctm.net

Don Alfonso 1890—Macau
Grand Lisboa Hotel
Avenida de Lisboa, Macau
telephone : +853.8803 7722

Fat Siu Lau
Rua da Felicidade
Downtown, Macau
telephone : +853.2857 3580
facsimile : +853.2857 3266
fsl1903@macau.ctm.net
www.fatsiulau.com.mo

Fogo Samba
Shop 2410,
Grand Canal Shoppes,
The Venetian Macao
Estrada da Baia de N. Senhora da
Esperanca, Taipa
telephone : +853.2882 8499
inquiries@venetian.com.mo
www.venetianmacao.com

Il Teatro
Wynn Macau
Rua Cidade de Sintra, NAPE, Macau
telephone : +853.8986 3663
facsimile : +853.2832 9966
inquiries@wynnmacau.com
www.wynnmacau.com

Kira
10/F, Crown Macau
Avenida de Kwong Tung at Avenida Dr.
Sun Yat Sen, Taipa
telephone : +853.2886 8868
facsimile : +853.2886 8666
enquiries@crown-macau.com
www.crown-macau.com

Le Bistrot
G/F, Block 27, Nova Taipa Garden, Taipa
telephone : +853.2884 3739
facsimile : +853.2884 3994
bistrot@macau.ctm.net
www.lebistrot-macau.com

Long Kei
7B Largo do Senado, Downtown, Macau
telephone : +853.2857 3970

Lord Stow's Bakery
1 Rua da Tassara, Coloane Town Square,
Macau
telephone : +853.2888 2355
facsimile : +853.2888 1066
lordstow@macau.ctm.net
www.lordstow.com

Lua Azul
3/F, Macau Tower, Largo da Torre de Macau
Downtown, Macau
telephone : +853.8988 8700
www.macautower.com.mo

Margaret's Café e Nata
Edificio Kam Loi, Nam Van, Macau
telephone : +853.2871 0032

Morton's of Chicago
Shop 1016, Grand Canal Shoppes,
The Venetian Macao
Estrada da Baia de N. Senhora da
Esperanca, Taipa
telephone : +853.8117 5000
inquiries@venetian.com.mo
www.venetianmacao.com

Nga Tim Café
8 Rua Caetano, Coloane Village, Coloane
telephone : +853.2888 2086

Okada
Wynn Macau
Rua Cidade de Sintra, NAPE, Macau
telephone : +853.8986 3663
facsimile : +853.2832 9966
inquiries@wynnmacau.com
www.wynnmacau.com

Portas do Sol
2/F, Hotel Lisboa
2–4 Avenida de Lisboa, Downtown, Macau
telephone : +853.2888 3888
www.hotelisboa.com

Restaurante Fernando
Praia de Hac Sa 9, Coloane
telephone : +853.2888 2264
facsimile : +853.2884 1591
fernandr@macau.ctm.net
www.fernando-restaurant.com

Restaurante Litoral
261A Rua do Almirante Sergio, Macau
telephone : +853.2896 7878
facsimile : +853.2896 7996
www.yp.com.mo/litoral

Robuchon a Galera
3/F, Hotel Lisboa
2–4 Avenida de Lisboa, Downtown, Macau
telephone : +853.2888 3888
www.hotelisboa.com

Tenmasa
11/F, Crown Macau
Avenida de Kwong Tung at Avenida
Dr. Sun Yat Sen, Taipa
telephone : +853.2886 8868
facsimile : +853.2886 8666
enquiries@crown-macau.com
www.crown-macau.com

MACAU: NIGHTLIFE

Bar Florian
Shop 1043, The Venetian Macao
Estrada da Baia de N. Senhora da
Esperanca, Taipa
telephone : +853.8118 9960
www.venetianmacao.com

Bellini Lounge
Shop 1041, The Venetian Macao
Estrada da Baia de N. Senhora da
Esperanca, Taipa
telephone : +853.8118 9960
www.venetianmacao.com

blue frog bar & grill
Shop 1037 The Venetian Macao
Estrada da Baia de N. Senhora da
Esperanca, Taipa
telephone : +853.2882 8281
facsimile : +853.2882 8289
info@bluefrog.com.cn
www.bluefrog.com.cn

Casablanca
1373–1369, Avenida Dr. Sun Yat Sen
Outer Harbour, Macau
telephone : +853.2875 1281

Champagne Bar
MGM Grand Macau
Avenida Dr. Sun Yat Sen, NAPE, Macau
telephone : +853.8802 8888
www.mgmgrandmacau.com

Cinnebar
Wynn Macau
Rua Cidade de Sintra, NAPE, Macau
telephone : +853.8986 3663
facsimile : +853.2832 9966
inquiries@wynnmacau.com
www.wynnmacau.com

Crystal Club
38/F, Crown Macau
Avenida de Kwong Tung at Avenida Dr.
Sun Yat Sen, Taipa
telephone : +853.2886 8868
facsimile : +853.2886 8666
enquiries@crown-macau.com
www.crown-macau.com

D2
2/F, AIA Tower, 251A–301 Avenida
Comercial de Macau, Macau
telephone : +853.2872 3777

Dom Pedro V Theatre
Largo de Santo Agostinho, Macau

Jazz Club
9 Rua das Alabardas, Macau
telephone : +853.2859 6014

Lumina Bar
5/F, Crown Macau
Avenida de Kwong Tung at Avenida
Dr. Sun Yat Sen, Taipa
telephone : +853.2886 8868
facsimile : +853.2886 8666
enquiries@crown-macau.com
www.crown-macau.com

M Bar
G/F, MGM Grand Macau
Avenida Dr. Sun Yat Sen, NAPE, Macau
telephone : +853.8802 8888
www.mgmgrandmacau.com

Macao Cultural Centre
Avenido Xian Xing Hai, NAPE, Macau
telephone : +853.2870 0699
facsimile : +853.2875 1395
enquiry@ccm.gov.mo
www.ccm.gov.mo

Macau Jockey Club
Estrada Governador Albano da Oliveira, Taipa
telephone : +853.2882 1188
facsimile : +853.2882 0503
www.mjc.mo

Moonwalker
Avenida Dr. Sun Yat Sen,
Outer Harbour, Macau
telephone : +853.2875 1326
facsimile : +853.2875 1327

Sky 21
21/F, AIA Tower, 251A-301 Avenida
Comercial de Macau, Macau
telephone : +853.2822 2122
info@sky21macau.com
www.sky21macau.com

The Venetian Arena
The Venetian Macao
Estrada da Baia de N. Senhora da
Esperanca, Taipa
telephone : +853.2882 8888
facsimile : +853.2882 8889
www.venetianmacao.com

Veuve Clicquot Lounge
MGM Grand Macau
Avenida Dr. Sun Yat Sen, NAPE, Macau
telephone : +853.8802 8888
www.mgmgrandmacau.com

MACAU: A SHOPPING SENSATION

Asian Artefacts
9 Rua dos Negociantes, Coloane
telephone : +853.2888 1022

Grand Canal Shoppes at The Venetian Macao
The Venetian Macao
Estrada da Baia de N. Senhora da
Esperanca, Taipa
telephone : +853.2882 8888
inquiries@venetian.com.mo
www.venetianmacao.com

Macau Wine Museum
Tourism Activities Centre
431 Rua Luis Gonzaga Gomes, Macau
telephone : +853.8798 4188
facsimile : +853.2870 6076

Pavilions
417 Avenida da Praia Grande
Downtown, Macau
telephone : +853.2833 3636
facsimile : +853.2832 3993

Wing Tai
1A Avenida de Almeida Ribeiro, Macau
telephone : +853.2857 3651
facsimile : +853.2834 6532

Wynn Esplanade
Rua Cidade de Sintra, NAPE, Macau
telephone : +853.2888 9966
facsimile : +853.2832 9966
inquiries@wynnmacau.com
www.wynnmacau.com

SPAS IN MACAU

Six Senses Spa
3/F, MGM Grand Macau
Avenida Dr. Sun Yat Sen, NAPE, Macau
telephone : +853.8802 3838
facsimile : +853.8802 3333
inquiries@mgmgrandmacau.com
www.mgmgrandmacau.com

Spa at Wynn Macau
Rua Cidade de Sintra, NAPE, Macau
telephone : +853.2888 9966
facsimile : +853.2832 9966
inquiries@wynnmacau.com
www.wynnmacau.com

Spa Philosophy
327–331 Avenida Xian Xing Hai
Nam On Garden, Macau
telephone : +853.2872 8330
facsimile : +853.2872 8331
info@spaphilosophy.com
www.spaphilosophy.com

The Spa at Crown
Crown Macau
Avenida de Kwong Tung at
Avenida Dr. Sun Yat Sen, Taipa
telephone : +853.2886 8886
facsimile : +853.2886 8666
enquiries@crown-macau.com
www.crown-macau.com

The Spa at the Mandarin Oriental Macau
956–1110 Avenida da Amizade, Macau
telephone : +853 793 4824
momfm-spa@mohg.com
www.mandarinoriental.com

MACAU'S CASINO SCENE

Crown Macau
Avenida de Kwong Tung at
Avenida Dr. Sun Yat Sen, Taipa
telephone : +853.2886 8888
facsimile : +853.2886 8666
enquiries@crown-macau.com
www.crown-macau.com

Grand Lisboa
2–4 Avenida de Lisboa, Macau
Telephone : +853.2828 2828

MGM Grand Macau
Avenida Dr. Sun Yat Sen, NAPE, Macau
telephone : +853.8802 8888
www.mgmgrandmacau.com

Sands Macao
203 Largo de Monte Carlo, Macau
telephone : +853.2888 3388
generalinquiries@sands.com.mo
www.sands.com.mo

The Venetian Macao
Estrada da Baia de N. Senhora da
Esperança, Taipa
telephone : +853.2882 8888
inquiries@venetian.com.mo
www.venetianmacao.com

Wynn Macau
Rua Cidade de Sintra, NAPE, Macau
telephone : +853.2888 9966
facsimile : +853.2832 9966
inquiries@wynnmacau.com
www.wynnmacau.com